On the Theory and
Archaeological Computing

Edited by

GARY LOCK and KAYT BROWN

Oxford University Committee for Archaeology
Monograph No. 51
2000

Published by
Oxford University Committee for Archaeology
Institute of Archaeology
Beaumont Street
Oxford

Distributed by

Oxbow Books
Park End Place, Oxford, OX1 1HN
(Phone 01865-241249; Fax 01865-794449)

and

The David Brown Book Company
PO Box 5605, Bloomington, IN 47407, USA

ISBN 0-947816-51-8

Produced by Production Line, Minster Lovell, Oxford
Printed in Great Britain by Redwood Books, Trowbridge

Contents

Contributors

Anthony Beck
Department of Archaeology
University of Durham
England
a.r.beck@durham.ac.uk

Kayt Brown
Oxford Archaeological Unit
Oxford
England
kayt.brown@oau-oxford.com

Patrick Daly
Institute of Archaeology
University of Oxford
England
patrick.daly@stx.ox.ac.uk

Hannah Forsyth
Faculty of Veterinary Science
University of Sydney
Australia
h.forsyth@vetsci.usyd.edu.au

Jayne Gidlow
Whitstable
England
jayne-gidlow@hotmail.com

Mark Gillings
School of Archaeological Studies
University of Leicester
England
mg41@leicester.ac.uk

Glyn Goodrick
Department of Archaeology
University of Newcastle upon Tyne
England
G.T.Goodrick@ncl.ac.uk

Francis Grew
Museum of London
London
England
fgrew@museum-london.org.uk

Jeremy Huggett
Department of Archaeology
University of Glasgow
Scotland
J.Huggett@archaeology.arts.gla.ac.uk

Gary Lock
Institute of Archaeology
University of Oxford
England
gary.lock@arch.ox.ac.uk

Rog Palmer
Air Photo Services
Cambridge
England
rog.palmer@dial.pipex.com

Ben Robinson
Peterborough Museum and Art Gallery
Peterborough
England
ben.robinson@peterborough.gov.uk

André Tschan
Institute of Archaeology
University of Oxford
England
andre.tschan@arch.ox.ac.uk

Acknowledgements

This collection of papers is loosely based on a session organised by the editors at the Fourth World Archaeological Congress held in Cape Town, South Africa in January, 1999. Jeremy Huggett was partly responsible for the initial idea and we are in his debt for without that discussion in Glasgow this would not have materialised. We would also like to thank the participants in the WAC session, and others who have responded to subsequent appeals for papers. Gary Lock would like to thank the University of Oxford for financial support to attend WAC4. Many thanks to André Tschan for providing the cover picture.

Gary Lock and Kayt Brown
Oxford, January, 2000

Acknowledgements

Introduction

Writing this immediately after the Millennial celebrations it would be difficult not to enter into the prevailing mood of looking both backwards and forwards at the same time. That is our only concession to media hype, however, as we do not intend offering our 'Top 10' of best computer applications in archaeology or to indulge in, almost certainly doomed, predictions of what we will be doing in five, ten or fifteen years time. Rather, this collection of papers offers a reflective, critical view of computer usage in archaeology and how it has impacted on the discipline.

More specifically we are interested in exploring the impact of computers on the theory and practice of archaeological enquiry. By practice we mean those daily practices which together create the discipline of archaeology individual to each of us. By theory we mean the framework of abstract principles, whether implicit or explicit, within which we perform practice, establish meaning and produce archaeological information. Neither of these definitions is straightforward or neat and tidy. Indeed, archaeology exists as an articulated set of sub-disciplines, a range of situations each with its own sphere of operation, its own set of real-world entities, conceptual models and procedures for discourse. Archaeologists working in a commercial field Unit, a university, a museum or a National Monuments Record will operate within different universes of theory and practice while at the same time be united in purpose by strands of commonality. It is these commonalities which create the identity of archaeology as a discipline, and our self-identities as archaeologists, while at the same time define the differences which make it such a rich and diverse subject.

Part of that diversity is the variation in concepts of theory and codes of practice within the sub-disciplines and at the higher level, so that any discussion of these issues becomes reductionist and generalising. People working within a Unit, for example, will have individual theoretical frameworks and ways of interpreting and carrying out working practices although it may be possible to generalise the practices of that Unit and, at a higher level, the practices of all Units. Theory and practice within individuals and at all levels of organisation also change through time. Twenty years ago, for example, developer-funded commercial archaeology was rare although it is now the driving force behind most excavation in many countries having a significant impact on excavation theory and practice (Chadwick, 1998).

One of the commonalities which permeates this diversity is the increasing use of computers. It must be remembered that archaeology exists within, and draws experience from, a wider social sphere and that technological osmosis is fundamental to disciplinary change. The very term 'computer' is now inadequate to describe the technologies necessary to deal with the recent, and increasing, Information Revolution. Some claim that Information is now so fundamental to social and economic structure that it defines the Age we live in (Webster, 1995). In this rapidly changing and increasingly technocratic world, Information

Technology (IT) has given way to ICT to emphasise the importance and integration of Communication. This has resulted in the emergence of the Network Society (Castells, 1996) which has implications for many aspects of daily life not least the theory and practice of archaeology. It is against this background and these wider areas of concern that we offer this collection of papers.

Of course, this book is part of a long tradition of publication concerned with computer applications in archaeology and it would be remiss of us not to try to explain its place within that literature. The obvious first reference point must be the annual meetings of CAA (Computer Applications and Quantitative Methods in Archaeology) which started small in 1973 and has now grown into a successful international conference. CAA's annual proceedings are a massive and important archive which reflects the rapid change within this sub-discipline and offers a wealth of detail about specific applications. As reflected in Scollar's 25th Anniversary review of papers at CAA (Scollar, 1999), however, the vast majority are technologically positivist, concerned primarily with description and rarely address the deeper questions attempted here. Other than CAA we must mention three collections of papers which are relevant to the development of many arguments presented in this volume. Although published a long time ago in computing chronology, the papers in Cooper and Richards (1985) still make interesting reading and raise many issues which retain currency today (as the volume's title suggests). A more pragmatic approach is taken by Ross, Moffett and Henderson (1991), who describe application areas within conceptual frameworks to provide 'usable' introductions to topics such as databases, statistics and graphics.

The most influential collection, however, is probably Reilly and Rahtz (1992), which, as a product of the World Archaeological Congress, reflects the global concerns of that body. It is interesting, and slightly ironic, that some of the most difficult issues are identified in the *Foreword* to that volume by Peter Ucko, who on his own admission doesn't operate at the cutting-edge of IT. It probably takes someone removed from the positivist hype that often surrounds gatherings of the techno-motivated (like any other self-interest group), to establish critical awareness and cut through to the underlying importance of what is going-on. Ucko suggests that the spread of these technologies will cause 'major social upheaval' within archaeology which may develop for the better or worse, and that research within computer applications will result in 'fundamental questioning of the principles and concepts which have long underpinned traditional archaeological enquiry and interpretation' (Ucko, 1992, viii). While we are not suggesting that this collection of papers will resolve these issues, the intention is to engage with them and explore interesting avenues of thought.

In many ways the first offering here, by Jeremy Huggett, acts as an Introduction to the volume. Jeremy expands on existing archaeological attitudes to computers and discusses the global technological paradigm and technological determinism in relation to archaeology. He questions some assumptions concerned with the adoption and increasing use of computers especially the so-called 'productivity paradox' – considering the massive investment in IT within most archaeological institutions, and the fact that most of us now spend a large part of our working day staring at a screen, are the claimed increases in efficiency and productivity real?

The second paper sees Jayne Gidlow exploring the apparent schism between the disciplinary aspects generally referred to as 'theoretical archaeology' and 'computer applications'.

Jayne relates the lack of interaction to a view of disciplinary change based on the paradigm shift and a misunderstanding of the potential of computers in the role of interpretation. She goes on to suggest more useful possible relationships between the two sub-disciplines.

The next six papers offer views on the impact of IT within particular specialisms, each embedded within the experience of an appropriate practising specialist. Hannah Forsyth reflects on the impact of computers on that most fundamental of archaeological activities, classification. She explores the notion that classification still operates through an analogy with science and suggests an alternative based on archaeology as text as a way of uniting classification and post— (modern, processual) theory.

Virtual Reality (VR) is certainly a technology that suffers from positivist hype and the paper by Glyn Goodrick and Mark Gillings should become seminal in establishing an understanding of what VR is and how it can be used in archaeology. They debunk popular misconceptions by exploring what reality means (virtual or not) and then assess the potential of VR to articulate with recent theoretical approaches to the past, particularly landscapes.

Francis Grew explores the relationship between field archaeology and museums through their common interest in the production and curation (respectively) of site archives. Based on his experience at the Museum of London he outlines the idea of 'Data Warehousing' and its implications for the working practices of both excavators and museum curators.

Excavation methodologies are long established and have been relatively slow to respond to computerisation. Anthony Beck critiques traditional methods and describes a new 'radical approach' being tried by Framework Archaeology. The novelty lies in the claimed 'democratisation of knowledge' that occurs within the excavation team through the reflexive Information System used for recording. Traditional working practices have been altered to benefit from the articulation of different software tools enabling 'ground-up' interpretation and information feedback.

Ben Robinson's topic is Sites and Monuments Records. His paper is illuminating for showing how the history of the *ad hoc* development of SMRs has created the challenges for today's IT in terms of standards and networking. It illustrates the tension within our endeavours between the legacy of the past, the constraints of the present and the potential of the future. A theme continued by Rog Palmer within the context of aerial survey and the interpretation of aerial photographs. Additionally, though, Rog emphasises the importance of human intuition, skill and decision making and questions whether and how these can be incorporated into the activities of mapping and analysis.

Finally, André Tschan and Patrick Daly ask whether there is such a thing as 'computer archaeology' and a 'computer archaeologist'. If IT is really well embedded within the working practices of archaeology this may seem a facile question to ask, although André and Patrick's analysis of the current disciplinary position suggests otherwise. They identify the need for an 'Information Systems approach' within a 'strategic framework' and offer models for both academic and public/private archaeology to achieve this.

Together we hope these nine papers raise important and interesting issues relating to the theory and practice of archaeological computing. As suggested above, archaeological computing will continue to develop through technological osmosis from the wider world of ICT although we owe it to the discipline and to ourselves to apply the technology through a filter of critical awareness.

Gary Lock and Kayt Brown

References

Castells, M. 1996. *The Information Age: Economy, Society and Culture. Volume 1. The Rise of the Network Society.* Oxford: Blackwell.

Chadwick, A. 1998. Archaeology at the edge of chaos: further towards reflexive excavation methodologies. *Assemblage*, 3, available online at http://www.shef.ac.uk/~assem/3/3chad.htm [accessed 7.1.00]

Cooper, M. and Richards, J. (eds) 1985. *Current Issues in Archaeological Computing.* Oxford: BAR S271.

Reilly, P. and Rahtz, S. (eds) 1992. *Archaeology and the Information Age: a global perspective.* London: Routledge.

Ross, S., Moffett, J. and Henderson, J. (eds) 1991. *Computing for Archaeologists.* Oxford: Oxford University Committee for Archaeology Monograph 18.

Scollar, I. 1999. 25 years of Computer Applications in Archaeology, in Dingwall, L., Exon, S., Gaffney, V., Laflin, S. and van Leusen, M. (eds) *Archaeology in the Age of the Internet. CAA97. Computer Applications and Quantitative Methods in Archaeology, Proceedings of the 25th Anniversary Conference, University of Birmingham, April 1997.* Oxford: BAR International Series 750, pp.5–10.

Ucko, P. 1992. Foreword, in Reilly, P and Rahtz, S. (eds), pp. vii–xi.

Webster, F. 1995. *Theories of the Information Society.* London: Routledge.

CHAPTER 1

Computers and Archaeological Culture Change

Jeremy Huggett

Archaeological Attitudes to Computers

The use of Information Technology is widespread throughout the archaeology of the 1990s to the extent that it is barely considered worthy of comment (unless someone is not using a computer). Undergraduate students of archaeology are increasingly computer-literate and expect to use IT in their work. The public face of archaeology represented through television programmes is often one of scientists labouring with instruments and data loggers producing plots and re-constructions with impressive sleight of hand. There is virtually no corner of archaeology that has not been touched in some way by IT. The management and protection of archaeological sites, the initial prospection and discovery of sites, the excavation, processing, analysis and interpretation of sites, and the theoretical frameworks within which all these activities take place have all been affected to some extent by the use of IT. The all-pervasive nature of IT is underlined by the fact that it is about more than just computers – Information Technology includes any technological device for transmitting, communicating, storing, transforming, and presenting information. However, computers are becoming ubiquitous within IT, and the recent history and present-day reality of IT is one of the convergence of the electronics, telecommunications and computing industries. Whether it is digital telephones, digital cameras, scanners, 2-D and 3-D digitisers, digital callipers, electronic distance meters, data loggers, or any of a whole host of other forms of increasingly 'smart' instrumentation, the computer is integral and fundamental.

For something that is so increasingly important to archaeology, it is curious that there has been so little discussion about why computers are used, in what contexts, and with what effect. This is probably to a large extent due to a not unreasonable supposition that since IT is playing an increasingly large role in everyday life, it would be more surprising if archaeologists were *not* making use of them. According to this argument the motivations behind computer usage in archaeology are self-evident. However, it also implicitly reveals a sense of powerlessness – it is as if we have no alternative but to adopt the new technology. What discussions there are about the use of computers in archaeology almost exclusively concentrate on computer-based techniques and their application in a wide range of areas and projects. Books on computers in archaeology are sometimes manuals or synthetic descriptions (rare examples include Richards and Ryan 1985, Ross, Moffett and Henderson 1991) or are more commonly edited collections of papers describing applications and techniques (for example, Martlew 1984, Cooper and Richards 1985, Reilly and Rahtz 1992, Lock and Stančič 1995). With the significant exception of contributions in Cooper and Richards (1985), computers, and the techniques and technologies surrounding them, are essentially taken for granted. Their benefits are invariably good, their negative effects (if they exist at all) are inevitably minor.

This focus on the tools and techniques in the archaeological texts represents the adoption of a technocratic approach, one which progresses little beyond looking at whether or not the techniques and technologies applied worked in the situation concerned, and whether the results were interesting from an archaeological perspective. In the process, assessments of the state of computer applications in archaeology tend to be shallow descriptive affairs, falling far short of equivalent assessments of, say, the introduction of new metalworking technology to some past society. Beyond the immediate realms of archaeology, approaches to the introduction and use of new technologies are infinitely richer and more complex in areas such as the history of science, sociology, philosophy, ethics, and business studies. The kinds of questions asked are more wide-ranging than those characterised above and yet have resonance in an archaeological context. For instance, who initiates, develops and applies the technology? What opportunities and barriers exist to access the technology? To what end and with what consequences is the technology applied? (after Webster 1995, 76). Such questions go far beyond those concerned primarily with the application of a tool and techniques and start to raise a series of political, social, and economic issues which archaeologists should feel comfortable with and yet which, strangely, have not been used to address the role of IT in archaeology. Ross, for example, asks

"Do computers change how archaeologists work? And, if, so, what do these new practices look like, in what areas have results been demonstrated, and how was that work done?" (1997, 162)

yet the answers are not forthcoming in an otherwise straightforward review of techniques and methodology. Similar reviews focus exclusively on application areas and discuss the various typologies of computer methodologies (for example, Scollar 1999, Kamermans and Fennema 1996, Moffett 1991). The emphasis is again placed on the development of tools, techniques, and methodologies, yet this is only a limited aspect of computer use.

Part of the problem may be that there are several attitudes to IT, often apparently contradictory and mutually exclusive. On one hand, there is the idea of the computer as no more than a tool, likened to an archaeological trowel or wheelbarrow, and yet unlike the latter, the computer is privileged with its own international annual conferences. The computer is seen as an instrument of revolution and change, but can also be a means of conservatism and control. The computer is neutral, but is also value-laden. It facilitates communication, yet can result in greater isolation. Which is right? Can it be all of these and more? In many respects, it is this very difficulty in tying down what the role of computers actually might be that causes the often ambiguous attitudes towards them. Much depends on experience and perception, and since analyses of computers in archaeology rarely progress beyond methodologies and application areas, it is hardly surprising that though the range of attitudes to computers can run the full gamut of emotions, more often than not reports about their application are positive, enthusiastic, even evangelical. No one likes to admit to failure. Yet everyone who has worked with computers knows that behind the formal, measured prose there was in all likelihood many hours of confusion, puzzlement, despair, anger, frustration, chaos, and perhaps disaster before the ultimate (inevitable) triumph of logic and order.

However, the real motivations behind the application of computers to archaeological situations are often difficult to find. It often seems as if the reasons for their use are self-evident and hence not worthy of mention, let alone discussion. The fact that a computer is used and results are achieved is justification in itself, and needs no further comment. The question is not so much *should* a computer be used, but *how* should it be used. The typical practical reasons for using computers – they help in data handling and data processing, for example – disguise more fundamental and implicit reasons which by their very universal nature may seem relatively insignificant within an archaeological context. Issues of efficient archaeological data handling naturally seem more important than the larger question of efficiency *per se*, for instance. Important questions are perceived to relate to the availability of software tools and their appropriateness or otherwise for the archaeological task, not to the underlying fundamental questions about the technology itself. While archaeology is hardly unique in this, it is an approach which leads to a lack of appreciation of the limitations of computers (a point made by Moffett 1989, 13, for instance), and, more importantly, by disguising the true, unspoken and implicit reasons and justifications for using computers, potentially leads to a misunderstanding and mis-application of computer technology. The application-driven approach may also lie behind the general lack of more sceptical examinations of computer applications, yet when questions such as 'should we use computers?' are asked, they are all too often perceived of as unimportant and their answers self-evident. They are not.

The reason such questions are important is because of the very ubiquity of the technology referred to above. It is increasingly part of, embedded in, and allied with much of what archaeologists do and the tools with which archaeology is done, and at the same time, it is widely used beyond archaeology as a defining factor in the new 'information age'. In such circumstances, we need to look beyond the techniques used to the effects of the technology itself. However, one problem is that such questions may not be seen to be the appropriate concern of archaeologists. This makes for an interesting parallel between archaeological computing and archaeological management – for example, Carman *et al* (1995, 9) suggest that discussions of management in the archaeological literature are limited, partly because it is thought to be about issues such as productivity and cost-effectiveness which are not considered relevant to archaeology. Yet the fact that the application of computers within archaeological organisations may have far-reaching implications (for example, Cooper and Dinn 1995, Hinge 1996) suggests that they should not be ignored in this way.

The New Technological Paradigm

Talk of a new age – a post-industrial or informational society – which, it is argued, will bring about major culture change in terms of values, attitudes, beliefs and methodologies, is predicated on a new technological paradigm based on information technology. According to Forester there are two reasons for this: first, it creates a new 'best practice' or set of ground rules, rapidly becoming the new 'common sense' and secondly, it calls for dramatic changes in organisational structures (1989, 1). Attewell and Rule comment that

"It is taken as self-evident that organisations computerise in order to pursue long-standing goals of efficiency and cost effectiveness. Rationalisation or the relentless effort to adopt the most efficient means to established ends, is seen as the hallmark of modern organisations. Computerisation is considered as the most eminently rational of present-day technological trends" (1994, 286).

Discussion of such ground rules and changes in organisational structures predicated on this new paradigm are extremely rare within the archaeological context (although see Cooper 1985, for instance).

A major characteristic of this supposedly rational trend is the speed with which it changes – the ground rules are effectively set in quicksand. It is commonly felt that technology is running ahead of society and that there is a constant need to catch up, seen in the almost instant obsolescence of IT equipment purchased today. Kallman and Grillo talk of the 'Order of Magnitude Effect', which suggests that for each ten-fold increase in speed our perception of what is going on changes dramatically –

"we can barely manage to learn the new technologies before they change, and as a result, we often pay scant attention to the consequences of their use" (Kallman and Grillo 1993, 25).

This has resonance with the way in which manufacturers use planned obsolescence to provide the illusion of progress. Only rarely is this rush to the future questioned, rarely is it pointed out that a 20% increase in processor speed does not result in a 20% increase in work completed, or that the feature-rich, power-hungry software of today is more often than not used to perform identical tasks to the leaner packages of five or even ten years ago.

Elements of this new rationality can be seen clearly in the blandishments of the computer and software manufacturers: Apple's emphasis on paradigm shift and revolution in their Ridley Scott directed '1984'-style advertisement for the Macintosh is a classic example. More recently, IBM's use of nuns, monks and anthropologists to advertise a range of laptop computers emphasises the use of the machine to bring everyone together and improve their lives immeasurably. Microsoft's advertisements seek to seduce us with images of access to a new world of limitless information through the use of their software. Whether it is hardware or software, the manufacturers promise it will change us for the better. The nature of that change has implications for archaeological users as much as anyone else.

Technological Determinism

Explaining Change

Clearly there is a general expectation that computers will bring change – whether it is improvements in the speed with which a task is accomplished, or the accomplishment of new tasks altogether. This emphasis on technological change as the cause of social change is a common form of determinism. Technology comes to identify an entire social world (Webster 1995, 10): for example, the Palaeolithic, Mesolithic, Neolithic, the Bronze and Iron Ages, all have their origins in the identification of technological change. This change is always perceived in one way or another as progress along an evolutionary social or economic trajectory, following a sequence of predictable development (for example, Heilbroner 1967).

Typical attitudes to new technology polarise into two categories: optimistic (pro-technology, liberal, progressive, positive) and pessimistic (anti-technology, reactionary, luddite, negative), for example, Rowe and Thompson (1996, 20–26). Nor are such attitudes new, or restricted to computers and information technology. An identical dichotomy in relation to technology existed at the time of the Enlightenment (Marx 1997, 13), when the new sciences were seen as a means of political liberation and social transformation while the counter-Enlightenment rejected the mechanistic ideas of Newton, Descartes, and others for the romanticism of Rousseau and Carlyle, for instance. Of course, characterising attitudes to technology in terms of pro- and anti-technology is clearly too simplistic, but the search for the middle-ground is not as straightforward as it might at first seem. Some would argue that technology is neither good nor bad, but neutral or benign. Here technology is seen as not worthy of particular notice because the effects on social or economic change are relatively small and well-understood (for example, Mesthene 1997, 66–7). Alternatively, Florman argues for the "tragic view" of technology, which recognises paradox and ambiguity but allies itself with those who "aware of the dangers and without foolish illusions about what can be accomplished, still want to move on, actively seeking to realise our constantly changing visions of a more satisfactory society" (Florman 1997). A variation on this theme is Kranzberg's First Law: "technology is neither good nor bad, nor is it neutral" (Kranzberg 1989, 30) which above all emphasises the unpredictability of technology. However, in many respects this so-called middle ground is populated by people of one or other persuasion – for instance, Mesthene (1997) clearly opts for a pro-technology stance, and Florman (1997) adopts what is still essentially a pro-technology standpoint. Rowe and Thompson (1996, 23) prefer to see attitudes to technology as ranging across a continuum, recognising that most commentators are both optimistic and pessimistic at different times and in relation to different aspects. They also identify a relationship between the level of analysis and the attitudes adopted: as the level of analysis reduces from the global to the particular, the level of optimism tends to rise and greater emphasis is placed on choice (Rowe and Thompson 1996, 26).

Essentially it seems to be very difficult to break out of a pro-technology, progress-driven mould, even whilst trying to adopt a more neutral, objective perspective towards computers and computing. To a considerable extent, this is due to the prevalence and largely tacit acceptance of a market-driven approach, in which efficiency, control, speed and cost-effectiveness are the primary considerations that have shaped attitudes towards computerisation. As Kling and Iacono argue, this means that most studies of computerisation ignore the ways in which people develop beliefs about what computing technologies are good for and how they should organise and use them (1990, 214). In particular, they claim that computerisation is socially charged through the activities of committed advocates and what they term 'computerisation movements' (Kling and Iacono 1990, 215; Iacono and Kling 1996, 88–90), more so than the adoption of other forms of office technology. These computerisation movements *"communicate key ideological beliefs about the links between computerisation and a preferred social order which help legitimise computerisation for many potential adopters. These ideologies also set adopters' expectations about what they should use computing for and how they should organise access to it" (Kling and Iacono 1990, 215).*

If this is indeed the case, then it is reasonable to draw two conclusions. First, if the adoption of computers is socially charged, then it becomes all the more important to understand the social and economic forces involved in order to fully appreciate the role and impact of the technology concerned and hence move beyond a technocratic approach. Secondly, if their argument is accepted it follows that we should expect the motivations and effects of the adoption and utilisation of computing technology to be disguised behind a welter of claims and counter-claims predicated upon the ideologies both of these computerisation movements (which may be archaeological, or imported from the wider world) and the producers of the hardware and software employed. It is necessary to see through and beyond these in order to examine the role and use of computers in archaeology.

The extent to which cultural change is driven by new technology is open to question, however. For example, some would argue that there is no such thing as technological determinism: "Technology does not determine society: it embodies it. But neither does society determine technological innovation: it uses it." (Castells 1996, note 2). Clearly other factors – political, social and economic – have a role to play in the explanation of change. For example, Hughes (1994) talks of 'technological momentum', a concept which falls somewhere between technological determinism and social constructivism while borrowing elements of both. However, 'non-technological' political, social and economic processes resulting in technological developments can equally be seen as a form of technological determinism (for example, Freeman 1987, 6). It is all too easy to intuitively conform to the popular experience of largely powerless consumers pulled along by the producers of Information Technology.

On the face of it, technologically deterministic explanations begin to look inevitable and unavoidable, but this need not be the case. While the demand-pull and technology-push forms of determinism in particular seem depressingly all-embracing, they make relatively little allowance for the political, social and economic dimensions – as Webster argues, technological determinism subordinates these dimensions to technology, whereas technology is in fact an integral part of them. For example, the motor car is more than a technological means of travel: it contains assumptions about family size, the value of personal ownership, the importance of status, attitudes to the environment, the role of public versus private transport, and so on (Webster 1995, 10). This leaves it open to examine the priorities and values expressed through the technology without necessarily employing arguments predicated on the technology itself, loosening the apparent stranglehold of technological determinism. However this can be taken too far: to treat technology as an independent variable by attempting to deconstruct these dimensions and extracting technology as a residual, non-social, neutral entity would itself lead to a form of technological determinism (Grint and Woolgar 1997, 14). It is not simply a question of recognising that the non-technical variables are important in understanding change, but equally, that technology is not a black box on which these other variables act. Indeed, as Scranton suggests, the study of technology consists of "an environment of serial indeterminacies" (1994, 149), where social, economic, political and technological factors play on a localised rather than global basis.

However, the expectation of change associated with information technology remains, and where there is such an expectation, technology and technological change are used in a circular fashion to predict change, describe change, and explain change, whether in archaeology or in society as a whole.

A Neutral or Value-Laden Technology?

Technological determinism can also be seen to appear on a smaller scale, in the form of the computer tools we use and their application to archaeological situations. To what extent are archaeological applications determined by the tools available, or the archaeological questions asked defined in terms of the tools applied? For example, most archaeological users of GIS seem to have research interests related to large-scale survey and landscape analyses rather than smaller scale within site analyses (Biswell *et al* 1995, 269). Is this coincidence, or is it related to the origins of the tools, or something else altogether? To what extent are perceptions of the data requirements for GIS behind their lack of use for intra-site studies (Huggett, forthcoming)? In much the same way, archaeological data are structured in relational databases, which enforce a particular view of the information contained within the tables.

There is a perception that computers are a malleable technology which fit into an environment rather than changing it (for example, Johnson 1994, 152). Chameleon-like, the computer takes on the role devised for it without changing the nature of that role. Malleable they may be, but the idea that they do not change the tasks they undertake is counter-intuitive, as is demonstrated by Hinge's analysis of the changing nature of work at the Museum of London (Hinge 1996), for example. Archaeologists are accustomed to accept that the data we work with are theory-laden (Reilly 1985) but often appear less concerned that the computers used to work with those data may themselves be value-laden. These values may well determine and shape certain applications – perhaps built into the software itself. The very nature of computers might favour certain values: for example, they could be seen as skewing analysis towards the quantitative – "if you can't measure it, it does not exist" (quoted in Johnson 1994, 161). Similarly, there is a certain inevitability about the types of applications that are generated by Geographical Information Systems. Wheatley (1996, 75) has observed that GIS-based archaeologies tend to focus on environments rich in economic or settlement evidence and avoid situations where it is scarce because of the ease with which GIS manipulate such data. In such circumstances, it is as well to remember Kranzberg's First Law: "technology is neither good nor bad, nor is it neutral" (Kranzberg 1989, 30). The tools may be content-free, in the sense that they can be applied within a whole host of different archaeological contexts, but they are not value-free.

Technological Utopianism

If many of the explanations of change are driven by the technology, many of the descriptions of change and predictions for future change are characterised by technological utopianism

(Kling 1996, Iacono and Kling 1996). Kling sees this as a style of writing that tends to be buoyant, expansive, breathless, enthusiastic, and polemical. It accentuates the positive and minimises conflict, emphasises benefits and trivialises concerns, and, as Kling argues, it side-steps difficult questions while creating a sense of excitement about the new (1996, 48). Inevitably this triggers anti-utopianism responses, "tragedies that serve as counterpoints to the technological utopians' inspiring romances" (Kling 1996, 51). In combination with computerisation movements, this becomes a highly potent force for legitimising the adoption of the new technologies.

Utopian analyses of information technology are perhaps less obvious in archaeological writing, but early papers introducing new computer movements such as artificial intelligence or GIS are sometimes utopian in character and result in correspondingly anti-utopian reactions (characteristic of some contributions to Cooper and Richards (1985), for example). Indeed, utopianism was recognised as a characteristic of the language of archaeological computing by Pryor (1986, 50) who distinguished between rosy optimism and reality in an early discussion of why archaeologists used computers. In fact, it seems more likely that archaeological writing about computers can be characterised not so much as utopian or anti-utopian, but as a form of 'social realism' (Kling 1996, 56), in which the emphasis is placed on empirical data about actual applications rather than deterministic logics. This reinforces the argument put forward above: that the emphasis of archaeological writing about computers is exclusively application-oriented and hence its assessments of computer usage are essentially flawed. Furthermore, the proposition that archaeologists write utopian analyses of computer use should not be rejected immediately – writing is socially charged, and Kling argues that utopian views of the world are an inevitable result of the need to justify positions, salaries, budgets, grants and the like. Whether or not archaeological writing about computers can be characterised as utopian, anti-utopian, or as social realism, the fact remains that archaeologists are not divorced from the wider world. Knowledge, opinions, and decisions will be based on the reports of business analysts, journalists, industry gurus, and the proponents of computer movements as well as on the experience of experts in the archaeological world.

Some Case Studies

To re-phrase Attewell and Rule (1994, 286), we can see that computerisation is an eminently rational trend in present-day archaeology, yet this very rationality is based, for good or ill, on essentially utopian and often deterministic views of the technology. Hence, when we investigate some of the justifications that might be put forward for computerisation, these are by their very nature optimistic in that they focus on perceived benefits. This applies whether they be productivity-related (efficiency, cost-effectiveness, etc.), or to solve specific issues (data handling, archiving, access, for example), or simply talk of the advantages to be gained from a specific application (development of bespoke software, the use of a particular tool or technology, for instance).

The Productivity Paradox

Most arguments for the adoption of computers and various software solutions rely in one way or another on the idea that the use of computers increases efficiency and productivity and hence (usually more peripheral) aspects such as job satisfaction. Can these assumptions be justified? One of the problems in approaching this within an archaeological context is that the motivations behind the adoption of the technology and its subsequent effects are rarely questioned. Some issues are more or less openly addressed (the augmentation of tasks leading to new opportunities, and benefits associated with information handling and creation, for instance), whereas others remain largely unspoken (efficiency, cost-effectiveness, and quality of work, for example). Why these latter justifications remain largely moot is unclear, but it seems likely to be associated with the sense of powerlessness amongst archaeologists and others in the face of the IT onslaught noted previously, and hence a reluctance to address the absence of proof (or at least, supporting empirical evidence) for the supposed benefits paraded by the various computerisation movements.

Actual data relating to productivity, where they exist, are rarely more than anecdotal. For example, the system developed for the Maxey excavation "led to substantial savings in time and effort, and its cost-effectiveness is assured" (Booth *et al* 1984, 87) and it was claimed that with computer data entry work that would have taken around three months took only days. A technological solution to digitising context plans led to a thirty to forty-fold increase in the number of plans an illustrator could process in a day (Templeton 1990). The automated artefact processing system developed by the All American Pipeline Project was claimed to be capable of measuring artefacts between 10 and 100 times faster than a human (Plog and Carlson 1989, 264).

Interestingly, there has been a good deal of concern outside archaeology that computers have not brought their much-vaunted claims to greater efficiency and productivity – hence the productivity paradox. For example, "we observe a downward trend of productivity growth starting roughly around the same time that the Information Technology Revolution took shape" (Castells 1996, 71). There are problems of measurement which affects the relia-bility of this picture, and much of the slowdown may be explained in part by the soaking up of productivity gains in manufacturing industry by the dramatic expansion of the service sector (for example, Castells 1996, 74; Landauer 1995, 73–77). One of the key issues to arise out of this debate is that introducing computers does not necessarily increase productivity, and that there are many social processes that reduce any potential gains (though these social processes may in themselves be desirable). For example, Attewell (1996) defines six such restricting social processes:

1. formalisation of communication (increase in typed communications at the expense of faster spoken communication);
2. quantity/quality trade-off (for example, improving the appearance of output rather than its substance);
3. expanding the volume of work ("computers may make information work easier to do, but they thereby increase the amount of such work to be done" (Attewell 1996, 232));

4. managerial control (the growth of Management Information Systems data and increasing levels of managerial employment. Computers may also move tasks 'up' an organisational hierarchy, such as word processing);
5. competition (information technology is used to increase the volume of business, but such expansion does not necessarily involve increased productivity as long as the growth is at competitors' expense);
6. demands for information (improvements in information availability lead to demands for more information placing greater burdens of information-work on organisations, the costs of which may not be passed on).

All of these features can be recognised in the modern archaeological world. Arguably, most of the developments in British archaeology in the face of competitive tendering and commercialisation could not have been accomplished without the use of Information Technology, but that does not mean that computers have increased productivity per archaeologist. The speed of artefact processing claimed by Plog and Carlson (1989) was not borne out in reality (Ackerly 1995), and given the level of investment and numbers of programmers required to maintain the system, it is doubtful whether it ever could have been as productive as was thought. The digitisation of context plans reproduced traditional on-site planning (Templeton 1990) and, in spite of the advantages in relation to the creation of structure and phase plans, it is doubtful that overall productivity was enhanced. In any event, even where productivity may be enhanced, it may be offset by increasing the overall workload. In areas such as CAD, the productivity gains are often negligible since much the same tasks are undertaken as were carried out prior to computerisation, and any enhancement of productivity is probably offset by the increased number of draft drawings, and time spent altering the infinite range of properties, colours, line thickness, hatch patterns, fonts and the like. In much the same way, written texts are worked and reworked with word processors, increasing the quality of appearance of the report, but not increasing the overall quantity of completed reports.

The nature of work may also change as a result of these activities. Task-shifting is a common characteristic in business, and may ultimately lead to job replacement. In archaeology, examples of task-shifting are starting to appear though not (yet) any clear examples of job replacement. For instance, Hinge identifies it as a significant aspect of change brought about by the introduction of a relational database system at the Museum of London (1996, 16–17). De-grading of previously skilled work is another characteristic which also has its parallels in archaeology – for example, the computer system used by the All American Pipeline Project was tedious and boring to use for trained archaeologists who reacted by developing sophisticated means of sabotaging the system (Plog and Carlson 1989, 263). Similarly, McVicar and Stoddart reported that the availability of on-site computer-generated stratigraphic sequences caused problems with the site supervisors who found it difficult to keep full control over the excavation when faced with stratigraphic inconsistencies revealed by the computers (1986, 226). A similar interpretation could be placed on the emphasis on user-friendly database interfaces which offer terminology control and hence inadvertently de-skill the data entry role.

The conclusion, then, is not so much that computers do not improve productivity, because in some circumstances they might, but that more often than not they have side-effects, some desirable, which may not have been predicted and which impact upon potential efficiency gains.

The Digital Data Mountain

For a number of years now, computers have been seen as a means of coping with the expanding quantities of data, particularly generated by excavations (for example, McVicar 1986). However, the shift to digital data processing led inexorably to larger quantities of data being collected in the first place, leading to a still greater data mountain (Moffet 1989). For a time, some sought to deal with this by using computer-based data compression methods (for example, Powlesland 1985, Huggett 1988). However, with the increasing power and capacity of personal computers, such concerns seemed to vanish. At the time, the concern was over the quantities of paper-based data which could be conveniently reduced in physical size through computerisation, but today the concern is increasingly to do with the preservation of the growing quantities of electronic data (for example, Condron *et al* 1999). Archaeological data archive projects have been set up both in the USA (Eiteljorg 1997) and in the UK (Richards 1997) to try to deal with issues of preservation and access. These are important and valuable programmes, but if we stand back and take a longer view then they may be indicative of a more worrying trend than simply the need to preserve digital data.

Metadata, data about data, is a concept that is increasingly appearing in archaeological parlance (Miller 1996, Wise and Miller 1997). Used to define the way data was originally described, it also enables its re-location by providing a high-level catalogue for resource discovery. But the term is significant: metadata means more data. The quantity of 'ordinary' data has grown to the extent that we now need still more data in order to understand and use the data we already have. This puts archaeological data on an exponential growth path – only half jokingly, people already refer to 'meta-metadata'. Archaeology thereby conforms to the First Law of Informational Entropy: information

"... multiplies in its raw form, and then goes through an interpretative process to create informational by-products, which in turn become more information, thus creating an exponential and ultimately infinite explosion of information" (Pearce 1997, 280).

Archaeology has always been data-rich, now, with computer mediation, the data are more immediate, arrive faster and in greater quantities than ever before. Access to these vast datasets is usually perceived as a positive benefit, but how are we to handle it? By creating more data? As humans we only have a limited capacity to handle information. Pushing those limits with technological support results in a reduced ability to recall and process what we do know, leading to information stress, information anxiety, data smog, and paralysis by analysis (Shenk 1997, Dertouzos 1997, 295–8). The desirability of increased access to information and its associated emphasis on Internet delivery only serves to exacerbate this situation. In many respects the post-processual emphasis on multi-vocality of the archaeological record (for example, Hodder 1997, 1999) may indeed be the only way to make sense of the data, albeit a conclusion arrived at from a practical rather than a theoretical perspective.

One thing we can be certain of, computer power will not restrict the exponential growth in information. Under Moore's Law computer power has continued to double every eighteen months for the last forty years and shows every sign of continuing to do so for the foreseeable future. In comparison, it has been estimated that knowledge doubles only every seventeen years and has done so since the time of Newton (Hamming 1997, 73). The solutions offered by technologists such as Dertouzos and Hamming involve the application of still more new technology in order to reduce the complexity, to summarise and simplify, but is this an appropriate archaeological solution? Responding to the growth in information by relying on corresponding technological solutions simply emphasises the powerlessness of the individual.

Great Expectations or Great Misconceptions

If it is the case that the application of computers gives rise to often unexpected side effects, it is also the case that they engender hopes of great improvements, revolutionary developments, liberating tasks, and hence raise expectations to higher levels than perhaps any other technology. This is not an especially archaeological characteristic, and largely conforms to the (over) optimistic claims of manufacturers. Even though, it often seems as if archaeologists throw away their critical faculties when faced with the promise of the new technology – we critically study the material culture of the past, but fail to apply those same analyses to modern technology. This may take many forms, ranging from the many detailed 'blue-sky' discussions of proposed software which for whatever reason are never developed, through overly optimistic descriptions of systems and software in which often large amounts of time and money have been invested, to associations between archaeological desiderata and software solutions that may turn out to be wholly inappropriate or misconceived.

In many respects, this is similar to the state identified by Grint and Woolgar as 'technological beguilement' (1997, 130), where it is the need to be seen to use the technology which seems to become all-important. To what extent therefore is archaeology becoming a 'technopoly'?

"Technopoly is a state of culture. It is a state of mind. It consists in the deification of technology, which means that the culture seeks its authorisation in technology, finds its satisfaction in technology, and takes its orders from technology" (Postman 1997, 25).

The technological solution is seen to be the rational one; to adopt a specifically non-technological approach can be seen as irrational and deliberately perverse. Hence though archaeologists and others

"... may believe they are acting rationally in adopting new technologies, their decisions actually reflect a pervasive mystique that what can be developed, must be developed." (Attewell and Rule 1994, 287).

Determinism therefore re-appears in the form of the computer-driven application which puts technological solutions before archaeological questions – a common criticism of the early stages of computer archaeology in which it was often felt that tools and techniques were in search of an application. This is one of the criticisms made of the use of computers in the All American Pipeline Project, a rare example in which the computer system developed for an archaeological project was openly discussed (Plog and Carlson 1989) and subsequently critiqued (Ackerly 1995). Allied to this technologically driven approach was the unthinking recording of data – Ackerly points to the 1350 gigabytes of data collected but comments that the usefulness of that data was never considered (1995, 600). This was a project that pushed the limits of technology yet which ultimately fell prey to the very technology which it depended upon. With the benefit of hindsight, Ackerly lists a catalogue of failures but includes specifically: the failure to anticipate the speed of technological evolution, the failure to appreciate the future necessity of constantly upgrading hardware simply to keep the data available, the failure to anticipate the need (and the expense) of the maintenance of custom software to the extent that the database can now no longer be retrieved (Ackerly 1995, 600–1). Nor does this even begin to deal with the technical problems associated with the recording and analysis of the data themselves. This very public airing of problems rings true across many projects – the same or similar problems are experienced albeit to differing degrees and some will have similarly resulted in ultimate failure, but in most cases the evidence for this is anecdotal. In a utopian environment, reports of failure are generally discouraged, or else causes other than those associated with the technology are sought (which usually means human failure).

If determinism is apparent in the applications of computer technology in archaeological projects, so too is utopianism. This often takes the form of overly optimistic or unrealistic claims being made about the relationship between computers and archaeological ends. For example it is curious that, in a series of statements about excavation methodologies in which computers are used to derive the reflexivity required about archaeological assumptions, the same reflexivity is not applied to the technology being adopted (Hodder 1997, 1999). Hodder argues that excavation methodology needs to be relational (to understand context and inter-dependencies in the data), inter-active (enabling the data to be questioned from different perspectives) and multi-vocal (allowing different people to participate in the discourse) (Hodder 1997, 694) and underpinning each of these aspects is computer technology. There is a strong impression that since information technology is perceived to offer relational computer databases, inter-activity, and multi-vocality, it therefore provides a series of apparently natural technological solutions to the problems posed, but the implications or appropriateness of these technologies are never questioned. For example, there are the apparent contradictions between the degree of flexibility and change desired on the one hand, and the use of a more or less standard relational database which performs standard relational database tasks on the other. Hodder talks of the database retaining multiple hypotheses in parallel so that analysis and interpretation can proceed in different ways according to different definitions, but at the same time talks of the need for codification and 'fixity' of the data (Hodder 1999, 120–121). The solution offered – "to embed the database within other information which contextualises its own production" – would seem to refer to a form of metadata held outwith the database which itself will be subject to contextualisation, simply emphasising the inherent contradiction. Similarly, inter-activity and multi-vocality are realised through the use of hypermedia (Hodder 1999, 125) without addressing any of the problems associated with the use of the technology – for example, the deluge of information presented to readers, the ease with which readers become lost and disoriented, and the limitations of the hypertext model. To some extent, this is behind Hassan's limited critique of the information technology used by Hodder (Hassan 1997). However, it is not just that hypertext and the Web constitute "an overload of unstructured information that eventually paralyses decision-making and interpretation" (Hassan 1997, 1024) – the technique itself does not do what is claimed for it. Structure and control over the text is still retained, albeit in a looser fashion than is traditionally the case, and the author still defines the kinds of pathways available to the reader (for example, Murray 1995, 139–40). The technology does not provide the support for the level of inter-activity and multi-vocality that Hodder seeks. Ultimately the danger is that this may become perceived as the failure of the technology, rather than a failure to properly specify the technology in the first place because of inflated expectations.

Technological determinism and utopianism are clearly characteristics of archaeological applications of information technology. As long as this remains the case, archaeologists will remain in thrall to the technology, and the technology will be blamed for shortcomings which may be archaeological rather than technological. It also has implications for the archaeological computing fraternity, caught up in any backlash.

The Road Ahead

The title of this concluding section deliberately recalls that of Bill Gates' utopian view of the future of information technology (Gates 1996) as a reminder that it is all to easy to fall into adopting a relentlessly utopian or alarmingly anti-utopian perspective when looking to the future. The problem is the very universality of the computer, which makes it a difficult technology to tie down – a fact that became all the more apparent with the so-called Millennium Bug and its potential impact on all kinds of technologies that seem on the face of it to have little to do with computers. This very pervasiveness leads inexorably to talk of such machines having a revolutionary impact on the world around us. Technological determinism and utopianism colour analyses and inhibit efforts to examine the world as it really is rather than as it is perceived to be. Moreover, this determinism and utopianism encourages the presumption that the effects of computer use are self-evident and necessarily beneficial.

A key aspect is summarised by the corollary to Kranzberg's First Law (defined above): "the same technology can have quite different results when introduced into a different cultural setting" (Kranzberg 1989, 30). This emphasises that just because computers or a software package is seen to have a particular effect in, say business management or on a factory production line, it may have quite different, and unpredictable, effects in an archaeological context. Not only that, but the results may be quite different for different contexts within archaeology as well. It is the unpredictability of Information Technology that is at the same time its strength and its failing. It is important to remember, however, that information technologies of the past did not somehow have their function coded into them: their eventual use arose out of successive interpretations and negotiations, not determinations (Grint and Woolgar 1997, 21). There is every reason to think that the computers of today are no different in this respect.

Strange as it may seem, we are still in the early stages of computerisation. It is rare for any innovation in information handling to take less than twenty-five years to become established – for instance, the telephone was demonstrated in 1876 but was not used routinely until the 1910s; typewriting was introduced in 1871 but not used commonly in business until 1910; reproduction of documents was invented in 1780 but routine copying of documents was only undertaken in the 1860s (King 1996, 250). Equally, the recent past of information technologies emphasises their unpredictability: the radio was originally intended to replace the telephone, the telephone was envisioned as a means of piping music to people in remote locations, the original record players could also record and these recordings were predicted to replace the letter, the magnetic tape cassette was invented for dictation machines but used for music recordings, and the television was originally intended as a means of two-way visual communication (Cringely 1996, 45). This suggests that there is still plenty of opportunity to understand and shape the impact of computers within the archaeological community – the die is not yet cast. However, archaeologists need to take account of the problems associated with technological determinism and technological utopianism, as well as the host of political, economic and social issues surrounding the introduction and use of computers within archaeology. This requires an understanding of the technologies which goes beyond assessments and descriptions of the tools and techniques applied. While Hodder is surely right to claim that computers have the power to transform our lives, unless archaeologists take control of the technology, understand it and mould it, it will indeed retain its power "to homogenise, to limit debate and diversity, to create a true 'end of history'" (Hodder 1998, 214).

Bibliography

Ackerly, N., 1995. '"This does not compute": the All American Pipeline Project revisited', *Antiquity* 69, pp. 596–601.

Attewell. P., 1996. 'Information Technology and the productivity challenge', in R. Kling (ed.) *Computerisation and Controversy: value conflicts and social choices* (Academic Press, New York, 2nd edn), pp. 227–238.

Attewell, P. & Rule, J., 1994. 'Computing and organisations: what we know and what we don't know', in C. Huff and T. Finholt (eds) *Social Issues in Computing: putting computing in its place*, London: McGraw-Hill, pp. 276–294.

Biswell, S., Cropper, L., Evans, J., Gaffney, V. & Leach, P., 1995. 'GIS and excavation: a cautionary tale from Shepton Mallett, Somerset, England' in G. Lock & Z. Stancic (eds) *Archaeology and Geographical Information Systems: a European perspective*, London: Taylor and Francis, pp 269–285.

Booth, B., Brough, R. & Pryor, F., 1984. 'The flexible storage of site data: a microcomputer application', *Journal of Archaeological Science* 11, pp. 81–89.

Carman, J., Cooper, M., Firth, D. & Wheatley, D., 1995. 'Introduction: Archaeological Management' in M. Cooper, A. Firth, J. Carman & D. Wheatley (eds) *Managing Archaeology*, London: Routledge, pp. 1–15.

Castells, M., 1996. *The Information Age: Economy, Society and Culture. Volume 1: The Rise of the Network Society* Oxford: Basil Blackwell.

Condron, F, Richards, J., Robinson, D. & Wise, A., 1999. *Strategies for Digital Data. Findings and recommendations from Digital Data in Archaeology: A Survey of User Needs*, York: Archaeology Data Service.

Cooper, M., 1985. 'Computers in British archaeology: the need for a national strategy' in M. Cooper, & J. Richards (eds) *Current Issues in Archaeological Computing* Oxford: British Archaeological Reports S271, pp. 79–91.

Cooper, M., & Dinn, J., 1995. 'Computers and the evolution of archaeological organisations', in J. Wilcock & K. Lockyear (eds) *Computer Applications and Quantitative Methods in Archaeology 1993*, Oxford: British Archaeological Reports International Series 598, pp. 89–94.

Cooper, M., & Richards, J., (eds), 1985. *Current Issues in Archaeological Computing*, Oxford: British Archaeological Reports S271.

Cringely, R., 1996. *Accidental Empires*, London: Penguin.

Dertouzos, M., 1997. *What Will Be: how the new world of information will change our lives*, London: Piatkus.

Eiteljorg, H., 1997. 'Electronic archives' *Antiquity* 71, pp. 054–7.

Florman, S.C., 1997. 'Technology and the tragic view', in A.H. Teich (ed) *Technology and the Future*, New York: St Martin's, (7th edn.), pp. 93–103.

Freeman, C., 1987. 'The case for technological determinism', in R. Finnegan, G. Salaman & K. Thompson (eds) *Information Technology: social issues*, London: Hodder and Stoughton, pp. 5–18.

Forester, T., 1989. 'Making sense of IT', in T. Forester (ed) *Computers in the Human Context: Information Technology, productivity, and people,* Oxford: Basil Blackwell, pp. 1–15.

Gaffney, V. & van Leusen, P., 1995. 'Postscript: GIS, Environmental Determinism and Archaeology' in G. Lock & Z. Stančič (eds.) *Archaeology and Geographical Information Systems: a European perspective*, , London: Taylor and Francis, pp. 367–382.

Gates, W., 1996. *The Road Ahead*, London: Penguin.

Grint, K. & Woolgar, S., 1997. *The Machine at Work: technology, work and organisation*, Cambridge: Polity Press.

Hamming, R., 1997. 'How to think about trends', in P. Denning & R. Metcalfe (eds) *Beyond Calculation: the next fifty years of computing*, New York: Springer-Verlag, pp.65–74.

Hassan, F., 1997. 'Beyond the surface: comments on Hodder's "reflexive excavation methodology"' *Antiquity* 71, pp. 1020–1025.

Heilbroner, R., 1967. 'Do Machines make History?' *Technology and Culture* 8, pp. 335–345.

Hinge, P., 1996. 'The other computer interface' in H. Kamermans and K. Fennema (eds.) *Interfacing the Past: Computer Applications and Quantitative Methods in Archaeology CAA95*, Analecta Praehistorica Leidensia 28, University of Leiden, pp. 15–20.

Hodder, I., 1997. '"Always momentary, fluid and flexible": towards a reflexive excavation methodology' *Antiquity* 71, pp. 691–700.

Hodder, I., 1998. 'Whose rationality? A response to Fekri Hassan' *Antiquity* 72, pp. 213–217.

Hodder, I., 1999. *The Archaeological Process: an introduction*, Oxford: Blackwell.

Hughes, T., 1994. 'Technological momentum', in M.R. Smith & L. Marx (eds) *Does Technology Drive History? The dilemma of technological determinism*, London: MIT Press, pp. 101–113.

Huggett, J., 1988. 'Compacting Anglo-Saxon cemetery data' in C. Ruggles & S. Rahtz (eds.) *Computer and Quantitative Methods in Archaeology 1987,* Oxford: British Archaeological Reports International Series 393, pp. 269–274.

Huggett, J., (forthcoming) 'Looking at intra-site GIS', in K. Lockyear (ed) *Computer Applications and Quantitative Methods in Archaeology 1996.*

Iacono, S. & Kling, R., 1996. 'Computerisation movements and tales of technological utopianism', in R. Kling (ed) *Computerisation and Controversy: value conflicts and social choices*, New York: Academic Press, (2nd edn), pp.85–105.

Johnson, D., 1994. *Computer Ethics*, New Jersey: Prentice Hall.

Kallman, E.A. & Grillo, J.P., 1993. *Ethical Decision Making and Information Technology*, New York: McGraw-Hill.

Kamermans, H. & Fennema, K., 1996. 'Preface', in H. Kamermans & K. Fennema (eds) *Interfacing the Past: Computer Applications and Quantitative Methods in Archaeology CAA95*, Institute of Prehistory, University of Leiden, pp. xi–xiii.

King, J., 1996. 'Where are the payoffs from computerisation?', in R. Kling (ed) *Computerisation and Controversy: value conflicts and social choices*, New York: Academic Press, (2nd edn), pp. 239–260.

Kling, R., 1996. 'Hopes and horrors: technological utopianism and anti-utopianism in narratives of computerisation', in R. Kling (ed) *Computerisation and Controversy: value conflicts and social choices*, New York: Academic Press, (2nd edn), pp.40–58.

Kling, R. & Iacono, S., 1990. 'Computerisation movements', in M.D. Erman, M.B. Williams, & C. Gutierrez (eds) *Computers, Ethics, and Society* New York: OUP, pp. 213–236.

Kranzberg, M., 1989. 'The information age' in T. Forester (ed.) *Computers in the Human Context: information technology, productivity, and people*, Oxford: Basil Blackwell, , pp. 19–32.

Landauer, T., 1995. *The Trouble with Computers: usefulness, usability and productivity*, Cambridge Massachusetts: MIT Press.

Lock, G. & Stančič, Z., (eds) 1995. *Archaeology and Geographic Information Systems: a European perspective*, London: Taylor and Francis.

Martlew, R., (ed) 1984. *Information Systems in Archaeology*, Gloucester: Alan Sutton.

Marx, L., 1997. 'Does improved technology mean progress?', in A.H. Teich (ed.) *Technology and the Future*, New York: St Martin's, (7th edn.), pp. 3–14.

McVicar, J., 1986. 'Using microcomputers in archaeology: some comments and suggestions' *Computer Applications in Archaeology 1995*, London: Institute of Archaeology, pp. 102–108.

McVicar, J. & Stoddart, S., 1986. 'Computerising an archaeological excavation: the human factors', *Computer Applications in Archaeology 1986*, Birmingham: University of Birmingham, , pp. 225–227.

Mesthene, E.G., 1997. 'The role of technology in society', in A.H. Teich (ed.) *Technology and the Future*, New York: St Martin's, (7th edn.), pp. 65–76.

Miller, P., 1986. 'Metadata for the masses' *Ariadne* 5. (http://www.ukoln.ac.uk/ariadne/issue5/metadata-masses/).

Moffett, J., 1989. 'Computer perceptions in archaeology 2: the Eddie Effect', *Archaeological Computing Newsletter* 21, pp. 9–15.

Moffett, J., 1991. 'Computers in archaeology: approaches and applications past and present', in S. Ross, J. Moffett and J. Henderson (eds) *Computing for Archaeologists* Oxford: Oxford University Committee for Archaeology Monograph 18, Oxbow Books, pp. 13–39.

Murray, D., 1995. *Knowledge Machines: Language and Information in a Technological Society* London: Longman.

Pearce, C., 1997. *The Interactive Book: a guide to the interactive revolution* Indianapolis: Macmillan.

Plog, F. & Carlson, D., 1989. 'Computer applications for the All American Pipeline Project', *Antiquity* 63, pp. 258–267.

Postman, N., 1997. 'Technopoly: the broken defences' in A. Teich (ed.) *Technology and the Future* New York: St Martin's Press, (7th edn.), pp. 25–41.

Powlesland, D., 1985. 'Random access and data compression with reference to remote data collection: 1 and 1 = 1' in M. Cooper & J. Richards (eds) *Current Issues in Archaeological Computing*, Oxford: British Archaeological Reports International Series 271, pp.23–33.

Pryor, F. M. M., 1986. 'Post-excavation computing: some whys and wherefores', in J. D. Richards (ed) *Computer Usage in British Archaeology: report of the joint IFA/RCHME working party on computer usage*, Birmingham: Institute of Field Archaeology Occasional Paper 1, pp. 45–50.

Reilly, P., 1985. 'Computers in field archaeology: agents of change?' in M. Cooper & J. Richards (eds) *Current Issues in Archaeological Computing*, Oxford: British Archaeological Reports International Series 271, pp. 63–78.

Reilly, P. & Rahtz, S., (eds) 1992. *Archaeology and the Information Age: a global perspective*, London: Routledge.

Richards, J., 1997. 'Preservation and re-use of digital data: the role of the Archaeology Data Service', *Antiquity* 71, pp. 1057–9.

Richards, J. & Ryan, N., 1985. *Data Processing in Archaeology*, Cambridge: Cambridge University Press.

Ross, S., 1997. 'Archaeology', in C. Mullings, M. Deegan, S. Ross & S. Kenna (eds) *New Technologies for the Humanities*, London:Bowker Saur, pp. 161–181.

Ross, S., Moffett, J. & Henderson, J. (eds), 1991. *Computing for Archaeologists* Oxford: Oxford University Committee for Archaeology Monograph 18.

Rowe, C. & Thompson, J., 1996. *People and Chips: the human implications of Information Technology*, London: McGraw-Hill, (3rd edn.).

Scollar, I., 1999. 'Twenty-five years of computer applications in archaeology', in L. Dingwall, S. Exon, V. Gaffney, S. Laflin & M. van Leusen (eds) *Archaeology in the Age of the Internet: CAA97 Computer Applications and Quantitative Methods in Archaeology*, Oxford: British Archaeological Reports International Series 750, pp. 5–10.

Scranton, P., 1994. 'Determinism and indeterminacy in the history of technology', in M.R. Smith & L. Marx (eds) *Does Technology Drive History? The dilemma of technological determinis*, London: MIT Press, pp. 143–168.

Shenk, D., 1997. *Data Smog: surviving the information glut*, London: Abacus.

Templeton, L., 1990. 'Archaeological illustration and Computer-Aided Design – to boldly go where no illustrator has been able to afford to go before …', *Archaeological Computing Newsletter* 24, pp. 1–8.

Webster, F., 1995. *Theories of the Information Society*, London: Routledge.

Wheatley, D., 1993. 'Going over old ground. GIS, archaeological theory and the act of perception' in J. Andresen, T. Madsen & I. Schollar (eds) *Computing the Past: Computer Applications and Quantitative Methods in Archaeology 1992* Aarhus: Aarhus University Press, pp. 133–138.

Wheatley, D., 1996. 'The use of GIS to understand regional variation in earlier Neolithic Wessex', in H. Maschner (ed) *New Methods, Old Problems: Geographic Information Systems in modern archaeological research*, Centre for Archaeological Investigations, Southern Illinois University Occasional Paper 23, pp. 75–105.

Wise, A. & Miller, P., 1997. 'Why metadata matters in archaeology' *Internet Archaeology* 2 (http://intarch.ac.uk/issue2/wise_index.html).

CHAPTER 2

Archaeological computing and disciplinary theory

Jayne Gidlow

The 1998 CAA conference in Barcelona, was the 26th annual meeting of archaeologists concerned with computer applications in the discipline. The first of these meetings thus took place around the same time that British archaeologist David Clarke published *Archaeology: the loss of innocence*, in which he talked of these emerging technologies and their potential to 'extend' our archaeological 'senses' (1973:88). Clarke himself sensed a role for technologies in creating new visions of archaeological data. Just as the microscope offered visual material to work with, that literally did not previously exist, so quantitative analyses by computer suggested new relationships of significance between what would otherwise be discrete archaeological phenomena.

Clarke chose this phrase 'The loss of innocence', to describe a discipline that had become interested in the processes of inference it used, in a quest for more robust explanations of archaeological data. Through a positivist process of elimination and a hypothetical imagination it would be possible to explain all manner of culture change. What archaeology needed, Clarke argued, were not just the new technological visions, but better mechanisms for explaining the patterns they produced. Clarke was working at a time when North American archaeology appears to be going through radical changes in approach: an idea subsequently reinforced through histories of archaeology (e.g. Earl and Preucel 1987; Trigger 1989). In a similar way, 'The loss of innocence', is considered a turning point in British archaeology (Malone and Stoddart 1998) and is often used as a referent for understanding disciplinary change (e.g. Preucel 1991).

But if the fusion of theoretical perspectives and technological analyses was vital for 'the loss of innocence', why is it that today archaeological computing and archaeological theory tend to operate within their own publications, journals and conferences? Digital archaeologies informed by a contemporary theoretical agenda have been attempted – but often result in philosophical problems of subjectivity (e.g. Gaffney and van Leusen 1995) and quantifying the social (Wheatley 1993; Thomas 1993:25).

This paper sets out to understand the separation of these activities and why they are often regarded as, and practiced as, discrete sub-disciplines. First, I outline some of the points of contradiction in the relationship between archaeological computing and theory in the context of disciplinary practice today. Second, I highlight two major factors in this impasse:

the use of the paradigm shift to understand disciplinary change and the perceptions archaeologists often have as to how computer processors transform their data. I suggest instead that archaeological texts concerning the interpretative implications of the visualising technologies in general, can provide a more useful reference for understanding the kinds of relationship that should exist between archaeological theories and computer technologies.

Attempts to reconcile the current theory/technology schism are being made by archaeologists working with computers. Gillings and Goodrick (1996) for instance, emphasise the 'sensuous' and 'reflexive' nature of computer models of archaeological sites and their ease of generation. They utilise VRML to allow movement around an object or 'through' a landscape, as a means of representing those contextual and multiple interpretations so vital to contemporary theoretical concerns. Likewise, the use of viewshed analysis has contributed to archaeological landscape studies (e.g. Wheatley 1993; Gillings & Goodrick 1996). Using GIS algorithms to calculate which areas can and cannot be seen from significant places, has assisted the move to understanding that social, rather than ecological relations shape landscapes (e.g. Llobera 1996). However, the majority of archaeological publications concerning computer modelling, still seem reluctant to see computer generated archaeologies as an appropriate context for reflexive interpretations. A tendency to focus upon reality, naturalism and adherence to quantitative data presentation, gives the impression that these are the qualities a 'good' archaeological computer model should possess (e.g. Fletcher & Spicer 1992; Reilly 1991, 1992; Wood & Chapman 1992). Subsequently, improvements in computer modelling often take the form of more 'realistic textures' for materials and a data set which better represents the physical characteristics of an archaeological site in its present state. This preoccupation with creating a model that accurately reconstructs a site 'as it really was', occurs at the expense of a dialogue with the relevant theoretical issues and overlooks the historical changes the archaeology in question must possess. At times, the partial nature of the archaeological record can seem erased by the wholeness of a vector database and its mathematical calculation of surfaces. Miller and Richards sum up the roots of this unease. They say:

"people expect computers to be right and the past is therefore presented as a known, and knowable, reality" (1995:20).

They quite rightly point out the contradictions involved in representing interpretations of archaeological sites as static computer models: particularly criticising certain industries use of such models to induce 'awe and wonder' (1995:21) from an audience.

Llobera senses similar concerns for GIS with regard to the manipulation of archaeological data. He says,

"This question depends upon whether GIS is considered a ready-made set of tools delivered to archaeologists, or as a (more dynamic) way of representing, storing and handling spatial information. If the latter view is adopted, GIS becomes subservient to any theoretical approaches we might choose to employ" (Llobera 1996).

These two statements sum up well the contradictions in working with an explicit theoretical agenda and using analytical computer software.

Inclusive, contextual and multiple archaeological interpretations in the digital environment also appear to be an anathema to the theoreticians (e.g. Tilley 1989; Thomas 1993). The Cartesian world of the CAD or GIS program seems supported by an ahistorical, rigid computer architecture, by the zeros and ones of binary calculations. Thomas says,

"The means by which we characteristically represent place, the distribution map, the air photo, the satellite image, the Geographic Information System, are all distinctively specular. They all present a picture of past landscapes which the inhabitant would hardly recognise" *(1993:25).*

The situation is exacerbated by the fact that the majority of contemporary GIS-based analyses do seem to resurrect the questions addressed using middle-range theory (Lock 1995:16) and mathematical modelling. That these powerful tools provide lightening quick statistical analyses, nearest neighbour analyses and environmental distribution variables appears to have provided a good enough reason to support a processual method of working. Digital elevation models for example, often rely upon that Cartesian basis (and upon a set of uniformitarian variables), before the business of interpretation can begin. Overlaying a social coverage upon that set of variables does not engage successfully enough with contested and partial versions of the past. Ultimately, there is a rarity of computer generated pasts in the context of a post-processual archaeology, giving the impression that digital processes hinder, rather than aid interpretative reports and narratives.

So it is no surprise that some tend to regard computer technologies as the tools of a pseudo-scientism; of a particular kind of archaeological knowledge that now has a considerable history of critique (e.g. Tilley 1989:105; Shanks and Tilley 1992:56–7). But such gulfs between different aspects of disciplinary practice are not inevitable. Rather, there are specific reasons why technologies remain tightly bound to the theoretical perspectives of processual archaeology.

In the 1960s, processual archaeology, in its quest for understanding the philosophical basis of the discipline, explained the changes occurring in archaeology as a 'paradigm shift', after the philosopher of science Thomas Kuhn (1962). Developed within the natural sciences, paradigm shifts understand that scientific practice takes place through a series of revolutions, whereby fundamental changes in the 'metaphysical realm' (Meltzer 1979:654) of a discipline, overthrow the aims and concerns of a former tradition. The influence o f the scientific revolution framework is strong in histories of archaeology, in their emphases upon disciplinary theory, or thought (e.g. Meltzer 1979; Trigger 1989; Preucel 1991; Shanks and Tilley 1992). Many of these archaeological histories are preoccupied with when and where paradigm shifts take place and include little or no discussion of their actual appropriateness to the discipline. In a thoughtful article, Meltzer notes that archaeologists who were contemporaries, could not seem to decide whether they were at the beginning, middle or end of a paradigm shift (1979:650).

Arguments for rigorous scientific method within archaeology had already been made in the 1910s (Wylie 1993) and 1930s (Smith 1997). However, the adoption of the paradigm shift framework to explain disciplinary transformation in the 1960s, appears to be the epistemological moment whereby theory became a 'self-conscious' overlay (with the status of a sub-discipline) to the data.

The concept of the paradigm shift has also brought together many different areas of thought under the heading post-processual archaeology; an idea once again fuelled by historians. Within conventional histories, the behavioural paradigm of processual archaeology is deliberately replaced by the textual paradigm of post-processual archaeology (e.g. Hodder 1985, 1999). This change in philosophical referents is understood to be the signifier of an archaeological paradigm shift. But a closer look at this revolution shows post-processual approaches confined to Scandinavia and the UK, with links to critical traditions in the US – hardly representative of all practicing archaeologists. Furthermore, in Britain, the acknowledgement of the political and contested nature of archaeological practice by post-processual academics, has had little or no effect on work practices and working conditions in commercial field archaeology. It is thus highly questionable to suggest that a revolution has actually occurred.

The processual archaeologists' use of technologies to create new visions of archaeological data is of particular concern to the post-processual critique. Technological analyses seem to perpetuate an uncritical belief in the process of hypothesis testing: the fundamental theoretical basis of processual archaeology. If the theoretical position of processual archaeology required value-free explanation via its metaphysic, then the technological tools of these enquiries appear to have been selected because they seem to demonstrate just such properties. The use of computer software that searches for patterns in data not only upholds a theoretical status quo, but also acts to define particular characteristics for that technology in an archaeological context. Characteristics of reductionism, generalisation and inflexibility which are at odds with post-processual approaches. Computers thus appear processual by design; complicit in the creation of a past that is simply, in the words of cyber-feminist Sadie Plant: 'Read Only Memory' (1997:56).

Ultimately, the paradigm shift paradigm only allows the theoretical perspectives of the discipline a sense of history. The archaeological historians have omitted technologies and in doing so, technological analyses appear to be ahistorical, when really they have been tied to a particular set of theoretical concerns. Lock (1995) notes the increased flexibility written into computer softwares and the IT revolution in general, as something which archaeologists have utilised. Relational databases and hypertext certainly post-date 1960s processualism. But over all, the current theory/technology schism indicates that computer architectures and their workings have not been sufficiently re-conceptualised with regard to post-processual approaches. This lack of re-conceptualisation (attributable in part to the paradigm shift framework), means that contemporary theory appears to some to be abstract and inconsistent with the 'real', quantifiable archaeological data. As a result, many archaeologists working with GIS and computer visualisation, often regard contemporary theory as either important, but potentially problematic (e.g. Llobera 1996), or simply unhelpful and unworkable (e.g. Maschner 1996).

A useful place to start looking for ways to encourage the interaction of theory and computing is in the texts of archaeologists concerned with the impact of technologies upon archaeological interpretation, rather than those concerned with the history of archaeological thought.

Stuart Piggott for example stressed the importance of illustrations in communicating and influencing archaeological interpretations in the nineteenth century. Consider that access to artefacts until the formalisation of museum collections, was primarily through the dissemination of technical drawings. The comparison of illustrations of ethnographic specimens of stone tools, with those of the formed stones of natural history, he says, "led perceptive scholars to define (these formed stones) for what they were, prehistoric artefacts ..." (1978:27–28).

David Van Reybrouck in a recent *Antiquity* article (1998), illustrates how distorting properties of the Camera Lucida affected drawings made of the Neanderthal skull in the 1860s and 1870s. The tendency for the lens to contort the edges of an image, meant that the exaggerated areas of the skull were the brow-ridges, occipital bun and chin: features used to describe and distinguish the otherness of Homo Neanderthalensis. Consider how the dissemination of knowledge by illustration, of an ancient skull fits with the radical new theory of evolution at that time, and the contribution of the Camera Lucida to the fundamentals of human origins, is highly significant. Penny Spikins (1996) explained how long-held beliefs about the settlement patterns of upland Mesolithic sites in Britain were imbued with convincing authority through the use of GIS analyses. But in her particular study area, it was modern domestic sheep that had caused the peat erosion attributed to Mesolithic gatherer-hunters. The point illustrated by these texts is that technologies are not just spectators of information inherent in the data: rather they are in the business of transforming what the archaeological record actually consists of.

As a contrast to the neutral gaze of the machine, Donna Haraway has suggested that:

"The 'eyes' made available in modern technological sciences shatter any idea of passive vision; these prosthetic devices show us that all eyes, including our own organic ones, are actual perceptual systems, building in translations and specific ways of seeing" (Haraway 1991:190).

For Haraway, technologies are 'diffractors' (Haraway 1997) rather than projectors of realities. Archaeological data is not immune from these diffractive devices, as there are literally 'thousands' of archaeologies (Shiffer 1988 c.f. Hodder 1999:8) and uses of the past in the present. Therefore, the conscious and deliberate selection of computer technologies by archaeologists to materialise their data, becomes instrumental to archaeology's claims to interpret and represent the past[1].

In conclusion, archaeological computing and disciplinary theory currently take place within their own publications, journals and conferences, because the paradigm shift framework links the use of technological analysis to a particular kind of theory, which seeks to explain the processes of cultural change in searching for patterns in data. The use of computers to do this has fixed many archaeologists perceptions as to the capabilities of digital technologies. The rift is reinforced by the idea that theory is the only truly mutable aspect of archaeological enquiry, the only sub-discipline really capable of revolution.

The philosophical traditions associated with post-processual archaeology realise that the use of computers is not a value-free project, but post-processualists tend to regard their quantitative-based architecture as a hindrance to the production of multiple pasts (but see Hodder 1999). There is often little will to engage in an informed discussion regarding digital technologies and a compliance in its separation from theoretical concerns. Likewise, computing archaeologists have problems inputting the social into their applications. When reflexive positions are taken, they are arguably subject to more robust degrees of criticism than ostensibly 'theory free' digital projects. But the very authority and integrity that digital analysis is supposed to possess is not supported by the examples concerning analogue technologies as cited above. Analogue and digital technologies essentially require their own sense of history within archaeological practice.

In 1973, David Clarke could not predict the technological explosion of the 1990s or the subsequent debates that still discuss his work. "Archaeology the loss of innocence", is now available in digital form, one of the only papers *Antiquity* considers important enough to publish on-line in its entirety (Clarke 1998). Historical relations to this article are altered once again. But this time it is definitely through a technology.

Acknowledgements

Thanks to Matt Leivers, Ingereth MacFarlane and Julia Roberts for their comments and discussion.

Notes

1. I refer here to personal experience whilst working with Namibian rock art. In that case, the impact of previous representations of the art (mostly by Europeans), has had a significant impact upon the interpretations concerning the Bushman societies who produced the art (Gidlow forthcoming). This history (of what can only be described as Eurocentric misinterpretation), influenced my choice of software, in deciding how to digitise these images. It therefore seemed totally inappropriate to reduce such a diverse archive to a manipulatable matrix of numbers, or to use the material as a demonstration of a powerful program to search for some normative pattern or process (*ibid.*). Furthermore, I believe that this argument should stand with reference to the representation and analysis of past landscapes and monuments.

Bibliography

Clarke, D. L., 1973. Archaeology the loss of innocence, *Antiquity* 47, pp. 6–18.

Clarke, D. L., 1998. Archaeology the loss of innocence, http://intarch.york.ac.uk/antiquity/hp/clarke.html

Earl, T. K., & Preucel, R. W., 1987. Processual archaeology and the radical critique, *Current Anthropology* 28.4, pp. 501–37.

Fletcher, M. & Spicer, D., 1992. The display and analysis of ridge-and-furrow from topographically surveyed data, in P. Reilly & S. P. Q. Rahtz (eds), *Archaeology and the Information Age: a global perspective,* pp. 97–122, London: Routledge.

Gaffney, V. & Van Leusen, M., 1995. Postscript-GIS, environmental determinism and archaeology, a parallel text, in G. Lock & Z. Stančič (eds), *Archaeology and GIS: a European perspective,* pp. 367–81, London: Routledge.

Gidlow, J. M. (forthcoming). Rock art and Bubble worlds, In Wheatley, D., S. Poppy & G. Earl (eds), *Proceedings of the Computer Applications in Archaeology,* United Kingdom Conference, University of Southampton, March 1998.

Gillings, M., & Goodrick, G., 1996. Sensuous and reflexive GIS: exploring visualisation and VRML, *Internet Archaeology* 1, (http://intarch.york.ac.uk/issue1/gillings.html)

Haraway, D. J., 1991. Situated knowledges: the science question in feminism and the privilege of partial perspective, in D. J. Haraway, *Simians, Cyborgs and Women: the reinvention of nature,* pp. 183–202, London: Free Association Books.

Haraway, D. J., 1997. *Modest_Witness@Second_Millennium.FemaleMan _Meets_OncoMouse*. New York: Routledge.

Hodder, I., 1985. Postprocessual archaeology, in M. B. Schiffer (ed), *Advances in archaeological method and theory,* 8 pp. 1–25.

Hodder, I., 1999. *The archaeological process*. Oxford: Blackwell.

Kuhn, T., 1962. *The structure of scientific revolutions*. Chicago: University of Chicago Press.

Llobera, M., 1996. Exploring the topography of mind: GIS, social space and archaeology, *Antiquity* 70, pp. 612–622.

Llobera, M., 1996. Living and dying on a grid-cell: a discussion on the theoretical basis for a humanistic approach to archaeological GIS, (paper presented at Theoretical Archaeology Group, in the session, Spatial technologies and archaeological reasoning).

Lock, G., 1995. Archaeological computing, archaeological theory and moves towards contextualism, in J. Huggett and N. Ryan (eds.), *Computer Applications and Quantitative methods in Archaeology 1994*, pp. 13–17, Oxford: Tempvs Reparatum. British Archaeological Reports, International Series, number 600.

Malone, A., & Stoddart, S., (eds), 1998. David Clarke's 'Archaeology: the loss of innocence' (1973) 25 years after, *Antiquity* (special section), pp. 676–7.

Maschner, H., 1996, Fishing for theory on a digital river to nowhere: GIS and modern archaeology, (paper presented at Theoretical Archaeology Group 1996, in the session, Spatial technologies and archaeological reasoning).

Meltzer, D., 1979. Paradigms and the nature of change in American archaeology, *American Antiquity* 44, 4 pp. 644–57.

Miller, P., & Richards, J., 1995. The good, the bad and the downright misleading: archaeological adoption of computer visualisation, in J. Huggett and N. Ryan (eds.), *Computer Applications and Quantitative methods in Archaeology 1994,* pp. 19–22, Oxford: Tempvs Reparatum. British Archaeological Reports, International Series, number 600.

Piggott, S., 1978. *Antiquity depicted: aspects of archaeological illustration*. London: Thames and Hudson.

Plant, S., 1997. *Zeros and Ones*. London: 4th dimension books.

Preucel, R. W., 1991. The philosophy of archaeology, in R. W. Preucel (ed.), *Processual and Postprocessual archaeologies,* pp 17–29, Carbondale: Southern University of Illinois Occasional paper 10.

Shanks, M., & Tilley, C., 1992. *Re-Constructing archaeology, theory and practice* (2nd Edition), London: Routledge.

Smith, P. J., 1997. Graham Clark's new archaeology: the Fenland Research Committee and Cambridge prehistory in the 1930s, *Antiquity* 71, pp. 11–30.

Spikins, P., 1996. The role of sheep in the early to late Mesolithic transition: a cautionary tale about GIS applications, (paper presented at the Theoretical Archaeology Group 1996, in the session, Spatial technologies and archaeological reasoning).

Reilly, P., 1991. Visualising the problem: advancing graphics systems in archaeology, in S. Ross, J. Moffett & J. Henderson (eds), *Computing for archaeologists,* pp. 131–52, Oxford: Oxford University Committee for Archaeology, monograph 18.

Reilly, P., 1992. Three-dimensional modelling and primary archaeological data, in J. Huggett & N. Ryan (eds), *Computer Applications and Quantitative methods in Archaeology 1994*, pp. 147–73, Oxford: Tempvs Reparatum. British Archaeological Reports, International Series, number 600.

Thomas, J., 1993. The politics of vision and the archaeology of landscape, in B. Bender (ed), *Landscape: politics and perspectives,* pp. 19–48, London: Berg.

Tilley, C., 1989. Archaeology as socio-political action in the present, in Pinsky, V. & A. Wylie (eds), *Critical traditions in contemporary archaeology*, pp. 104–116, Cambridge: Cambridge University Press.

Trigger, B., 1989. *A history of archaeological thought*, Cambridge: Cambridge University Press.

Van Reybrouck, D., 1998. Imaging and imagining the Neanderthal: the role of technical drawings in archaeology, *Antiquity* 72, pp. 65–64.

Wheatley, D., 1993. Going over old ground: GIS, archaeological theory and the act of perception, in J. Andressen, T. Madsen & I. Scollar (eds), *CAA92, Computer applications and quantitative methods in archaeology,* pp. 133–138, Aarhus: Aarhus University Press.

Wood, J., & Chapman, G., 1991. Three-dimensional computer visualisation of historic buildings with particular reference to computer modelling, in P. Reilly & S.P.Q. Rahtz, (eds), *Archaeology and the Information Age: A Global Perspective,* pp. 123–146, London: Routledge.

Wylie, A., 1993. A proliferation of new archaeologies: Beyond objectivism and relativism, in N. Yoffee & A. Sherratt (eds), *Archaeological theory: who sets the agenda?* pp. 20–26, Cambridge: Cambridge University Press.

CHAPTER 3

Mathematics and Computers:
The Classifier's Ruse

Hannah Forsyth

Archaeological classification has always been structured upon the phenomenological comparison of attributes. In this context, the increased use of statistics and the subsequent development of computerised classification techniques seems a valuable progression. However, in the larger context of theoretical debate and the exploration of classificatory paradigms, mathematics and computers have been used as a conservative force. Archaeologists, in the area of classification, have used mathematics and computers to avoid considering and exploring various classificatory models and ideas.

When we consider the culture of Archaeology, we see pragmatism as a system of apparently self-evident morality. Further, when we consider the increasing role of computers and statistics in classification methodologies, we see a persistence of conservatism, self-justification and a refusal to consider the application of post—theory1 in one of the most central and basic of all archaeological practices, classification. Theory, and post—theory in particular, is suspected of having little or nothing to offer pragmatic processes of archaeological practice.

Classification's basic form, in archaeology, has not really changed this century. Despite methods such as Spaulding's (Spaulding, 1953) and Brainerd and Robinson's statistics (Brainerd, 1951; Robinson, 1951) and Wheat, Gifford and Wasley's type-variety systems (Wheat, Gifford & Wasley, 1958), and variations thereafter, classification's paradigm of attribute-based similarity, regardless of whether derived intuitively or statistically, remains in its 19th century form. In Ford and Spaulding's debate (1953 1954), Spaulding's defence of his statistical system included its lack of difference from that which Ford defended (Spaulding, 1954, 306). It has been only with the development of post–theory that an opportunity for experimental paradigmatical and methodological changes in classification have been available to archaeologists. I will argue that the increasing popularity of numerical taxonomy and other statistical systems, essentially maintaining the status quo, have defended archaeological classification from, not merely experimental methodology, but theory itself.

A Morality of Practice

In considering mainstream archaeology's tendency to dismiss theory in general and post—theory in particular, it is useful to take a look at the titles of the literature used. Evidently book titles are not simply signs of the contents of the book, but encompass the concepts of the discipline that constitute the successful marketing of the contents as a product. As such, book titles may be a useful method for discussing the culture of the discipline of archaeology. First, Yoffee & Sherratt's *Archaeological theory: who sets the agenda?* (Yoffee & Sherratt, 1993), suggests by its title a number of impressions; a question of 'who', of schools of thought, of power relations and a powerful and perhaps dangerous theoretical structure being constructed by influential agenda-setters. It implies that these agenda-setters may be of a school (i.e. the 'who') that is somehow wrong, powerful, perhaps dangerous or, as we shall see from the content of the book, immoral. The underlying tone is one of fear of who is doing what with theory in archaeology.

Archaeological theory: Progress or Posture? (Mackenzie, 1994) is a title in which 'posture' implies many words but few that are useful. This is evidently pointed at theory (as opposed to practice) in which sector of archaeological inquiry 'many words' are likely to proliferate, in opposition to the practicality and implied usefulness of practice. At first glance it appears safe to assume that the content will demonstrate that theory equals posture. We should not forget, however, that the title is for marketing purposes and this is particularly evidenced in this case where a much gentler approach to theory is taken inside the cover. In fact, the introduction, in a convolution of the cover-title, is rather entitled 'Progress and posture in Archaeological theory'. Why would a relatively even-handed book have a title seemingly significantly more provocative than its contents? Rather obviously, provocation sells better, but more particularly, a book holding a position in opposition to theory has a particular appeal to archaeologists.

A book title particularly relevant to this paper, Adams & Adams' *Archaeological Typology and Practical Reality* (Adams & Adams, 1991) suggests (and corresponds to) an in-depth study of typology which will probably necessarily incorporate theory but which will (implying contrast to other works containing theory) be based on common sense or practical reality. This betrays a sense in which theory, even in application to methodology, is imprac-tical and that this book has something else to offer, using a theoretical framework to bring some common sense to thinking about classification. The significance of common sense is profound in the context of a morality of practice and pragmatism.

Yoffee and Sherratt in their Introduction (Yoffee & Sherratt, 1993), make explicit this morality of practice and pragmatism and its opposition to post—theory in archaeology. They refer to "the suspicion that some post-processualists aren't interested in the practice of archaeology at all" (*ibid*, 5). Interestingly, the reason why this is a problem is not clari-fied in the context of an argument, but appears in itself to be self-evident in its immorality. Yoffee and Sherratt do also make explicit their view that post-processual archaeology is immoral, through an argument that suggests that post—theory validates world views that lead to violations of human rights (*ibid*, 7). The morality of practice continues to emerge through their criticism that post—archaeologists are neither "concerned with specific cases and concrete problems" nor interested in "practical and substantive arguments" (*ibid* 7). Finally, in the most forceful statement of the article that somewhat clarifies the perceived threat behind the fear, Yoffee and Sherratt pronounce; "The ideological danger posed by the grimmest processual scientism pales in comparison to the threat of those who seek to undermine the framework of traditional archaeological *practice* and who, at their most systematically critical, are indeed nihilists" (*ibid*, 8, italics added).

Yoffee and Sherratt's arguments, presented in emotive and moralistic terms, contain few (to use their own words) "specific cases and concrete problems" nor "practical and substantive arguments". Rather, their arguments are riddled with logical fallacies. The significance of this aspect of this particular article is that the force of the argument would appear not to require those characteristics they themselves call for in archaeological theory and practice. Its morality, it would seem, is self-evident. The article's assumption is that all archaeologists would adhere to their view of practice and its moral significance. The apparent non-adherence to this and the supposed consequent immorality of the post—archaeologists may be explained by the influence of 'outsiders', foreigners to archaeology; those post—theorists from other disciplines. This provides an impression that by exploring ideas from outside of the archaeological community, the post—archaeologists are being, in fact 'unarchaeological' (*ibid*, 7). Yoffee and Sherratt call for a "contextually relevant" theoretical structure, that is, one that is constructed solely from within the discipline, defending archaeology, in a manner of speaking, from the barbarian. This need to defend archaeological territory is also couched in a moralistic, almost patriotic call. Yoffee and Sherratt say that "archaeologists can not be excused the responsibility for setting our own theoretical and contextually appropriate agenda" (*ibid*, 8).

Considering archaeology's morality of pragmatism, it is unsurprising that archaeological classifiers have chosen to shift the battleground in the crusade against post—theory to an area of practice. It explains why discourse on the subject is shifted from the theoretical to the practical; specifically to the use of statistical methodology in classification, as shall be seen. The question is more than why practice is perceptually opposed to theory (see Mackenzie, 1994). It is why a morality of practice is more particularly opposed to post—theory in favour of a self-perception of an archaeology that is, at least partially, a science.

Post— and Classification

This opposition to post—theory in the area of classification, is based on a number of perceived (and perhaps actual) threats to traditional archaeological classification. They include; (i) that the concept of 'data' is mythological; (ii) that an emphasis on the cultural origin of archaeological material produces unachievable aims for classification; (iii) that the presence of archaeological investigation implies an unknowable past; (iv) that the practice of archaeology may be based on an analogy to text rather than the present analogy to science.

The practice of classification (as opposed to identification of objects within the context of an existing classification) generally occurs prior to any interpretation, or testing of theory against 'data' that forms the mythology of 'data' depicted by post-processualist archaeologists (Hodder, 1984, 27, 29–30; Trigger, 1992, 65; Shanks & Hodder, 1995a, 11). That is, classification and classified objects *are* the data. An application of anti-objectivism to classi-fication would seem to undermine the basic formulation of data and the basis of archaeological interpretation.

The reminder for archaeologists that archaeology is a cultural and social product (Hodder, 1984, 25; Shanks & Tilley, 1987a, 66) also reminded archaeologists of attempts at 'paleo-psychology'[2] (Hodder, 1984, 25; Binford, 1965, 203–210). That is, the attempt to elucidate the mental templates of social organisations through classification, that have been scattered throughout the past century of classification theory (see Krieger, 1944, 272; Ford, 1954; Spaulding, 1954; Phillips, 1959; Gifford, 1960; Rouse, 1960; Chang, 1967; Shanks & Hodder, 1995b, 31). Although this is not immediately apparent from Shanks and Tilley's approach to classification in *Reconstructing Archaeology* (Shanks & Tilley, 1987a; 154–5), the issue may be one of a distinguishment of archaeological objects from geological and biological (naturally occurring) phenomena.

The issue is also one of archaeology as a product of the cultural and social context of the archaeologists, or the present. The literature suggests that this idea is in fact the simplest for non-post-processual archaeologists to integrate into the discipline. Critics of the post—approach to archaeology often say that this is a 'useful' point brought out by the post-proces-sualists (for example, Kohl, 1993, 13). In the practice of classification it is 'useful' in that it doesn't necessarily obstruct the comparison of objects using their attributes, and it is non-threatening in that it can be adopted alongside a view that the past is partly knowable, with the consequence that practice need not change (see Trigger, 1992, 73).

The threat posed by a post—approach to archaeology and classification in particular relate in part to its apparent opposition to practice, its apparent lack of practical application but most significantly, its potential to undermine the basic structure of a classificatory concept that is analogous to the sciences. It is not that archaeological classifiers are necessarily loyal to the practices of science, but, rather that archaeological classification has always been constructed along the same premises. A threat to those premises has the potential to under-mine all archaeological work that has gone before, particularly in consideration of the basic role of classification in the discipline since its conception. The fear of undermining past archaeological practice is expressed in Yoffee and Sherratt's Introduction, interestingly in relation to its academic prestige; "Practical and substantive arguments are not held to carry conviction – this despite a century of progress in archaeological knowledge that ought to have made archaeology an ornament of modern academic life as it is a subject of public fascination" (Yoffee & Sherratt, 1993, 7–8).

Perhaps by an accident of history, the archaeological academy has selected science as its classification-methodological analogy. That is, the concepts and methods associated with classification methodology resemble those of the sciences rather than, say, the methods employed in the comparison and analysis of textual material. The post-processualist revision of archaeological conception to suggest an analogy with textual analysis rather than with scientific method, amongst others, poses a threat to traditional archaeological method. It is this consideration of archaeology as text that has direct relevance for classification, even though, in application, Shanks and Tilley use textuality to mean 'interpretative' (Shanks & Tilley, 1987a). The other implications of a textual classification are discussed later.

The Perceptual Impact of Mathematics and Computers

The past century of 'progress' in archaeological classification theory and methodology has primarily involved the appropriation of methodologies from the sciences. Most relevant is the appropriation of numerical taxonomy from Sokal and Sneath's proposal for the classification of biological species (Sokal and Sneath, 1963; Sokal, 1966) although prior and similar methods had been developed (Kroeber, 1940; Brainerd, 1951; Robinson, 1951; Spaulding, 1953). It seems reasonable to suspect that archaeological and scientific objects have a single significant feature in common that has caused the analogy of method to seem self-evident; their physicality. It is in this area that the acknowledgment of a cultural and social source for the archaeological object becomes problematic for the classification method in that it makes doubtful the analogy that holds the method in place.

Increasingly, from the introduction of numerical taxonomy, archaeological classification has used computers and statistics. While many of the advantages of the method that were asserted initially by advocates from within archaeology (Clarke, 1968, 517; Sabloff & Smith, 1969, 278) have since been rejected as unrealistic[3] (Adams & Adams, 1991, 291), it is still claimed, and may well be true, that statistical approaches to the classification of archaeological material are useful. Nevertheless, the perceptual impact of the variety of statistical approaches now available to archaeologists is far more significant than the ability to do what archaeologists have always done using computers.

There is no doubt that computers, mathematics and statistics in classification in archaeology have changed little in terms of both the concept and practice of classification in the discipline, a fact supported by both opponents and proponents of the methods (Spaulding, 1954, 306; Clarke, 1968, 513; Ford, 1954; Adams & Adams, 1991, 275). What it has achieved is a greater depth of thought in relation to attributes; what they are considered to be, how they relate to one another, how they impact and form our perception of the object and how they affect the classification of a selection of objects (Clarke, 1968, 520–525; Hodder, 1984, 28; Clegg, 1995, 370). Due to this, the method has the potential for achieving a greater understanding of the ways archaeologists and others classify material of a social and cultural origin. Unfortunately, instead, statistical approaches treat these attributes as if they were the genes that, compared to the genes of other objects, can determine an objective relationship between them (Clarke, 1968, 517; Clarke, 1972, ch6; cf Sokal, 1966, 2).

By ensuring that archaeology's emphasis in classification is on the phenomenological, the 'basic' and apparently axiomatic similarity of physical attributes of the material, the archaeologist/classifier can consider the issue of cultural products irrelevant. But the use of statistics and computers succeeds in evading the post—problem in other ways. It substantiates the impression of archaeology as a practical science through aesthetic and methodological impressions and through comparative nomenclature. Methodologies adopted directly from scientific disciplines create a transparent affiliation. But the use of computers and statistics means publications can be filled with algorithms, data in the form of numerical representations, graphs and scattergrams which create an aesthetic scientism and an image of objectivity in the same way that a lab coat can represent scientific credibility in advertising (see Madsen, 1991, 33; Adams & Adams, 1991, 274–275). It further introduces into delineations of methodology, words such as 'multivariate' and 'polythetic', which have the advantage of terminology specific to the more recent period of statistical classification (the one that can be more associated with computers) and a resemblance to scientific disciplines[4].

These impressions of scientism are particularly useful in the opposition to post— theory through their use of computer technology. The strength of this seemingly incidental equipment is in its relative novelty. Computers almost invariably create an impression of the 'cutting edge', and the literature surrounding their application often separate themselves from traditionalist methods, although concurrently justifying it through its similarity (for example Doran & Hodson, 1975,5). Given that novelty creates the impression of the most progressive thought and, as has been seen, archaeology possesses a pervading morality of practice, the effectiveness of the modernity of computer technology is that it is practical and new and therefore more likely to represent real progress than that which is theoretical and new, which may be likely to represent 'posture'.

What has been achieved through these impressions? In relation to classification, archaeology, within its self-perception as a practical discipline with a history of appropriating its methodologies from the sciences, has perpetuated a methodological analogy with science. In so doing, it has not addressed the possibility that classification theory and method may operate under a different analogy, and it particularly has not developed any response to the post— proposal of an archaeology more analogous to the interpretation of text. It has rather shifted the battleground to the more familiar area of practicality, identified itself further with science and neglected to identify the possibility that classification may be more than what it is generally understood to be. Ellen identified "that there are substantive areas and dimensions of classificatory space which remain unexplored (and perhaps unexplorable) by our present limited techniques" (Ellen, 1979, 6–7). These areas may be unexplorable, but archaeologists are yet to find out.

The Unexplored and perhaps Unexplorable

If we were to take Hodder's analogy of text (Hodder, 1986, 34; Hodder, 1989, 68–69) further than it is taken in Shanks & Tilley's application to classification (Shanks & Tilley, 1987a, ch7, 154, 155), we can see possibilities that classification can be more than its definition; that is, the comparison of attributes to determine phenomenological similarity (Adams & Adams, 1991, chs 3 & 5). Instead of, as in Clarke's discussions on the subject (Clarke, 1968, 520–525), attributes that conceptually resemble genes, attributes may resemble characters that constitute culturally-recognisable words, assemblages forming sentences and paragraphs until finally a partially-read novel emerges, revealing with it a language and grammar with which to read further. Such a thing may be improbable or impossible, and yet archaeologists are yet to discover even their own grammar and language that is used, not in terms of classificatory nomenclature, but in terms of the choices consistently made in the selection, prioritisation and association of attributes.

In this context the 'order' of the attributes would be as significant as their presence or absence. For example, if we were to compare the word DANGER to the word GARDEN in terms of their attributes alone they would register as statistically identical. And they would similarly be identical to the (non) word RDEGAN. Moreover, through a comparison of their attributes alone, these different words would be considered to possess the same significance, the same meaning, regardless of cultural origin or language.

Of course, objects are not really words. Yet, if we consider the ways that we classify objects in our own society it seems reasonable to believe that some attributes are more significant than others. Some years ago I experimented with using numerical taxonomy on material from my own house which revealed that a particular coffee cup more closely resembled a particular candle-holder than any other coffee cup. I know what it is, but why? Is it not that some attributes are more significant than others? Could it not be that on occasions a single attribute, rather than as many attributes as possible signifies what an object is? Could a candle-holder be what it is because its cavity is the right size for a candle and that is all?

The implications of this are various. Archaeological classifiers may have access to various attribute-languages that may suggest classifications other than the phenomenological theme; not in terms of non-physical attributes, but in terms of their selection and prioritisation according to their (non-physical) cultural significance. On the other hand, access to this may be illusory. What is certainly suggested is that there may be a variety of ways to look at the classification of objects, a variety of analogies to form its basis and definition. Since the admission that numerical taxonomy and statistical, even computerised classification methods can not identify and compare all attributes, where is the literature that studies the way that attributes are selected, the traditions and ideas that contribute to the way archaeologists look at their objects of study? If there is a variety of ways of conceiving and defining archaeological classification, the "past century of progress" has identified only one.

Archaeology's morality of pragmatism, and pragmatism's perceptual opposition to theory, in combination with the sense of threat perceived by archaeologists in the post—literature, has led to an implicit defensive action. This action is designed to use progressive technology, along with existing method, to perpetuate a conservative classificatory ideology. As suggested by Ellen (Ellen, 1979, 6–7), other ideas or models, unexplored areas of classificatory space, may in fact be unexplorable. However, there is no justification to be found in information technology for a failure to attempt to explore it.

Notes

1. I have chosen to refer to various forms of post-theory (post-modernism, post-structuralism and post-processualism) in the form of 'post—' as the archaeological literature is often unclear which it refers to. Where it is clearly post-processualism I have used that word.

2. This perception is not unwarranted. Ironically, despite criticisms that post-processual archaeologists make archaeology meaningless, book titles from this school tend to suggest an increase in meaning, supported by content that often (in different terminology) advocates the elucidation of mental templates. (Consider book titles, all by Ian Hodder, *Interpreting Archaeologies, finding meaning in the past,* (1995), *The Archaeology of Contextual Meanings,* (1987), *The Meaning of Things,* (1989), *Reading the Past,* (1986).)

3. Originally it appeared that to use statistics to follow the same classificatory procedures as have always pervaded archaeology, seemed to quantify and make objective a comparison of all the attributes of a collection of material. It is generally asserted in more recent literature that objectivity is impossible and that, as there are an infinite number of attributes for any object, it is similarly impossible to notice, let alone document and compare them all. It was also often (and frequently still is) claimed that at the very least the method compares more attributes than would be detected intuitively (an over-simplification of the term 'polythetic' which in fact refers to the treatment of the attributes rather than the number of them). However, it is difficult to ascertain how many attributes might be compared

intuitively, and it in fact seems likely that the skilled use of intuition might detect and compare significantly more attributes than could be listed quantifiably (Dixon, 1981, 257; Bastick, 1982, 2–3, 12, 331; Adams & Adams, 1991, 46).

4. Interestingly those two words also resemble the words used to denote multiplicity and polysemous meaning in post literature, while definitively connoting objective and scientific analysis of data. As the words were introduced to archaeological discourse prior to the influence of post—theory in archaeology, the resemblance (although not necessarily their continuance) must be considered coincidental.

Bibliography

Adams, W.Y., & Adams, E.W., 1991. *Archaeological Typology and Practical Reality: A Dialectical Approach to Artifact Classification and Sorting*, Cambridge: Cambridge University Press.

Bastick, T., 1982. *Intuition: How we Think and Act*. New York: John Wiley & Sons.

Binford, L. R., 1965. Archaeological Schematics and the Study of Culture Process, *American Antiquity* 31.2, pp. 203–210.

Brainerd, G. W., 1951. The place of Chronological ordering in Archaeological Analysis, *American Antiquity* 16.4, pp. 301–313.

Chang, Kwang-chih, 1967. *Rethinking Archaeology*. New York: Random House.

Clarke, D. L., 1968. *Analytical Archaeology*. London: Methuan & Co Ltd.

Clarke, D. L., 1972. *Models in Archaeology*. London: Methuan & Co Ltd.

Clegg, J., 1995. *Mathesis Drawing*. Sydney: Clegg Calendars.

Dixon, N. F., 1981. *Preconscious Processing*. New York: John Wiley & Sons.

Doran, J. E. & Hodson, F. R., 1975. *Mathematics and Computers in Archaeology*. Edinburgh: Edinburgh University Press.

Ellen, R. F., 1979. Introductory Essay, in Ellen, R. F. & Reason, D., (eds), *Classifications in their Social Context*. London: Academic Press, pp. 1–32.

Ford, J. A., 1954. Comment on A.C. Spaulding, Statistical Techniques for the Discovery of Artifact Types, *American Antiquity,* 19.4, pp. 390–391.

Gifford, J. C., 1960. The Type-Variety method of ceramic Classification as an indicator of Cultural Phenomena, *American Antiquity*, 25.3, pp. 341–347.

Hodder, I., 1984. Archaeology in 1984, *Antiquity*, 25, pp. 25–31.

Hodder, I., 1986. *Reading the Past*. Cambridge: Cambridge University Press.

Hodder, I., (ed) 1987. *The Archaeology of contextual meanings*. Cambridge: Cambridge University Press.

Hodder, I., 1989. Postmodernism, poststructuralism and postprocessual archaeology, in Hodder, I., (ed) *The Meaning of Things: material culture and symbolic expression*. Boston: Unwin, pp. 64–78.

Hodder, I., Shanks, M., Alexandri, A., Buchli, V., Carman, J., Last, J & Lucas, G.,1995. *Interpreting archaeology: finding meaning in the past*. New York: Routledge.

Kohl, P. L., 1993. Limits to a post-processual archaeology (or the dangers of a new scholasticism), in Yoffee & Sherratt (eds), *Archaeological Theory: who sets the agenda*, pp. 13–19.

Krieger, A. D., 1944. The Typological Concept, *American Antiquity*, 9.4, pp. 271–288.

Kroeber, A. L., 1940. Statistical Classification, *American Antiquity*, 6.1, pp. 29–44.

Layton, R., 1992. *Australian Rock Art: A New Synthesis*. Melbourne: Cambridge University Press.

Mackenzie, I. M., (ed), 1994. *Archaeological Theory: Progress or Posture?*, Avebury, Aldershot.

Madsen, T., 1991. The Use of Multivariate Statistics in Scandinavian Archaeology, in Bock, Hans-Hermann & Peter Ihm (eds), *Classification, Data Analysis, and Knowledge Organisation: Models and Methods with Applications*. Springer-Verlag, pp. 330–342.

Phillips, P., 1959. Application of the Wheat-Gifford-Wasley taxonomy to Eastern Ceramics, *American Antiquity*, 24.2, pp. 117–125.

Robinson, W.S., 1951. A Method for Chronologically Ordering Archaeological Deposits, *American Antiquity*, 16, pp. 293–301.

Rouse, I., 1944. On the Typological Method, *American Antiquity* 10.2, pp. 202–204.

Rouse, I. 1960. The Classification of Artifacts in Archaeology, *American Antiquity* 25.3, pp. 313–323.

Sabloff, J. A., & Smith, R. E., 1969. The Importance of both Analytic and Taxonomic Classification in the Type-Variety System *American Antiquity* 34.3, pp. 278–285.

Shanks, M & Hodder, I, 1995a. Processual, postprocessual and interpretative archaeologies, in Hodder *et al* (eds) *Interpreting Archaeology: Finding Meaning in the Past*, pp. 3–29.

Shanks, M & Hodder, I, 1995b. Interpretative archaeologies: some themes and questions, in Hodder *et al* (eds) *Interpreting Archaeology: Finding Meaning in the Past*, pp. 30–36.

Shanks, M. & Tilley, C., 1987a. *Reconstructing Archaeology: Theory, Methods and Practice.* Cambridge: Cambridge University Press.

Shanks, M. & Tilley, C., 1987b. *Social Theory and Archaeology*. Cambridge: Polity Press.

Shanks, M. & Tilley, C., 1989. Archaeology into the 1990's, *Norwegian Archaeological Review*, 22.1, pp. 1–12.

Sokal, R. R., & Sneath, P. H. A., 1963. *Principles of Numerical Taxonomy.* San Franciso: W.H. Freeman and Co.

Sokal, R. R., 1966. Numerical Taxonomy, *Scientific American*, 215.6, pp. 2–12.

Sokal, R. R. & Rohlf, F. J., 1969. *Biometry*, San Franciso: W.H. Freeman & Co.

Spaulding, A. C. M., 1953 Statistical Techniques for the Discovery of Artifact Types, *American Antiquity*, 18, pp. 305–313.

Spaulding, A. C. M., 1954. Reply to Ford, *American Antiquity*, 19.4, pp. 391–393.

Thomas, D. H., 1978. The Awful Truth about Statistics in Archaeology, *American Antiquity*, 43.2, pp. 231–244.

Trigger, B., 1989. *A History of Archaeological Thought*. Cambridge: Cambridge University Press.

Trigger, B., 1992. Post-Processual developments in Anglo-American Archaeology, *Norwegian Archaeological Review*, 24.2, pp. 65–76.

Wheat, J. B., Gifford, J. C., & Wasley, W. W., 1958. Ceramic Variety, Type Cluster, and Ceramic System in Southwestern Pottery Analysis *American Antiquity* 24.1, pp. 34–47.

Yoffee, N., & Sherratt, A., 1993. *Archaeological theory: who sets the agenda?* Cambridge: Cambridge University Press.

CHAPTER 4

Constructs, simulations and hyperreal worlds: the role of Virtual Reality (VR) in archaeological research

Glyn Goodrick and Mark Gillings

Introduction – Thinking about VR

Since the late nineteen eighties, Archaeology, in common with many disciplines in the Humanities and Social Sciences, has been openly advocating the use of VR techniques as a means of revolutionising the way in which we engage with and re-present the past. The following paper seeks to explore the relationship that has developed between the techniques we loosely group under the banner of 'Virtual-reality modelling' and Archaeology. We intend to argue that there currently exist a number of fundamental limitations inherent in the dominant archaeological understanding of VR, which if left unchecked are destined to exert a profound (and highly restrictive) influence upon the shape of this growing partnership.

Archaeologists use VR without adequately understanding what precisely it *is*. It is almost as if the ubiquity of all things virtual in contemporary society has lulled researchers into treating VR as a taken-for-granted. There is also a tendency to design applications shaped by what we *think* VR can, or should, routinely do, rather than the things it actually can. The lack of readily accessible practical techniques geared around the specific requirements of archaeology aggravates this situation. It serves to portray VR as resource intensive and technically sophisticated. Above all inaccessible. It is our assertion that in much the same way as GIS before it, VR has been portrayed as a neutral set of computer-based tools that can be transplanted wholesale into the archaeological context. The process of integrating VR has been seen as non-problematic and as a result the application of VR in archaeological research has been severely under theorised. In the present paper we intend to foreground and explore precisely these issues:

- What is VR?
- How can archaeology utilise VR?
- Can VR be made accessible?

As will become clear, in attempting to take a step back and examine the theoretical and practical issues associated with the technology, three important strands need to be traced and explored.

The first can be thought of as the theoretical underpinnings of VR itself, the conceptual 'baggage' that the techniques bring with them into the discipline of archaeology. Penny has recently argued that current implementations of VR depend upon culturally acquired knowledge in order to be intelligible. In particular, modern, Western, male-gendered cultural knowledge (Penny 1993: 17).

The second strand concerns the relationship between VR as a set of practical approaches and developments in archaeological (and broader disciplinary) theory. Examples of the latter include the increasing popularity of Phenomenological perspectives and a host of recent debates concerning perception, experience and understanding on the human scale (e.g. Ingold 1992; Tilley 1994; Thomas 1996; Barrett 1994; Edmonds 1999).

The final strand is concerned not with the role VR can play in realising existing theoretical perspectives, but the implications it has for encouraging new lines of thought – developing new heuristics for thinking about and interpreting the past. For example, in claiming to be taking an embodied perspective when we explore a virtual world, we are faced with the question as to the source of the virtual body we are encased within and virtual eyes we see through. In addition, we also have to consider the role of virtual constructs and models as a unique (and increasingly profligate) form of material (or perhaps im-material) culture, gaining their own biographies as they are viewed, incorporated and re-worked in a variety of social and virtual contexts.

Taking all of these themes together, the aim is to discuss VR not as an emergent technology on the cusp of impacting upon archaeology, but instead as a technology already useful and embedded within the wide arena of everyday archaeological practice. In this way we hope to illustrate how VR can be profitably integrated at all levels of the archaeological process.

What's in a name?

It is perhaps ironic that much of the ambiguity surrounding VR is a direct consequence of the inherent imprecision of the term 'virtual-reality'. By far the majority of archaeological discussions treat VR as self-evident. Rarely has the question *what, precisely, does it mean to describe something as 'virtually'-real?* been brought to the fore (cf. Gillings and Goodrick 1996; Pringle and Moulding 1997; Gillings *in press* b). Within archaeology, by far the most widespread definition has been that offered by Reilly in his seminal work on Virtual-archaeology (Reilly 1991). This emphasises the role of the VR-model as a döppelganger. In effect a sophisticated form of archaeological illustration or reconstruction drawing. In this model the relationship between the model and reality is tangible – the model represents some object, structure or thing which is real and 'out-there'. The degree of realism inherent in such a model lies somewhere on a sliding scale dictated by the quality and quantity of information that has gone into its creation. Such models are quantitative insofar as the greater the amount of information and effort put in, the closer the match between the VR-model and the reality it purports to represent. This definition lies at the heart of the only major publication on VR and archaeology, Forte's 'Virtual Archaeology' (1996).

Other definitions have sought to challenge this orthodoxy, stressing the infinitely more complex and nuanced relationship that exists between an archaeological VR-model and reality. For example, in their detailed exploration of the relationship between VR-models and archaeological illustration, Pringle and Moulding have emphasised that all archaeological illustrations are inherently selective and creative. If VR-models are to be employed, or portrayed, as a form of archaeological illustration, then by default these must equally be selective and creative (Pringle and Moulding 1997:22). The resultant awkwardness of the term 'virtual-reality' prompted the authors to promote the rather more anodyne term 'synthetic environment', derived from the field of military visualisation. Other authors have sought inspiration in the approaches advocated by critical theorists such as Baudrillard, directly challenging the notion that there exists any measurable link at all between a VR-model and the 'thing' it purports to represent (Baudrillard 1983; Gillings 1999; for a review of such perspectives in the context of photographic reproduction see McQuire 1998: 92–104). Once again, such discussions prompted the advocacy of yet another term to replace virtual reality, in this case 'hyperreal simulation'.

It would appear that a number of conflicting notions have been tendered as to what precisely VR is. The fundamental distinction between these competing definitions of VR lies in the claimed relationship that exists between reality and the simulation:

- Concrete relationship: the model strives to replicate an objective external reality and the faithfulness or 'accuracy' of the model can be measured and quantified (Reilly 1991, Forte 1996).
- Tenuous and profoundly ambiguous relationship: the only reality at question is that created by the model itself (Gillings 1999; *in press* b).

To shed more light upon this we must now turn to look in more detail at the vexed relationship between 'reality' and any given virtual construct.

Relationships with the real

"The object of this book... is to offer the reader the most faithful re-presentation of the ancient world possible: highly realistic in information and with a high scientific content." *(Forte 1996: 10)*

"'Virtual reality is as real as a picture of a toothache" (Penny 1993:19).

The rather stark alternatives presented above, namely: concrete, quantifiable relationship; tenuous, if any relationship; are no doubt useful points of departure. However, they are also inherently restrictive as they both fail to adequately consider the nature of the archaeological process of reconstruction and interpretation that underlies any attempt to fashion a virtual model. Our VR-models are based upon remains that have been carefully and often meticulously recorded and recovered. By the same token those remains are fragmentary, physically incomplete and shorn of any 'thick' social context. All archaeological interpretations and reconstructions blend the piecemeal physical remains of the past with the dominant disciplinary views on the topic – informed speculation that is always open to challenge, revision and change [1]. To deny either the empirical basis of archaeological VR-models (e.g. Gillings 1999), or the creative essence of the archaeological process (e.g. researchers such as Forte with their frequent claims of faithfulness and repeated calls to the authority of science) is to yield a partial and potentially restrictive definition of what archaeological VR should be.

At this point it is profitable to look in more detail at what we mean by 'realistic'. It seems clear that many of the difficulties we encounter in adequately defining VR, are as much to do with our understanding of terms such as 'real', 'faithful' and 'authentic' as with virtuality itself. A detailed discussion exploring precisely this issue has recently been offered by Gillings (*in press* b). Whilst it is not our intention to repeat these debates wholesale here, it is useful to summarise briefly the main points of his argument.

The point of departure for this work is the claim that when the 'realism' of a VR-model is judged, it is rarely against the physical world of things and processes, but instead against photographs. Within the realm of archaeological-VR, for realism one is actively encouraged to read 'photo-realism'. Despite the relatively simple incorporation of sound, VR is a profoundly visual medium and this emphasis upon verisimilitude is a powerful example of the influence exerted by the theoretical underpinnings VR brings with it into the archaeological context (Penny 1993:17). The reality or authenticity of a given model is reduced to little more than a direct correlation with visual approximation. Simply put, the more it resembles the thing it purports to represent, the more realistic it is deemed to be. Such an equation reflects a profoundly *ocularcentric* approach to the world, an approach which reifies vision as the prime means by which people understand and evaluate their world (Jay quoted in Gregory 1994: 340–1). It must be realised that this trend represents only one means of evaluation, one which it could be argued, is profoundly historical and peculiar to modern western society.

Rather than stressing the issue of visual approximation alone, it may be more profitable to follow instead the phenomenologist Kimberly Dovey in asserting that authenticity is not *solely* a property of form, but is instead a property of *process* and a relationship, or connectedness, between people and their world. This is not to deny the importance of verisimilitude, but to effectively de-centre it, casting visual approximation as but one factor influencing the faithfulness of any representation. Central to Dovey's argument is the assertion that authentic meaning cannot be created through any manipulation of mere form alone, as authenticity is the very source from which form gains meaning (Dovey 1985:33). The critical difference therefore between an original (for example Stonehenge) and its representation (English Heritage's Virtual Stonehenge [2]) is not in any detail of form but in the richness of environmental, or experiential, depth that attend the original object or landscape.

This notion of experiential depth is critical and has a parallel in Benjamin's ideas regarding what he termed the 'aura' of a work of art (Snyder 1989: 162–3; Caygill *et al.* 1998: 134–7). The aura is that facet which is lost when an artwork is reproduced. It relates to factors such as the location and history of the artwork and the way in which it has gradually become embedded in social practice. In a study of the famous re-creation of the Lascaux cave rock-art, Lascaux II, Diamond has explored this issue of aura through a discussion of the process of 'sacralisation'. This is a profoundly cultural phenomenon whereby certain things and places undergo a complex process of social constitution, what we might think of as 'aura evocation', so as to define them as 'authentic' and 'worth-seeing' (1996: 6). Coupled to this idea of aura, a reading of Heidegger's notion of 'gathering' is perhaps also pertinent. This serves to emphasise the way in which things and locales gain meaning through the unique way each gathers the world around itself (Thomas 1996: 49).

What can be extracted from such discussions is the realisation that authenticity is as much about process, biography and embeddedness as it is about the mere visual approximation of form. Taking these discussions to their logical conclusion, the critical point to emphasise is that VR representations, however stunning and detailed their appearance, can *never* be wholly authentic. Saying that a given re-creation is inauthentic is not to say that it is either actively deceiving us or that it is not useful. Virtual-representations can serve to facilitate new modes of engagement and interpretation through laying emphasis upon this notion of *process* rather than critical attention to details of form. As a result, the importance of ensuring that a sense of frustration is encountered within a model at not being able to see over a section of wall to the other side, becomes as critical as the attention that has gone into 'realistically' weathering the texture of the stones blocking the view.

This has profound implications for how we treat VR-models in archaeology. Far from wholly objective döppelgangers, forever straining to replicate some source reality as faithfully as possible, VR-models should instead be seen as constructs which can never be wholly authentic. Archaeological applications of VR which are driven by a continual desire to increase computing power in an attempt to increase visual detail, amount to little more than tail chasing. Exhausting, frustrating and ultimately pointless. This is not to claim that such approaches should be neglected. There are of course instances where a high degree of detail and photo-realism is desirable, for example the creation of a heritage display. Instead this should be seen as but one application amongst many rather than the sole driving force behind the realisation of VR in archaeology. This issue of the breadth and contingency of VR will be discussed in more detail in the next section.

To conclude this brief examination of the 'reality' of VR, it is interesting to look at one area where the relationship between the virtual and the 'real' becomes even more tenuous. This is in the realm of simulations undertaken of phenomenon which exist beyond the physical world of things and objects. Virtual navigation tools have been developed which enable complex data spaces to be navigated using spatial and geographical metaphors (Harvey *in press*). This immediately prompts the question as to how we determine the reality or accuracy of such virtual-simulations and renditions? For example, we may want to use VR techniques and the familiar metaphors of the city and route-map, to facilitate the routine navigation of a large archive or database. A good example would be a museum catalogue. Equally, we may want to aid the interpretation of a complex, unwieldy Harris matrix by re-expressing it in a three-dimensional form. In each case we are constructing a virtual simulation where no tangible, physical, *three-dimensional* original exists.

So what is VR?

As intimated in the introduction, the term VR is inherently slippery. Archaeology is not the only discipline that has found it hard to establish an adequate definition which does not rigidly prescribe and limit its potential application. In seeking to forge an adequate definition, a recent debate undertaken within Geography, resulted in the collection of a host of definitions, derived from fields as diverse as aesthetics, computational science, cartography and common-sense (see Brodlie *et al. in press*). Rather than attempting to assess the relative merits of any one definition against the others, the authors sought instead to extract a series of common threads from these varied understandings. Two conclusions emerged from this exercise:

Firstly, at the most basic level VR comprises a form of Human-Computer Interface (HCI). This differs from traditional interfaces in that rather than keeping the user and representation separate (as for example is the case with an on screen GIS-derived distribution map), it contains the inherent ability to collapse the user into a given representation. The second factor that became clear was that the precise degree of collapse achieved by any given VR-model (what we might think of as 'realism') was not dictated by any fixed rule or rigidly defined threshold, but instead by the requirements of the precise use to which the model was being put.

These conclusions can be summarised as follows. Assigning a generic definition is a relatively straightforward task: VR is a form of HCI. More precise definitions are varied and dictated by fitness for purpose (ibid.).

To illustrate these points more clearly, the intention may be to use VR to train surgeons in a complicated operation, whereby one slip could result in the death of the patient. In this instance you ideally want the level of collapse between user and representation to be as full as possible (Brodlie *in press*). The trainee surgeon must be immersed in the simulation to such an extent that they believe a slip could prove fatal. The fact that such levels are already routinely obtainable is shown by the physiological symptoms of stress suffered by airline pilots using flight simulators, which are equal to or even greater than those shown during ordinary flights.

In contrast, if your interest is in examining the progressive shuttering effects (visual-permeability) a linear arrangement of standing stones pose to vision whilst moving along a putative processional way, simple geometric archetypes and a low level of collapse may well suffice (Gillings *et al. forthcoming*). Despite the wildly different levels of realism and technical sophistication involved, or expected, both of the examples constitute VR. Where they differ is in the desired degree of collapse between user and representation that is effected.

Developing a framework for the realisation of VR and archaeology

What should be clear from the discussions undertaken above is that in order for archaeology to develop a useful framework for VR applications, the following factors must be acknowledged and addressed:

- To make best use of VR archaeology needs to establish what VR is.
- Any single, prescriptive definition of VR runs the risk of being inherently restrictive. Descriptions of VR must acknowledge instead the intrinsic flexibility, contingency and fitness for purpose that make it unique.
- Issues such as realism and authenticity need to be confronted and examined as a critical stage in re-thinking existing orthodox views of VR.

At present we appear to have two options. One is embedded in the field of semantics – to discard the term and replace it with something more appropriate. This is the course advocated by researchers such as Pringle and Moulding and, in earlier discussions, Gillings. Alternatively we can accept the term VR, but ensure that researchers understand from the outset what it actually is and what it is capable of doing.

We intend to advocate the latter course of action. Retain the term VR whilst emphasising that it is not simply about the creation of sophisticated pictures. Whilst verisimilitude may well be important in certain contexts, there is much more to authenticity than the visual approximation of form.

Using VR – Yearning for a tomorrow that may never come

So far discussion has focused upon the conceptual issues which underlie all applications of VR in archaeology. Before we go on to look at how VR can be profitably integrated into everyday archaeological practice, it is interesting to examine how VR is currently being used by archaeologists.

It could be argued, that to date, the lack of any clear idea as to what VR represents, coupled with a tendency to describe VR not in terms of its present functionality, but in terms of some projected, future functionality, has served to greatly restrict the range of uses to which models have been put. The former ambiguity has resulted in the acceptance of an uncritical orthodoxy which promotes the view that VR-models are sophisticated end-products, in much the same way as reconstruction drawings. The latter tendency to characterise VR in terms of some projected, idealised functionality, has been described by Simon Penny as a unique type of yearning, whereby society tends to describe VR as if it could already yield wholly convincing, fully immersive virtual experiences, indistinguishable from everyday life (Penny 1993). Such a tendency to describe VR-models as wholly convincing, fully embodied experiences of place and structures is implicit in the subtitle of Forte's volume – Great Discoveries *Brought to Life* Through Virtual Reality (1996 *emphasis added*). It is also enshrined in the numerous claims that VR enables archaeologists to 'walk back into the past' and 'see the past through the eyes of the original people' (e.g. Bintliff 1997; and the 'monk's eye view' of Furness Abbey suggested by Delooze and Wood (1991)). Describing the application of VR in these terms invariably leads to disappointment and disillusion when the VR model always fails to live up to such a grand billing. It also encourages researchers not to look critically at what VR can achieve at present, but to seek recourse in the even further future, when the deficiencies inherent in the current models will no doubt be rectified and addressed. This attitude is both enshrined within, and serves to fuel, the calls for ever greater sophistication and computing power inherent in the idea of perfect verisimilitude we have argued is of limited use when considered in isolation.

In much the same way that a web-page can be treated as a traditional document, a VR-model can be treated as a reconstruction drawing. In each case to promote such an attitude is to heavily restrict the potential of the medium and deny what it is that makes it unique. Web-pages offer a completely new way of presenting and engaging with data that far transcend the limitations of the printed page. By the same token VR-models are more than technologically intensive reconstruction drawings. This latter point that has been made forcibly by

Pringle and Moulding (1997). To realise that at present, VR-models do not provide archaeologists with the chance to experience wholly authentic landscapes and structures on a human scale is not to say that they do not already provide us with a set of powerful practical adjuncts to theoretical approaches such as Phenomenology. Far more challenging than a process of continual speculation, is to take VR technologies as they are now and begin to look at how they can already serve to enhance and enrich archaeology.

Synergy: VR as an adjunct to existing approaches

Viewshed analysis, i.e. mapping the total area visible from a fixed point in a landscape, has become a standard technique for the investigation of complex inter-site relationships. In recent years the original map-based techniques pioneered by researchers such as Renfrew (1979) have been greatly enhanced by the introduction of a range of GIS-based viewshed analyses (for a thorough review see Gillings and Wheatley *in press*). Despite the care taken within such studies to acknowledge factors such as viewer height and maximum observable distance, the intrinsically precise and absolute zones produced by viewshed analyses have largely side-stepped the myriad factors that govern the theoretical visibility of a given object (Higuchi 1983). Enhancements, such as the 'fuzzy' viewsheds proposed by Fisher (1994) which explicitly incorporate the notion of a fall-off in object-background clarity with distance are useful, but tend to simulate the subjective by objectively degrading the analysis. At the end of the day the highly nuanced and fundamentally human act of seeing is still reduced to the delineation of aseptic zones on a flat projected mapsheet.

Two fundamental problems have served to limit the use of our own powers of observation as an analytical adjunct to the precise zones delineated by the viewshed analysis. Firstly, although we may be able to visit a site and record our observations, the observations

Figure 1. The 'stitching' of multiple photographic images to produce a single panoramic view. In this instance images are of the Carrawburgh Mithraeum.

themselves can rarely be reproduced in any meaningful, flexible way. The use of video or sequences of photographs constrains the observer to follow a heavily prescribed sequence of visual cues. Unlike the original observer they are not free to simply look around. Secondly, the majority of sites, landscapes and vegetation patterns either no longer exist, or have been substantially altered from their original state.

One solution is to combine the viewshed with a VR-based panoramic viewing technique such as the Bubbleworld. The term Bubbleworld was first coined by Goodrick in 1996 to describe a cylinder, sphere, or 'bubble', of photographic images that could be wrapped around a fixed view point, and viewed freely from that point (Goodrick 1999). The stages in the creation of a Bubbleworld are straightforward. A series of overlapping photographs are taken at all angles around a viewpoint, Figure 1. The photographs are then stitched together to create a single composite cylindrical or spherical view, Figure 2. The stitching and processing software is readily available and requires no specialist skills in its application. Although freely distributed viewers were originally required to view such panoramas, Bubbleworlds can now be accessed over the Internet and viewed using Java applets downloaded with the image file, Figure 3.

The strengths of the technique lie not only with its relative simplicity and Internet based accessibility. As well as integrating modern photographs into a scene, photographs can also be taken within virtual constructs and stitched together to form wholly synthetic Bubble-worlds. Traditional VR models contain both geometric information (the constituent polygons and primitive shapes), and many detailed images (encoding surface textures). Enabling a user to freely interact with any complex model in real time (i.e. to look-around) requires considerable processing power to render the required stream of images and handle the often very large files. This often precludes the distribution and routine access of even modest virtual worlds using more egalitarian technologies such as the Internet. In contrast,

Figure 2. The resultant cylindrical image of the Carrawburgh Mithraeum.

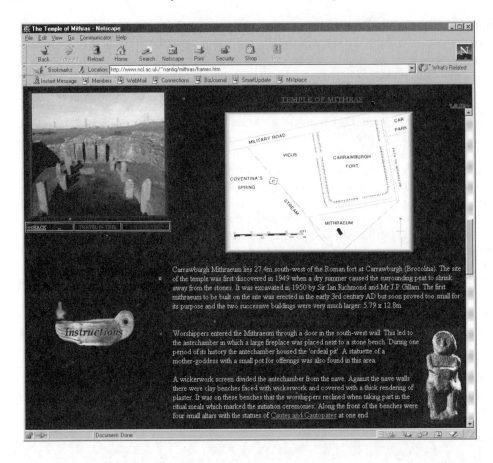

Figure 3. Viewing the resultant Bubbleworld using a specially designed Java applet.

Bubbleworlds are stored and distributed as single pre-rendered images, and are often held within remarkably small files, Figure 4. Viewing is simply a matter of warping a single image to fit a two-dimensional screen, a task which can be undertaken in real time using entry level PC's.

Generating Bubbleworlds within 3D modelling packages enables the archaeologist to reconstruct hypothetical structures, landforms and vegetation patterns. As we are dealing with a single image, rather than a virtual world, the addition of features such as tree lines, buildings and other objects can be undertaken using simple graphics packages, without the need to employ any complex 3D modelling programme. It also enables a number of variables directly affecting vision to be controlled. For instance it is possible to generate atmospheric effects such as fog, haze or smoke or compare the view at dusk or dawn. We can even adjusting the depth of field of the rendered image to mimic eye conditions such as long or short sightedness. It is even possible to view the world at night, draping a star map over the model set to replicate the correct starfield for any given date. By combining photographic,

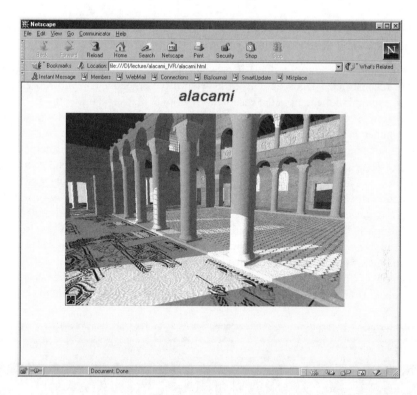

Figure 4. The Alacami, a stunningly detailed three-dimensional reconstruction of a late Roman basilica church in southern Turkey, constructed by Richard Bayliss of the University of Newcastle upon Tyne. This figure illustrates the ability of Bubbleworlds to deliver highly complex and detailed virtual environments whilst minimising bandwidth requirements [3].

virtual and star-almanac data we can explore possible astrological alignments very quickly and easily without the need to produce complex models.

Examples of the application of Bubbleworlds already abound. In her work in Namibia, Gidlow is using photographic Bubbleworlds, what she terms interactive hyperimaging systems, to explore the context and meaning of rock-art sites (Gidlow *in press*). In attempting to develop teaching materials for human and physical Geography, Dykes has developed a variant on the Bubbleworld (termed 'geo-referenced digital panoramic imagery') which combines an on-screen map interface with a series of panoramic wrap-around views that can be accessed for a number of marked viewing points on the map (Dykes *in press*).

The use of panoramic viewing techniques enables us to reproduce existing viewsheds and recreate lost viewsheds, in a way that is both tangible and immediate. It is important to stress that the Bubbleworld is not intended as a replacement for GIS-based approaches such as viewshed analysis, on the contrary it instead acts as a complementary technology, adding an element of qualitative interpretation to the quantitative process of map analysis, in a highly synergistic and productive way.

Exploration: the potential of VR to realise existing theoretical approaches to the study of the past

It is a commonplace assumption that VR provides archaeologists with a unique opportunity to explore reconstructed landscapes from a perspective embedded *within* representations, rather than external to them, as is the case with traditional maps and drawings. By restricting the observer to sedately paced surface movement we can extend this to read not only *embedded* but *embodied*, seeing not from the detached vantage point of the neutral scientific observer, but from the perspective of an individual located and implicated within the landscape/structure being explored. As such, there is enormous potential to use VR techniques to provide a much needed practical dimension to the more phenomenological lines of enquiry being advocated within landscape research (e.g. Tilley 1994). Rather than exploring the ways in which people constitute and are in turn constituted by their physical worlds through hybrid photographic and textual accounts of modern day landscapes, VR offers the unique opportunity to construct such travelogues (complete with photographs if desired) in carefully simulated past environments.

An example of how VR techniques are currently being utilised to explore such embodied perspectives can be seen in the studies being undertaken at Thornborough, a Neolithic

Figure 5. The VRML model of part of the Thornborough monument complex.

monument complex in North Yorkshire, England. The Thornborough complex comprises a unique configuration of ceremonial sites including three massive henge sites built on a plain flanking the river Ure. The monuments survive today as shallow earthworks and cropmarks.

Researchers have suggested that the precise siting, orientation and internal design of these henge monuments is the result of a careful process of cosmological reference and planning. Their layout and organisation is bound up in the specific ceremonies undertaken at the site, themselves intimately linked to patterns in the night sky and the movements of stellar constellations (Goodrick and Harding *in press*). The precise relationship between the monuments, the wider landscape and the night sky, is being explored through VR constructs, which are being used to investigate how the monuments frame and structure experience, revealing or concealing the movement of celestial bodies. A series of methodologies were developed around the VRML Internet-based modelling standard. This involved the further development of existing techniques, for example the construction of virtual topographic models on the basis of a GIS-based digital elevation model (DEM) and the construction of structural components of the monuments using AutoCAD. It also entailed the development of new methods, primarily to facilitate the draping of the night sky over the model, using star maps generated in low-cost astronomical mapping programmes. In practice the various data sets were merged by hand and a public domain virtual person was added to give the model a sense of scale. The result is a VR-model of part of the Thornborough complex that can be explored and investigated in real time, allowing the visual relationship between the constellations, the landscape, and monuments to be investigated, Figure 5. Further developments will include the addition of an interface to enable us to interactively modify the model, for instance changing the date or time and the corresponding star-field configuration.

A second example is taken from the ongoing programme of research at the late Neolithic henge monument of Avebury, Wiltshire. The surviving earthworks and stone settings at Avebury are fragmentary, partial and confused by the presence of a modern village within the confines of the site. In an attempt to interpret the complex arrangements of ditch, bank and standing stones as a profoundly physical, three-dimensional entity, a programme of VR modelling has been underway since 1997 (Pollard and Gillings 1998). Central to the project has been the development of accessible fieldwork techniques for the collection of three-dimensional information. In effect routine practical methods for collecting primary VR data that can be used to provide carefully scaled input data for a series of VRML-based simulations of the site (Gillings *in press* a). As stones are surveyed they are integrated into the model, replacing archetype stone simulations which mark original stone positions. As the recording of more of the extant stones progresses the ratio of archetypes to surveyed stones will fall, with those remaining occupying the settings of stones long since destroyed. These models are being used to explore a number of questions about the role and morphology of the site. For example, due to mediaeval and early modern disturbance, the precise relationship between a linear avenue of standing stones (the West Kennet Avenue) and the southernmost entrance of the henge is ambiguous. The configuration marked out by concrete posts today is but one of two very different possible re-constructions based upon the original excavation records, which differ in how the visual relationship between an individual approaching the henge and the internal settings of the monument was choreographed –

concealment or revelation. By creating two virtual entrances, the implications for vision and movement of each of these possible configurations is being explored, Figure 6, (Wheatley and Earle, *in press*).

Figure 6. The VRML model of the junction between the West Kennet Avenue and southern entrance of the henge site of Avebury. This is currently being used by Wheatley and Earle to examine ambiguities in the existing excavation record. The cylinders indicate the positions of possible stone-settings in this badly disturbed area of the site (image taken from Wheatley and Earle, *in press*).

Innovation: VR and the development of new theoretical approaches

"What if virtual reality was developed in a culture with a different attitude to the body?" *(Penny 1993: 17)*

Applications of VR such as those above are both stimulating and challenging. However in claiming to be taking an 'embodied' perspective we are faced with the question as to whose body are we actually inhabiting? For example, in creating a VR model of Avebury are we really collapsing the neutral, external, scientific observer with the representation or simply changing their existing male, western, academic viewing perspective? Any attempt to tailor the viewing body to some notional archetype suffers from the same issues concerning authenticity as the quest for verisimilitude discussed earlier. In addition, in a discussion of the relationship between the body and virtual simulations, Penny (1993) has argued that the virtual-body VR presents us with is culturally specific, intimately bound up with modern western conceptions of space, perspective and relative scale. This not only has important implications for the way in which contemporary, non-western societies engage with *our* virtual realities, but also raises serious questions about the use of VR as a mechanism for exploring the perceptions of such societies, and those of the long dead peoples of the past.

The techniques we are currently exploring take a different approach to this issue of embodiment. Rather than seeking to colour *how* you observe in a given VR simulation, emphasis is instead placed upon colouring *what* is observable. We have termed this process Gummidging, taking our inspiration from the character Worzel Gummidge in the books of Barbara Euphan Todd. Gummidge was a scarecrow who, when faced with a new or tricky situation, had the singular talent of being able to change the specific head he was wearing to assume a new set of characteristics, preconceptions and behaviours. In such a formulation the notion of a single, monolithic VR model, is replaced by a multiplicity of models viewed, in effect, through the computer-based equivalent of the rose-tinted spectacles of a particular individual, interest group or social gathering. This is in many ways similar to the VR concept of the Avatar turned in on itself. In defining an Avatar one defines the outward appearance of your virtual representative within the VR world, Gummidging attempts to define how you perceive the world. This can be illustrated using an example. In the work currently underway at Avebury, we are interested in exploring ideas of ancestor worship, and control over access to the monument in late Neolithic ritual practice (for discussions see Barrett 1994; Pollard and Gillings 1998; Parker-Pearson and Ramilisonina 1998; Gillings and Pollard *in press*). Through Gummidging we are currently constructing not one VR-model but three Virtual-Aveburys:

- An Avebury of exclusion, whereby physical access to the henge and associated Avenue of standing stones is blocked (and perhaps the size of the stones and earthworks are exaggerated).
- An Avebury of inclusion, whereby access to the Avenue and earthen bank is permitted but access to the henge itself is restricted.
- A Shamanistic/Ancestral Avebury, whereby access to the henge is permitted but the stones are replaced by anthropomorphic representations (and perhaps restrictions upon flying above the surface of the ground are lifted).

Work is currently underway to use this technique of Gummidging to explore the Avebury of the Antiquarian imagination. Here the irregularity suggested by the surviving earthworks and stone settings are replaced by a monument of certainty. The sarsens became a series of formally planned fixtures in a circular context shaped by rigid geometry – the Palladian ideal – a symmetrical, bilaterally balanced, thoroughly Georgian monument (Gillings and Pollard *in press*).

Archaeology in VR – im-material culture studies?

So far we have talked about the role of VR in archaeology, in effect how VR can be used to influence the ways in which archaeologists approach, record and interpret the past. One of the interesting factors to emerge from the discipline of Geography is the notion that in a number of contexts this relationship can be reversed. Rather than VR in Geography, Geographers are already undertaking demographic and social analyses of virtual meeting places and worlds. A good example is the work being undertaken at sites such as Alphaworld (http://www.awcommunity.org/). As an aside it is interesting to note that these virtual cities already have their own museums, folklore and derelict structures (Dodge *in press*; Kitchin *in press*). Archaeology has a well established tradition of utilising computer-based simulations for educational purposes, and virtual-reconstructions and real-time web-based excavation projects will no doubt continue this trend. More intriguing is the notion of virtual-constructs themselves as a form of material culture unique to the late twentieth century. Like artefacts, VR-models can generate lengthy, and often complex biographies. A form of material culture that needs to be studied, curated and examined. Building upon the earlier discussion concerning the 'aura' of virtual-simulations, although the original aura of a place or structure is lost upon its reproduction, this is not to say that VR-models cannot in time generate new and wholly different auras as they are experienced, altered and incorporated into a host of virtual-settings and social contexts (Baudrillard 1997: 10–11). Gathering, in effect, new things and worlds around them. This was certainly the hope in a recent discussion of one of the stone settings making up the monument at Avebury. Here, publication of a detailed account of the biography of the stone was accompanied by the distribution of its VRML simulacrum on the World Wide Web with the aim of stimulating a new chapter in this biography (Gillings and Pollard *in press*).

Conclusion: Where do we go next?

It is perhaps inevitable that a discussion such as this ultimately fails to provide any neat solutions or concise developmental trajectories. As will hopefully have become clear, given the inherent slipperiness, contingency and flexibility of the term VR itself, this is perhaps to be expected. Rather than seeking to offer another conceptually tidy (but ultimately restrictive) bounding definition, the present discussion has instead attempted to stress the breadth and flexibility of VR.

What we hope to have illustrated is that at present, VR is under theorised and shrouded in an opaque mist of ambiguity and mis-representation. By fore-grounding issues such as authenticity and the status of reality, and the crucial need to develop accessible practical techniques grounded in the current capabilities of VR, we hope to have drawn attention to the relevant issues and acted as a stimulus to the debates that will be instrumental in forging a profitable relationship between archaeology and the technology.

Notes

1. For an example of this complex dialectic between fragmentary empiricist data and informed speculation see the Peel Gap case-study undertaken by Gillings and Goodrick (1996).
2. Virtual Stonehenge can be accessed from the following URL:http://www.intel.com/cpc/explore/stonehenge/index.htm (accessed 10/6/99).
3. When the rendered CAD model of the Alicami was converted into VRML, the resultant file occupied 15MB of disk space before any texture details were added. This rather sparse VRML model ran at an astounding 1 frame per 40 minutes on a 400Mhz Pentium PC! In contrast the highly detailed Bubbleworld file is of the order of 500Kb.

Bibliography

Barrett, J., 1994. *Fragments from Antiquity: An archaeology of Social Life in Britain, 2900–1200 BC.* Oxford: Blackwells.

Baudrillard, J., 1983. *Simulations.* New York: Semiotext(e).

Baudrillard, J., 1997. Objects, Images, and the possibility of Aesthetic Illusion. In N. Zurbrugg (ed.). *Jean Baudrillard, Art and Artefact,* pp. 7–18, London: Sage.

Bintliff, J., 1997. The Role of Science in Archaeological Regional Surface Artefact Survey. In D. Dirksen & G. von Bally (eds). *Optical technologies in the Humanities,* pp. 9–28, Berlin: Springer.

Brodlie, K., (in press). Web-based virtual environments. In P. Fisher & D. Unwin (eds). *VR and Geography.* New York: Taylor & Francis.

Brodlie, K., Dykes, J., Gillings, M., Haklay, M., Kitchen, R. & Kraak, M-J., (in press). Geography in VR: introduction. In P. Fisher & D. Unwin (eds). *VR and Geography.* New York: Taylor & Francis.

Caygill, H., Coles, A. & Klimowski, A., 1998. *Walter Benjamin for Beginners.* Cambridge: Icon Books.

Delooze, K. & Wood, J., 1991. Furness Abbey Survey project: the applications of computer graphics and data visualisation to reconstruction modelling of an historic monument, in Lockyear, K. & Rahtz, S. (eds), *Computer Applications and Quantitative Methods in Archaeology 1990,* pp. 141–148. Oxford: British Archaeological Reports (Supp. Series 565).

Diamond, S. J., 1996. *Replicating Rock Art: the European Appropriation of a Palaeolithic Past at Lascaux II.* Unpld. MA Dissertation: University of Southampton.

Dodge, M., (in press). Explorations in Alphaworld: the Geography of 3D virtual worlds on the Internet. In P. Fisher & D. Unwin (eds). *VR and Geography.* New York: Taylor & Francis.

Dovey, K., 1985. The quest for authenticity and the replication of environmental meaning. In D. Seamon & R. Mugerauer (eds), D*welling, place and environment: towards a phenomenology of person and world,* pp. 33–49. Dordrecht: Martinus Nijhoff Publishers.

Dykes, J., (in press). Building Information Rich Environments using Geo-referenced Digital Panoramic Imagery: some thoughts, examples and experiences. In P. Fisher & D. Unwin (eds). *VR and Geography.* New York: Taylor & Francis.

Edmonds, M., 1999. *Ancestral Geographies of the Neolithic.* London: Routledge.

Fisher, P.F., 1994. Probable and fuzzy models of the viewshed operation. In Worboys, M &. F. (ed). *Innovations in GIS: selected papers from the First national Conference on GIS Research UK,* pp. 161–75. London: Taylor & Francis.

Forte, M., (ed) 1996. *Virtual Archaeology: Great Discoveries Brought to Life Through Virtual Reality.* London: Thames and Hudson.

Gidlow, J., (in press). Rock art and Bubble Worlds. In D. W. Wheatley (ed), *Proceedings of the 1998 Computer Applications in Archaeology United Kingdom Conference.* Southampton Archaeology Monographs series, Oxford: Oxbow Press.

Gillings, M., 1999. Engaging place: exploring the potential of VR in experiential landscape studies. In Dingwall, L., Exon, S., Gaffney, V., Lafflin, S. & van Leusen, M. (eds). *Computer Applications and Quantitative Methods in Archaeology: Proceedings of the 25th Anniversary Conference, University of Birmingham, April 1997,* pp. 247–254. Oxford: British Archaeological Reports S750.

Gillings, M., (in press a). Plans, Elevations and Virtual worlds: the development of techniques for the routine construction of hyperreal simulations. In J. Barcelo (ed), *Virtual Reality Applications in Archaeological Research.*

Gillings, M., (in press b). Virtual archaeologies and the hyperreal (or, what does it mean to describe something as *virtually*-real?). In P. Fisher and D. Unwin (eds). *VR and Geography.* New York: Taylor & Francis.

Gillings, M. & Goodrick, G. T., 1996. Sensuous and Reflexive GIS: exploring visualisation and VRML. *Internet Archaeology* 1, (http://intarch.ac.uk/)

Gillings, M. & Pollard, J., (in press). Non-portable stone artefacts and contexts of meaning: The tale of Grey Wether (museums.ncl.ac.uk/Avebury/stone4.htm). *World Archaeology* 31(2).

Gillings, M. & Wheatley, D. W., (in press). Seeing is not believing: unresolved issues in archaeological visibility analysis. In B. Slapsak (ed). *On the good use of GIS in Ancient Landscape Studies 2.* Brussels: EC.

Gillings, M., Goodrick, G. T., Pollard, J. & Wheatley, D. W., (forthcoming). *Processional and post-processional archaeology: understanding the West Kennet Avenue, Avebury.*

Goodrick, G., 1999. VRML, Virtual Reality and Visualisation: The best tool for the job? In Dingwall, L., Exon, S., Gaffney, V., Lafflin, S. & van Leusen, M. (eds). *Computer Applications and Quantitative Methods in Archaeology: Proceedings of the 25th Anniversary Conference, University of Birmingham, April 1997:* 266–268. Oxford: British Archaeological Reports S750.

Goodrick, G., & Harding, J., (in press). VRML reconstruction of the Neolithic monuments complex of Thornborough, North Yorkshire – a phenomenological investigation of the night sky. In J. Barcelo (ed.), *Virtual Reality Applications in Archaeological Research.*

Gregory, D., 1994. *Geographical Imaginations.* London: Blackwells.

Harvey, F., (in press). Visualising data quality through interactive metadata browsing in a VR environment. In P. Fisher and D. Unwin (eds). *VR and Geography.* New York: Taylor & Francis.

Higuchi, T., 1983. *The visual and Spatial Structure of Landscapes.* Massachusetts: MIT Press.

Ingold, T., 1992. Culture and the perception of the environment. In E. Croll and D. Parkin (eds). *Bush base: forest farm*, pp. 39–56. London: Routledge.

Kitchin, R., (in press). There's no there there: virtual reality, space and cartography. In P. Fisher and D. Unwin (eds). *VR and Geography.* New York: Taylor & Francis.

McQuire, S., 1998. *Visions of Modernity.* London: Sage.

Parker Pearson, M. & Ramilisonina., 1998. Stonehenge for the ancestors: the stones pass on the message. *Antiquity* 72 (276), pp. 308–326.

Penny, S., 1993. Virtual Bodybuilding. *Media Information Australia* 69, pp. 17–22.

Pollard, J. & Gillings, M., 1998. Romancing the Stones: towards an elemental and virtual Avebury. *Archaeological Dialogues 5(2),* pp. 143–164.

Pringle, M. J., & Moulding, M. R., 1997. Applications for Virtual Reality, and associated Information technology, in the illustration of archaeological material. *Graphic Archaeology*, pp. 22–33.

Reilly, P., 1991. Towards a Virtual Archaeology, in Lockyear, K. & Rahtz, S. (eds). *Computer Applications and Quantitative Methods in Archaeology 1990,* pp. 133–40. Oxford: British Archaeological Reports (Supp. Series 565).

Renfrew, C., 1979. *Investigations in Orkney.* London: Society of Antiquaries.

Snyder, J., 1989. Benjamin on reproducibility and aura: a reading of The Work of Art in the Age of its Technical Reproducibility. In G. Smith (ed.). *Benjamin: Philosophy, Aesthetics, History*, pp. 158–174. Chicago: University of Chicago Press.

Thomas, J., 1996. *Time, culture and identity.* London: Routledge.

Tilley, C., 1994. *A Phenomenology of Landscape.* Oxford: Berg.

Wheatley, D. W. & Earle, G. (in press). Will the real Avebury please stand up? VR as an analytical tool for interpretative archaeology. In D. W. Wheatley (ed.). *Proceedings of the 1998 Computer Applications in Archaeology United Kingdom Conference.* (Full title to be confirmed) Southampton Archaeology Monographs series, Oxford: Oxbow Press.

CHAPTER 5

From museum store to data warehouse: archaeological archives for the twenty-first century

Francis Grew

Background: attitudes towards IS/IT within museums and archaeological field units in England

Since the mid-1980s there has been extensive use of computer systems within archaeological field units in England. In 1985 a survey was conducted of computer usage in British archaeology generally, and about 25 units in England were found to be users at that time (Richards 1986, Appendix 1). When the survey was updated just three years later, the figure had risen to nearly 40 (Booth, Grant & Richards 1989, Appendix 1). The situation today is clear in outline if not in detail. It can be reasonably assumed that most field units are computerised to some degree – though it should be noted that the most recent survey shows as many as six of the 38 field units which responded to the questionnaire in fact use no computers at all (Condron *et al* 1999, 22–3, Table 5.7; see also Table 5.3 (p 18). This also highlights the very poor response rate (< 30%) from such organisations.

As Richards has pointed out (1991, 172–3), the impetus towards computerisation in the 1980s came from the availability, for the first time, of cheap microcomputers and business software, rather than from a desire to build upon the type of data analysis, usually statistically based, that had been pioneered on university mainframes during the previous decade. Initially, therefore, the emphasis was on word-processing for reports and on simple databases, principally for context-level information, artefacts and environmental evidence (Grant 1986, 17–19; Ross 1991, 3). More recently, attention has turned towards imaging and digital photography; and towards surveying, planning and mapping, chiefly by means of CAD technologies (Beck, this volume). Geographical Information Systems are gradually being introduced by field units for the purpose of intra-site analysis, but for a number of reasons the rate of adoption has been much slower than it has been among the national agencies that use GIS primarily for cultural resource management (Harris & Lock 1995, 350, 356)

It is consistent with the role of a field unit that efforts seem generally to have been targeted toward devising systems for recording and analysing data, as a means of preparing written reports, for instance, rather than in structuring data for public presentation or long-term archiving. Whereas at the national level the emphasis has been on developing standards and vocabulary lists to describe site types and monuments (Stewart 1999, 20; Quine 1999a), so far as field archaeology goes, the impression is of numerous independent developments closely linked to local methodologies and requirements (Booth 1995, 6–7). Many different programs are currently in use for a wide range of different, but often overlapping, functions (Condron et al 1999, 63, Table 8.1; William Kilbride, *pers comm*). Significantly, there are no standard commercial applications for handling archaeological data, although there are some proprietary standards for non-digital site recording that have received broad acceptance (for example, Museum of London 1994) and a few computer packages that have been developed by individuals or organisations and are now used more widely within the profession. Arguably the most comprehensive and widely applicable of these is the *Integrated Archaeological Database System* that was originally created by the Scottish Urban Archaeological Trust (Rains 1995); but mention should also be made of *G-Sys*, which was developed initially for the West Heslerton project (Powlesland 1998, Sections 2.6.9, 3.2), and of the Central Excavation Unit's *Delilah*, which is now out-dated but was used by a number of field units in the late 1980s and early 1990s (Booth, Grant & Richards 1989, Appendix 3).

During the past few years there have been several initiatives aimed at producing high-level catalogues of archaeological data and making these available over the Internet. The National Monuments Record and the various local Sites and Monuments Records contain a vast corpus of information, built up over 20 years or more, and in many cases plans are already well advanced to provide web access (Beagrie 1994, 33–4; RCHME/EH/ALGAO 1998). Here the information inevitably relates more to sites and topographical data than to artefacts, say, or to archives more generally. Arguably the most important new initiative, at least so far as digital archives are concerned, is the creation of the Archaeology Data Service (ADS), funded by the Joint Information Systems Committee of the Higher Education Funding Council (Richards 1997; http://ads.ahds.ac.uk/). ADS's role is not principally to hold excavation archives themselves, but rather to develop a searchable catalogue with metadata records that summarise the resources available and allow the enquirer to contact the appropriate archive repository – at present mainly by 'traditional' means, but in the future directly on-line.

In England, museums are the ultimate repositories for most archaeological site archives – but, as a recent survey has shown (Swain 1998, 24–33), the rate at which archives are deposited by excavation units varies considerably from place to place. In Oxfordshire, for instance, most archives have already been deposited, whereas in the City of York hardly any have. There are many different reasons for this, ranging from the physical storage capacity of a particular museum to the ability of the excavation unit itself to provide quasi-museum functions. The length of time it takes to analyse and publish the results, especially of large projects, is often the single most important factor that impedes deposition.

As in field archaeology, there was a steady adoption of computer technology in museums during the 1980s and 1990s (see, for example, Roberts 1986, 15–16), though the rate of progress varied enormously between institutions. Leaving aside the standard 'office' functions, word-processing, financial control etc, the emphasis was principally on collections management: inventorying collections, controlling the movement of objects and administering loans (ibid, 43, Table 18B). At least one of the reasons, perhaps the main reason, for this particular emphasis was the need to respond to a series of reports by government organisations, such as the National Audit Office, that were highly critical of museums' ability to account for their collections (Booth 1995, 4). The extent of computerisation today is evident from a survey conducted in 1998, where just ten of the 290 institutions responding to the questionnaire reported that they had no computer facilities at all (Dawson & McKenna 1999, 51). Even though many of those which failed to respond, predominantly small or very small institutions, can be assumed to have no computerised systems either, the figures nevertheless demonstrate the extent to which automation has penetrated the large and medium-sized museums that house the bulk of archaeological archives. Significantly, however, from the point of view of archaeology, whereas 212 of the respondents stated that they ran a collections database, just 28 had GIS or CAD facilities (ibid, 52).

In tandem with the emphasis on collections management, museums have, from the start, had an interest in using and refining standard term lists and procedures. This originated in the work of the Information Retrieval Group of the Museums Association (IRGMA) in the late 1960s, but standards development continues to be pursued with enthusiasm, principally under the leadership of the Museum Documentation Association (mda) (for the early history of computerised documentation in UK museums, see Roberts 1984, 137–9; Roberts 1985, 21–2). The mda (*sic*) (http://www.mda.org.uk) is funded partly by government through the Museums & Galleries Commission and partly on a commercial basis through sales of its products and services.

In 1987 the mda released MODES (*Museum Object Data Entry Software*), a purpose-built collections management application targeted principally at the needs of the smaller museum (Gill 1996, 41). MODES has now been installed at well over 200 sites in the UK and development has passed from the mda itself to a User Association (Dawson & McKenna 1999, 19; http://www.mdocassn.demon.co.uk/modeswin.htm). Conversely, many of the larger museums in the late 1980s and early 1990s developed entirely in-house systems based on Oracle, Informix or similar multi-purpose relational database engines (Dawson & Gill 1996, 11, 49–56.). These often failed to meet expectations and in most cases have now been replaced by large-scale commercial museum applications with an international customer base (for example, *Collection*, *MicroMusée* or *Multi MIMSY*; Dawson & McKenna 1999, 18-19). For sales in the UK these applications are mostly tailored to comply with the mda's *Spectrum* (MDA 1997a), a set of standards and guidelines for good museum practice.

Unfortunately, nearly all these museum systems currently share serious limitations when it comes to accommodating archaeological archives. As the very name, *Museum Object Data Entry Software*, implies, the emphasis tends to be on artefacts rather than on sites or environmental material, and on single entities or groups of entities that have simple relationships. Consistent with this, the two main foci of development at the present time are on an *Archaeological Objects Thesaurus* (MDA 1997b) and on the critical problem of documenting adequately the transfer to museums of the physical and intellectual ownership of archaeological archives (Longworth 1998).

These differences in the application of IT thus reflect real differences in 'culture' between museums and field archaeologists. But perhaps this very disparity will be turned to our advantage if we can draw out the strengths from both sides and combine them dynamically so as to create what might be termed *data warehouses*. This concept of data warehousing, a system of information management that originated in the need to engender more informed decision-making in large organisations (see, for example, Laudon & Laudon 1997, 218–20). It is based on the presumption that data initially produced at a local, *operational*, level will in fact have much wider applicability and will become a source of creative ideas, once it has been consolidated and combined, Table 1. The process of 'warehousing', in effect, establishing and maintaining a 'living archive', will typically involve the organisation of the data into a single structure whose particular design (tight or loose, hierarchical or networked) will depend on the function it is to serve.

Table 1. Characteristics of the data warehouse. Based on the definition by Laudon & Laudon (1997, 219, Table 7.2), adapted and applied to archaeology

Operational data *[Produced by field units]*	Data warehouse data *[Created and maintained by museums or archives]*
Current only	Recent and historical
Stored in multiple environments	Stored in a single environment
Rapidly changing, with an emphasis on creation	Slowly changing, with an emphasis on maintenance
Used by the creator	Used by others
Isolated, with consistency within but not between databases	Connected, with defined links between units of information
Organised from an operational or functional view – for instance, by the individual site, artefact specialism or report goal	**Organised around major informational themes – for instance, periods, processes or activities**

To develop archaeological archives in this way, we should therefore:

• build on traditional archaeological expertise in studying material 'in bulk', and in developing spatial and temporal models;

• build on museum skills, as revealed traditionally through the medium of the gallery or exhibition, in providing access and in combining archaeological material with other forms of data, thereby enhancing its potential significance.

The challenge we face is how to create an environment, or, perhaps, formal structures, within which these can be achieved. Most archaeological fieldwork in England is developer-funded within the confines of PPG16 and MAP2, and has the aim of recording the site before redevelopment and of producing an academic report. Most museums are central or local-government funded, and have a remit for collections management, display and education.

How, therefore, can we bring the two together, so that archaeological data can be created in a way that guarantees preservation and access?

Archaeological archives in Greater London

The general picture that I have outlined is mirrored at the local level by the situation in Greater London. In the 1970s and 1980s well over 1,500 sites were excavated (Schofield & Maloney 1998; Thompson, Westman & Dyson 1998), and during that period the archives remained entirely with the field units that produced them. In 1992 the decision was taken to transfer all this material to the curatorial department of the Museum of London. Of the 1,500 or more site archives only about 350 contain any digital data; though since most of these concern deeply stratified sites in central London, rather than suburban or semi-rural ones in Greater London, the number of individual records is very large. Nearly all the structured data relates to artefacts, rather than to site records or environmental material, though there are large numbers of reports in word-processed form.

The Museum has purchased Multi MIMSY (see above) as its primary tool for managing and cataloguing its collections (Roberts 1999). Multi MIMSY is a large-scale Oracle-based application, developed by Willoughby Associates of Chicago, Illinois (http://www.willo.com/; see also Keene, Grant & Warren 1996), and we propose to develop this as the principal repository for both site, artefact and 'ecofact' data. Additional applications will probably be required to provide GIS-type functionality and a front-end public interface. So far, 140,000 artefact records have been migrated to Multi MIMSY, together with top-level information, addresses, names of excavators, short abstracts etc, relating to about 4,000 sites. We are currently working on the specifications for a series of extensions to the system. One of these will provide facilities for handling those categories of material, pottery, building materials or animal bone, for example, that are generally not recorded by archaeologists as individual objects but as ware-, form- or species-groups (often in a statistical manner; see below). Another extension will make it possible to place an individual object within the particular scheme of stratigraphic 'phasing' that has been applied to the site; or, conversely, to assemble all the objects that relate to a given 'phase' (for the phasing methodology employed in relation to many of the sites that now form part of the Museum of London's collection, see Williams 1991, especially 191 (Fig 10.1), 192–3; also Museum of London 1998, Section 2.1.18).

In addition to managing archives created in the past, the Museum of London is prepared to accept archives generated in the future by professional fieldwork in any of the 32 boroughs that comprise Greater London. But whereas previously our role was essentially passive, as a store for archaeological material, we now see ourselves taking a more active role in archive creation, in line with our commitment not only to preserve but to provide access. An essential tool for implementing this new role is our *General standards for the preparation of archaeological archives deposited with the Museum of London* (Museum of London 1998), which was issued to all archaeological contractors in October 1998 after a period of consultation with English Heritage, the contractors themselves and others. This document itemises, first, the categories of data that the Museum requires to be supplied in digital form for access or management purposes and, secondly, the procedures to be adopted for formatting and transferring any other categories of digital data that were created during the course of the project.

Digital archives: preservation issues

Let us now consider some of the issues arising from the use of digital media for the purposes of ensuring long-term *preservation* of archives.

First it is essential to distinguish resources that were created originally in digital form, from digitisation, for preservation purposes, of resources that were created on paper. These raise different questions for the archivist. In the latter case, digitisation of paper records, he or she must consider the relative value of other preservation media, such as microfilm or microfiche. Many of these 'traditional' media have the advantages of low creation costs, proven archival stability and easy maintenance. Sometimes, indeed, it may even be appropriate to produce hard copies of material produced purely digitally and archive it, say, on microfilm. This would be consistent with the trend in many major libraries and record offices towards 'a hybrid approach that marries microfilm for preservation and digital imaging for access' (Kenney 1998, 4).

Most of the problems that arise when attempting to preserve digital archives are a consequence of the rapid evolution of the medium and of the highly competitive commercialism of the computer industry. It is by now commonly recognised that the approach taken to preservation cannot be dependent to any great extent on particular physical media (Garrett & Waters 1996, 5). There will be few 3.5 inch disk drives in the mid-21st century. What is perhaps less commonly recognised is that dependence on a particular software format can be just as risky. Simple 'bit copying' of data from one physical medium to another, a process often termed *refreshment* (ibid, 5–6; ADS 1999, Section IV.A), presupposes the future existence of applications to manipulate it. At present, however, the lack of compatibility between applications produced by rival manufactures, and in some cases the limited backward compatibility even between releases of the same application, suggest that this is likely to be a false assumption.

Consequently, most archives are now turning to a policy of *migration* (*ibid*): the wholesale transfer, when required, of data from one hardware/software configuration to another or from one generation of computer technology to another. For migration to be possible, data must be transferred to the archive in readable form, *with documentation to explain what it is* (see below). After studying the documentation, and having decided whether the data are in a format that is 'current' or in one that already requires migration, the archivist can either read it into 'live' systems, so that it will be automatically carried forward as the repository's own applications are upgraded, or maintain it off-line in a way that still guarantees preservation. In practice, I believe the decision whether to keep data on or off-line should be informed mainly by storage and access needs, rather than by different approaches to preservation. Off-line data requires just as careful, perhaps more careful, management, simply because its readability is not tested by large numbers of users.

One particular aspect of migration that has perhaps been inadequately recognised is that it is rarely a 'loss-less' process (Bearman 1996, 149). A resource that has been created digitally may have meaning, and, in some cases, 'added value', enshrined in its very structure as much as in its individual data elements. Just as the choice of a scale for drawing reflects a conscious decision about the function of the illustration, so a database is invariably an implementation of a particular conceptual model (Burnard 1991, 100–101) – the strategy that determines the collection and analysis of the data. This original model may no longer be apparent if the data is transferred uncritically to a different application. Take as an example a database table of the type regularly used in England to record the pottery from an excavation (Orton, Tyers & Vince 1993, 57–64). Records with fields such as 'Fabric' (the 'ware' or type of pottery), 'Form', 'Rim Diameter', 'Estimated Vessel Equivalent' (the degree of completeness, reckoned as a percentage) and 'Weight' could, *prima facie*, be absorbed easily within a standard museum cataloguing system. Before migration could take place, however, it would be essential to establish whether each record related to an individual sherd, to a group of sherds from the same vessel or to groups of sherds from vessels of the same fabric and form (ibid, 58). This is, after all, a *statistically-based* recording system, geared more to answering high-level questions about date, trade and status (ibid, 23) than to contextualising the individual pot. But while the precise method-ology should have been made *explicit* in documentation accompanying the table (see above), it might also be *implicit* in the way that particular table articulated with other tables in the database: it might, for instance, be related more closely to higher-level records than to single-context or individual object ones. In preparing for migration we should, therefore, have to decide how essential it was to replicate the *meaning of the database* as well as the meaning of the data itself.

From issues relating to the preservation of digital archives generally, we can turn to consider standards for file and data formatting – a further set of problem areas. For the reasons stated above, the aim should be to avoid complexity and proprietary standards, though in practice this is hardly ever possible. The British Library has issued guidelines that enable data compilers to 'score' their methods and formats for 'risk', taking account of factors such as the type of material (text, image or map, for instance) and the algorithm (proprietary or non-proprietary, compressed or uncompressed) (Bennett 1997; see also Brown, et. al. 1999, Section 6.2, for file formats recommended by the Archaeology Data Service).

Unfortunately, there are very few non-proprietary, international standards that have received common acceptance. For text we have ASCII, and for simple description of text documents we have RTF or HTML, SGML and so forth – all of which are ASCII files with visible control codes. Word-processor files are not suitable for preservation of text, except in carefully managed environments. For raster graphics there is uncompressed TIFF – in fact a proprietary format but so widely licensed and comparatively simple in structure as to be regarded as a safe choice for preservation (PRO 1998, 45). For databases, some would argue the same for DBF – another widespread, though proprietary, standard although it is doubtful whether DBF can cope with the complex archaeological databases that are now being created.

In some key fields, which are of particular concern to archaeologists, the *only* available standards are proprietary. These fields include CAD, where it looks as though the DWG and DXF formats developed by Autodesk (http://www.autodesk.com/) have become the *de facto* standards, and GIS, where the Arc/Info or Shapefile formats developed by ESRI (http://www.esri.com/) will probably predominate, at least for the time being (used for management of GIS data by the Archaeology Data Service, for example; Gillings & Wise 1998, 53–4, Section 6.3.3.1). An important new format is Adobe's PDF, which allows documents to be viewed as they were intended to be printed, ie as images, yet at the same time provides facilities for word-searching in the manner of a word-processor file or database. PDF is proprietary, but the standards specification has been placed in the public domain by the owners and it is being rapidly adopted by major archives such as the Public Record Office – as yet, though, mainly for access purposes (PRO 1998, 46).

And, finally, even when the choice has been made about the file format, there are additional issues to be considered, especially if the task is to digitise images (Chapman 1998, 47–55). What is the optimum resolution for scanning? If the aim is preservation, a very high resolution will normally be required – but can this be matched with the capacity of the software and hardware infrastructure? If the image is in colour, what colour space should be used? RGB, which relates to projected, on-screen colour or CMYK, which is a printer's format?

It will be clear, therefore, that I have substantial reservations about the usefulness of certain types of digitisation – *if the purpose is principally, or entirely, preservation of data that was not created in digital form*. At the Museum of London, our general policy on accepting and maintaining digital archives is as follows:

We do not propose to digitise manual records 'en masse' for the purpose of preservation *alone*. We will continue to use traditional preservation media such as microfilm.

While encouraging field units to deposit all data that has been created digitally, we take a 'rule of thumb' approach to file and data formats, but are prescriptive as regards documentation. Broadly speaking, we plan to archive data on the systems which we have selected to become the standard for our organisation, thereby ensuring automatic 'refreshment', or appropriate 'migration', as hardware or software is upgraded. At the present time, the principal applications are Microsoft Office products (for word-processing, spreadsheets and small databases), Oracle and AutoCAD. For purposes of transfer, however, depositors may present data in many other additional formats. Our *Standards for the preparation of archives* list is, firstly, a series of acceptable formats, ie those from which data can easily be 'migrated' to the supported applications I have mentioned, and, secondly, our requirements for metadata (Museum of London 1998, Section 2.7.3). The metadata record provides essential documentation of the data itself, filenames, version numbers, software used, creators, date of creation and so forth, and must be provided as plain ASCII text (for current initiatives on the development of metadata for *preservation*, rather than access, purposes, see Day 1998a; summarised, particularly with regard to the preservation of images, in Day 1998b.)

We request that archival-quality hard copies are deposited for some resources that have been created in digital form. Sometimes, for example, in the case of site drawings, this is because we feel that in the absence of a universal and stable standard we cannot otherwise guarantee the long-term preservation of essential site records. Otherwise, it is because data has been created by applications that are so specialised that we are unable to support them ourselves. In those instances, national research institutions may often provide satisfactory alternative facilities for archival storage – for example, English Heritage's Ancient Monuments Laboratory in regard to geophysical surveys (see http://www.eng-h.gov.uk/SDB/ for on-line access to the English Heritage Geophysical Survey Database).

Digital archives: access opportunities

It is time to turn from preservation issues to the opportunities that digital archiving provides for access. Let me start by stating three premises that underlie our policy towards the London Archaeological Archive:

First, that there is a wide range, and significant number, of people wishing to use it, in some form. These include academics, students, amateur and professional archaeologists in London and abroad, and the general public. These potential users currently make written or telephone enquires, or visit the museum in person.

Second, that information within an archaeological archive can be reworked in innumerable different ways. A single publication or gallery exhibit, however 'definitive', often only reflects *one story*, one view of the available data (Hodder 1989, 271–3; Davis 1997, 85, 88-93).

Third, that data locked within archaeological archives can be enriched by combination with resources outside. This process gives greater significance to, and provides a context for, the archaeological finds themselves. Obvious examples of such resources are documents or historical photographs. Less commonly used at present, perhaps, are environmental or conservation surveys and oral history.

When we match these premises against the potentials of digital archives, especially when available in hypertext form and suitable for web delivery, we find a remarkable degree of synergy (Landow 1997, 33–48; see also Hodder 1999, 126–7; 180–4):

First, there is the potential for facilitating both multi-user access and remote access. For some users the digital records may become the sole and sufficient method of accessing the site archive, whereas for others they may provide a means of selecting material and preparing for a visit in person.

Second, there is the potential for using sophisticated tools for handling and analysing data. These include search mechanisms and 'intelligent agent' software; viewers for images; and Geographical Information Systems.

And, third, there is potential for creating gateways into other resources – links to record offices, libraries or other archives. In the case of London, for instance, digitisation will for the first time make it possible to link easily the site records held by the Museum with the records for the same sites held by the Greater London Sites and Monuments Record.

Consequently, whereas I am cautious about digitisation for the purposes of preservation, I am extremely optimistic about digitisation for the purposes of providing access – though, as Peter Ucko has stressed (1992, x–xi; see also Hodder 1999, 185–7), care must be taken to ensure that it does not inadvertently lead to disenfranchisement by reason of the vastly unequal availability of computer technology in different countries of the world and among different sections of the world's population.

It is in line with our intention to promote greater usage and to take a more active role in specifying the form in which archives are to be deposited, that our *Standards for the preparation of archaeological archives* (Museum of London 1998, Section 2.7.1) makes the provision of some categories of digital data mandatory – principally to support current or future access initiatives. One such category is locational data, in the form of precise National Grid co-ordinates for each excavation trench or building survey, to serve as the foundation of a Geographical Information System. Another category comprises the basic catalogues of 'finds', whether recorded as individual items or in ware-, form- or species-groups, so that these can be integrated with the main Museum catalogue to facilitate inter-site study, as well as searching across both the archaeological and the non-archaeological collections.

Finally, I should like to return to metadata. I have already indicated its importance for documenting the creation of digital data and enabling the future management of it. Yet metadata is also a valuable tool for resource discovery, and for this reason we require depositors to provide a metadata record for the entire site archive – not merely the digital components of it. This takes the form of an abstract, that is, a text description consisting normally of between 100 and 500 words, and a 'site authority' database entry, which details the site address, the excavator, the date of excavation and other basic information. This abstract and entry are broadly compatible with the draft CIDOC *Core Data Standard for Archaeological Sites and Monuments* (Quine 1999b, 100–111; http://www.natmus.min.dk/cidoc/archsite/coredata/arch1.htm), though our concern for documentation of the archive rather than of the monument(s) to which it may relate, will inevitably lead to some differences in emphasis.

Our metadata entry is, at the same time, comparable with the Archaeology Data Service's standard for describing site archives, which is in turn an implementation of the Dublin Core, an international metadata standard that has been developed specifically for the purposes of facilitating resource discovery (Miller 1999). The way is open, therefore, for researchers to use top-level data for London sites in combination with any other type of resource, worldwide, that adheres to the Dublin Core standard. I believe we can look forward to the rapid extension of current metadata, keyword and indexing systems to encompass topics of particular archaeological concern, such as buildings, periods and processes, and in the UK a number of working parties are already in session. In the meantime, as a first step, my colleague, Andrew Roberts, has been working with ADS to integrate the Museum's 4,000 'site authorities' both with extracts from the Greater London Sites and Monuments Record and with records for over 700 sites in the city of York, held by the York Archaeological Trust. The catalogue, which is fully searchable, is now available on the ADS website (http://ads.ahds.ac.uk/catalogue/).

Conclusion

As recently as ten years ago most museums in England would probably have been regarded as little more than stores for artefacts from excavations. Their role was passive rather than active. Archives were poorly understood and little used. Information Technology provides many new opportunities – especially for facilitating access and developing new user groups. It also provides tools for new types of data analysis and for the creation of data that can be used in many different ways. If museum curators and field archaeologists can work together to produce archives that fulfil the needs and ambitions of them both, we shall indeed create 'data warehouses' that befit the twenty-first century.

Acknowledgements

For comments on an early draft of this paper I am grateful to Andrew Roberts and Hedley Swain at the Museum of London; and for information on specific points to William Kilbride at the Archaeology Data Service. Especial thanks are due to Gary Lock and Kayt Brown for providing the opportunity to present the paper at WAC4 in January 1999; for much helpful advice; and for exceptional patience in awaiting the completion of the final draft.

Bibliography

ADS 1999. *Guidelines for depositors* (Version 1.1). Archaeology Data Service, York.
  URL: http://ads.ahds.ac.uk/project/userinfo/deposit.html

Beagrie, N. 1994. Museum collections, national archaeological indexes and research: information resources, access and potential, in, Denford, G.T. (ed) *Museum archaeology: what's new?* The Museum Archaeologist (Society of Museum Archaeologists) No. 21, pp. 28–34.

Bearman, D. 1996. Preserving digital information: a review, *Archives and Museum Informatics*, 10 No.2, pp. 148–53.

Bennett, J C. 1997. *A framework of data types and formats, and issues affecting the long term preservation of digital material*, British Library Research and Innovation Report No. 50.
  URL: http://www.ukoln.ac.uk/services/elib/papers/supporting/pdf/rept011.pdf

Booth, B. 1995. Has archaeology remained aloof from the information age?, in Huggett & Ryan (eds), pp. 1–12.

Booth, B K W., Grant, S A V., & Richards, J D. (eds) 1989. *Computer usage in British archaeology*, second edition. Institute of Field Archaeologists Occasional Paper No. 3.

Brown, A., Brown, D., Coles, G., Dawson, D, Dodd, A., Gardiner, J., Lock, G., Longworth, C., Merriman, N., Miller, P., Murray, D., Reeve J., & Wise, A. 1999. *Digital archives from excavation and fieldwork: guide to good practice*. Arts and Humanities Data Service, ADS, York. URL:
  http://ads.ahds.ac.uk/project/goodguides/excavation/

Burnard, L., 1991. Analysing information for database design: an introduction for archaeologists, in Ross, Moffett & Henderson (eds), pp. 99–109.

Chapman, S., 1998. Guidelines for image capture, in NPO/RLG, pp. 39–60.

Condron, F., Richards J., Robinson, D. & Wise, A., 1999. *Strategies for digital data*. Archaeology Data Service, York. URL: http://ads.ahds.ac.uk/project/strategies/

Davis. 1997. Sites without sights: interpreting closed excavations, in J H Jameson (ed), *Presenting archaeology to the public: digging for truths*. London, pp. 84–98.

Dawson, D., & Gill, T., 1996. *The MDA survey of information technology in museums, 1996–97*. Museum Documentation Association.

Dawson, D., & McKenna, G., 1999. *mda Survey of information technology in museums 1998*. mda *Information* Vol. 4 No. 1. URL: http://www.mdocassn.demon.co.uk/info41.htm

Day, M., 1998a. *Metadata for preservation*. UK Office for Library and Information Networking CEDARS Project Document No. AIW01. URL: http://www.ukoln.ac.uk/metadata/cedars/AIW01.html

Day, M., 1998b. Issues and approaches to preservation metadata, in NPO/RLG, pp. 73–84.
  URL: http://www.ukoln.ac.uk/metadata/presentations/rlg-npo/warwick.html

Dingwall, L., Exon, S., Gaffney, V., Laflin, S., & van Leusen, M., (eds) 1999. *Archaeology in the age of the internet* (CAA 97), Oxford: British Archaeological Reports International Series No. 750.

Garrett, J., & Waters, D., (eds) 1996. *Preserving digital information: report of the Task Force on archiving of digital information* (Commission on Preservation and Access, Washington D C, and Research Libraries Group) URL: http://www.rlg.org/ArchTF/index.html

Gill, T., 1996. *The MDA guide to computers in museums*. Museum Documentation Association.

Gillings, M., & Wise, A. (eds), 1998. *GIS guide to good practice*. Archaeology Data Service, York.
  URL: http://ads.ahds.ac.uk/project/goodguides/gis/

Grant, S., 1986. Summary and recommendations, in Richards 1986, pp. 13–31.

Harris, T M., & Lock, G R., 1995. Toward an evaluation of GIS in European archaeology: the past, present and future of theory and applications, in G. Lock and Z. Stančič (eds), *Archaeology and Geographical Information Systems*. London, pp. 349–365.

Hodder, I., 1989. Writing archaeology: site reports in context, *Antiquity* 63, pp. 268–74.

Hodder, I., 1999 *The archaeological process: an introduction*. Oxford.

Huggett, J., & Ryan, N., (eds) 1995. *Computer applications and quantitative methods in archaeology 1994*, Oxford: British Archaeological Reports International Series No. 600.

Keene, S., Grant, A., & Warren, J., 1996. Multi-talented, in *Museums Journal*, 96 No.8 (August 1996), pp. 26–7.

Kenney, A R., 1998. Guidelines vs. Guidance for digital imaging: the opportunity before us, in *Guidelines for digital imaging: papers given a conference in Warwick 28th–30th September 1998*. National Preservation Office and the Research Libraries Group, pp. 4–9.

Landow, G P., 1997. *Hypertext 2.0: the convergence of contemporary critical theory and technology*. Baltimore.

Laudon, K C., & Laudon, J P., 1997. *Essentials of management information systems: organisation and technology*. Prentice-Hall (2nd edn).

Longworth, C., 1998. SPECTRUM archaeology guide, in *Papers from the Standards in Action workshop*. mda *Information* Vol. 3 No. 1. URL: http://www.mdocassn.demon.co.uk/info31cl.htm#Archaeology

Miller, P., 1999. The importance of metadata to archaeology: one view from within the Archaeology Data Service, in Dingwall *et al* (eds), pp. 133–6.

MDA 1997a., *Spectrum: the UK museum documentation standard*. Museum Documentation Association.

MDA 1997b. *MDA archaeological objects thesaurus*. Museum Documentation Association URL: http://www.mdocassn.demon.co.uk/archobj/archcon.htm

Museum of London 1994. *Archaeological site manual* (3rd edn). Museum of London.

Museum of London 1998. *General standards for the preparation of archaeological archives deposited with the Museum of London*. Museum of London. URL: http://www.museumoflondon.org.uk/MOLsite/forum/dep0.html

NPO/RLG 1998. *Guidelines for digital imaging: papers given at the conference in Warwick 28th–30th September 1998*. London. National Preservation Office and the Research Libraries Group.

Orton, C., Tyers, P., & Vince, A., 1993. *Pottery in archaeology*. Cambridge, Cambridge University Press.

Powlesland, D., 1998. The West Heslerton assessment, *Internet Archaeology*, 5, Autumn/Winter 1998. URL: http://intarch.ac.uk/journal/issue5/index.html

PRO 1998. *Guidelines on the management and appraisal of electronic records*. London, Public Record Office, 1998.

Quine, G., 1999a. The role of data standards in digital access and interchange, in Dingwall *et al* (eds), pp. 129–32.

Quine, G., 1999b. The CIDOC standard: an international data standard for recording archaeological sites and monuments, in H J Hansen and G Quine (eds), *Our fragile heritage: documenting the past for the future*. Denmark: National Museum of Denmark, pp. 105–11.

Rains, M J., 1995. Towards a computerised desktop: the Integrated Archaeological Database System, in Huggett & Ryan (eds), pp. 207–10.

RCHME/EH/ALGAO 1998. *Unlocking the past for the new millennium: a new statement of co-operation on Sites and Monuments Records in England. Royal Commission on the Historical Monuments of England*, English Heritage and the Association of Local Government Archaeological Officers.

Richards, J D., (ed) 1986. *Computer usage in British archaeology*. Institute of Field Archaeologists Occasional Paper No. 1.

Richards, J D., 1991. Computers as an aid to post-excavation interpretation, in Ross, Moffett & Henderson (eds), pp. 171–86.

Richards, J D., 1997. Preservation and re-use of digital data: the role of the Archaeology Data Service, *Antiquity* 71, pp. 1057–9.

Roberts , D A., 1984. The development of computer-based documentation. In J M A Thompson (ed), *Manual of curatorship*, pp. 136–41.

Roberts, D A., 1985. *Planning the documentation of museum collections*. Museum Documentation Association.

Roberts, D A., (ed) 1986. *The state of documentation in non-national museums in southeast England*. Museum Documentation Association Occasional Paper No. 9.

Roberts, D A., 1999. Inspiring a passion for London, *Library Technology*, 4.4 (August 1999), pp. 62.

Ross, S.,1991. Introduction: computing, digging and understanding, in Ross, Moffett & Henderson (eds), pp. 1–9.

Ross, S., Moffett, J., & Henderson, J.(eds), 1991. *Computing for archaeologists*. Oxford: Oxford University Committee for Archaeology Monograph No. 18.

Schofield, J., & Maloney, C., (eds) 1998. *Archaeology in the City of London, 1907–1991: a guide to the records of excavations by the Museum of London and its predecessors*, Archaeological Gazetteer Series, vol 1. Museum of London.

Stewart, J., 1999. Has 25 years of computing provided greater physical and intellectual access to archaeology? in Dingwall *et al* (eds), pp. 19–23.

Swain, H., 1998. *A survey of archaeological archives in England*. English Heritage and Museums & Galleries Commission.

Thompson, A., Westman, A., & Dyson, T., (eds) 1998. *Archaeology in Greater London, 1965–1990: a guide to records of excavations by the Museum of London*, Archaeological Gazetteer Series, vol 2. Museum of London.

Ucko, P., 1992. Foreword, in P Reilly and S Rahtz, (eds), *Archaeology and the information age: a global perspective*. London: One World Archaeology No. 21, vii–xi.

Williams, T., 1991. The use of computers in post-excavation and publication work at the Department of Urban Archaeology, Museum of London, in Ross, Moffett & Henderson (eds), pp. 187–200.

CHAPTER 6

Intellectual Excavation & Dynamic Information Management Systems

Anthony Beck

Introduction

"It is valuable for any discipline to take stock from time to time to ask what has been achieved and what further aims and objectives can be set. To address this latter point, it is necessary to decide what the discipline is fundamentally about, and how it compliments other areas of research and scholarship." (O'Connor, 1998, 1)

Use of Geographical Information Systems (GIS) and other computerised visualisation and analysis mediums is no longer news. GIS techniques have been applied to the archaeological record for nearly two decades, hardware and software have matured and costs have fallen to the extent that most archaeological units, all universities and even individuals have access to a GIS engine. However, the problems confronted in this paper lie not in individuals analysing information, but in how data collection and analysis can be integrated and disseminated to improve research frameworks, theory and methodology. Biswell *et al* (1995) and Harris and Lock (1990) also discuss these issues.

Biswell *et al* effectively encapsulate the problems of trying to implement GIS technology within the post *PPG16* contractual archaeology arena in the United Kingdom. They state that most GIS analysis has occurred at the landscape level. This is explained by the fact that the initial uptake of GIS was within academic environments, where there is a larger bias towards landscape studies, and that most analytical modules within GIS are designed for landscape analysis (particularly within raster models).

Landscape analysis, however, clearly generalises primary archaeological data, a process that is necessary in order to examine the data without being swamped by information, a position analogous to the creation of mapping at different scales by organisations such as the Ordnance Survey. This generalisation can be viewed as a means of creating a whole new data set or theme. Landscape analysis using GIS is possible, therefore, because the researcher creates the theme with the appropriate prior knowledge to make the analysis possible. This is in sharp contrast to analysis of information at an intra-site level. Here the researcher will normally have no control over how the information is collected and consequently will find research hampered by a large and complex paper record that is difficult and time consuming to integrate for GIS analysis.

On the other hand, Harris and Lock (1990) focus upon long term and immediate problems concerning aspects of data, dissemination and implementation. GIS should not be thought of as a 'quick fix' to one's spatial data problems (Stine and Decker, 1990, cf. Berry, 1987). The approach of 'ad-hocism' has been rampant within archaeological applications of GIS, and is a common occurrence with software systems generally. Mature broad-based analyses occur only when both the software and the implementing industry reach a threshold of confidence and maturity with the application. The identification of organisational maturity and commitment to improvement within the higher echelons of archaeology is flagged as a significant friction to successful implementation of the technology (Campbell and Masser, 1993). This is exacerbated by the limited computer skills of most UK archaeologists. Harris and Lock (1990) also lament the potential 'loss' of information from past excavations, a problem which has long hounded archaeology, but is still of major import. Is it practical or even possible to convert past archives into a digital format? Do we convert them all or a representative sample? How is this sample defined? More importantly who is to pay, what standard should it be converted to and will it actually be useful? The Archaeology Data Service (ADS) is already tackling some of these issues (Richards, 1997).

Though such problems have been recognised for some time, the successful implementation of data collection systems that realise the high quality data needed for intra-site GIS analysis are the exception rather than the rule. The design and implementation of such systems is an expensive exercise because of the ramifications that extend beyond the traditional modes of data collection. The post-PPG16 'polluter pays' environment, within which all UK archaeological units currently function, further exacerbates this situation. The shift from research led excavations, with core funding, to developer led excavations, based upon competitive tendering, has diminished the opportunities within which an initially expensive and radical approach to archaeological data collection can be realised. There is a feeling held by many UK archaeologists that most developers class archaeological deposits as a contaminant problem. This often results in the lowest bid winning regardless of the quality of ensuing research and polarises contractual and academic archaeologists even more (Chadwick, 1998: 4; Powlesland, *pers. comm.*).

The successful implementation of the computerised component within the post-PPG16 contractual environment is only one facet to the problem. Archaeological information is of a different nature to data collected by most other users of GIS tools due to its 'fuzzy', subjective and interpretative components. These have theoretical ramifications. Hodder has been a champion of research and theory driven excavations and his description of the organisational rationale behind the approach used at Çatalhöyük (Hodder, 1999) has some common themes with the development of the approach in this paper. This is particularly pertinent when considering how one is able to engage with the archaeological resource and the questions this could raise. A cautionary note is struck by Chadwick (1998), however, who gives a general critique of theory driven excavation practices. He is also critical of how Hodder's approach can be incorporated into contractual archaeology when considering the differential pressures that exist between that world and academic environs.

Background

Computers within field archaeology offer a particular challenge to traditional work practices and, with some notable exceptions, it is still rare for projects to have an integrated computerised approach. Even when this occurs it is even rarer for the data set to be fully articulated (Gillings, 1994). A situation that is true within contractual, academic and research environments. The approach to computers, software and computerised information systems in the field is at best fragmented and poorly documented with little effort having gone into co-ordination or dissemination of techniques and approaches. Yet, such information systems, coupled with effective methods of dissemination, could empower any archaeologist by allowing them access to a well-documented, integrated data set.

GIS are heralded as one of the most effective tools to analyse the information resource although few people have seen results of these groundbreaking approaches that form anything better than 'pretty computer generated pictures', never mind the raw data which was used to create them. It is my contention that computer applications have been allowed to run amok with scant regard for theory, practice, data (quality and longevity) and the reality of present day contractual scenarios.

The Framework Archaeology Commitment and Ethos

"I know of no general attempt to assess the relevance of recent theoretical debates to the practice of field archaeology; all too often they seem to be regarded as irrelevant, while work in the field continues in a determinedly empirical and un-selfcritical manner" (Champion 1991: 151)

Theory driven excavation is becoming part of reality, moving beyond academia and slowly filtering into the contractual environment. Although, as Chadwick states (1998, 5) there is still a gulf, and an increasing one at that, between problem-orientated, theoretically informed research projects and development-led, data gathering excavations. UK archaeologists working within the contractual arena are beginning to critically re-appraise excavation and management methodologies to incorporate post-processual and contextual theories (Andrews, Barrett and Lewis, *in prep.*).

Framework Archaeology is a recently established joint venture between the Trust for Wessex Archaeology and the Oxford Archaeological Unit. In the autumn of 1998 Thames Water Utilities Ltd (TWUL) cleared drying beds at Perry Oaks Sludge Works and, in collaboration with the British Airports Authority (BAA), commissioned Framework Archaeology to undertake the archaeological rescue works (Andrews and Barrett, 1998). Framework Archaeology has become the sole contractor for all works associated with BAA and part of the working partnership established between them and other contractual partners is a commitment to team working and quality management. This investment has allowed Framework Archaeology to re-evaluate its recording and working procedures, the result of which is a complete re-appraisal of the approach to the archaeological record. Gill Andrews, acting as the project consultant, and John Barrett, acting as the project academic advisor, are primarily responsible for specifying this approach. John Lewis and Ken Welsh designed the recording system in response to the specification, which was refined and implemented by the project team. Furthermore, BAA as the principal team co-ordinator have adopted a revolutionary stance in their responsibility to the archaeological record, reinforcing their commitment to team members.

Academic aims and the approach

The stated aim of the project is:

" to move beyond the recovery and description of archaeological remains as they are distributed across the landscape and to create an understanding of the history of human habitation." (Andrews and Barrett, 1998)

Theoretically, such an approach involves considering how barriers and space were used in the landscape, how cultural, social and other values can be extrapolated, and how these ideas fit into ideological, political and economic themes. Further thematic modes of conceptualisation are encouraged as a means to understand the inter-relationship of various practices, producing a series of social contexts with meaning and value. Such aspects include the archaeology of production and consumption, of ritual and of land use (*ibid.*).

There are many problems in achieving these goals within an excavation context, primarily what information should be recorded and how? It is relevant to note that the archaeological industry in the UK is very fortunate in having a committed workforce that includes a high proportion of graduates, although the pressures of modern contractual practice have devalued many excavators' roles to that of labourers whose opinions may be ignored (Chadwick, 1998: 4). The research-centred approach, however, needs interpretation to occur in the field to realise its potential, a 'ground up' philosophy that is intended to re-empower the field archaeologist. Communication between the excavation team is, therefore, vital. During the excavation, the role of the academic advisor has not been to direct the project's thought processes but rather to act as a stimulus by injecting current theoretical and thematic information.

The practical ramifications

As part of the field operation of Framework Archaeology it was decided that a two stage sampling procedure would be adopted. Stage 1, defined as *Landscape Generic*, is a consistent control sample taken across all landscape deposits followed by more intensive sampling where the understanding of the deposition process can be refined. This produces a series of grouped contexts that reflect deposition events. The generic sample is analysed *in-situ* following the research criteria and the results of this analysis influence the excavation methodology of Stage 2, defined as *Landscape Specific*. The research criteria frame project thinking in two ways. Firstly, they enable regional patterns to be recognised as the archaeological character of the landscape is established together with an understanding of the structural principles of its inhabitation. Secondly, they enable comparisons in terms of both landscape characterisation and the history of inhabitation in the larger research area and neighbouring regions.

Intellectual debate during excavation is necessary in order to realise these goals and as the Perry Oaks site became more complex, information feedback was essential to maintain the intellectual process. This is a primary ethos of the project and a notable departure from tradition. To a certain extent during any excavation this debate already occurs, though not in an

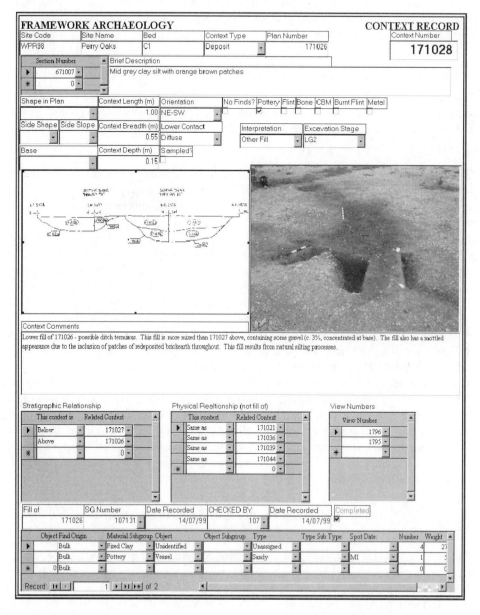

Figure 1. An example of a context sheet as fed back to the field.

overt form and the recording process and its slow or non existent feedback loop limits the extent to which this is productive – a testament to the field practitioners' tenacity rather than a pro-active approach concerned with intellectual input.

Furthermore, the question of 'what to record' has been re-assessed and in order to achieve the theory-driven goal a question centred approach is necessary. This requires a re-appraisal of what information should be recorded at the cut, deposit and grouping levels. The context sheets have been re-designed in response to the information deemed necessary, Figure 1.

The approach and end product definition

"Archaeology embodies a tension between theory and practice. On the one hand, the practice of digging demands a down-to-earth logic. On the other hand, archaeology more than most other disciplines depends on theoretical imagination in order to breathe life into dry-as-dust traces." Hodder, 1993)

The end product of Framework Archaeology excavations is the creation of a data model that fulfils the project aims outlined above. In order to do this the project team requires constant feedback at the context, Landscape Generic and Landscape Specific levels. This promotes an understanding of the processes that created the archaeological deposits at any level and situates ourselves within the landscape of this emerging model, both spatially and temporally.

The Perry Oaks project has also initiated a review of current working practices as delineated within the *Management of Archaeological Projects* (MAP2) (English Heritage, 1991) because the boundaries between what is commonly referred to as excavation and post-excavation have become blurred by necessity. The feedback mechanisms require that information traditionally exploited in the post-excavation phase is made available during excavation in order to understand the site processes. All artefacts and environmental samples are processed, assessed and entered into the database, allowing dynamic analysis of the archive as it grows. The evidence from these data sets (dates, social and economic indicators, etc.) are fed back into the excavation process, another movement away from traditional approaches without which the project aims could not be fulfilled effectively. Furthermore, the creation of 'interpretative groupings' on site has allowed a further post-excavation procedure to be conducted during excavation, allowing the creation of landscape themes and Virtual Reality (VR) reconstruction. This dynamic data set is used to influence excavation within the Landscape Specific phase in conjunction with an understanding of the current corpus of archaeological parallels.

The analytical model and data integration

Archaeology has to deal with a remarkable variety of differing information types (Ryan, 1991) with the typical Archaeological Information System (AIS) using CAD, image editing, database, document and presentation software. Each package is chosen specifically for its ability to handle a certain aspect of the record although, unfortunately, the lack of integration between these packages inhibits the ability to articulate all aspects. Ryan (*ibid.*) and Nickerson (online) advocate solutions to this problem through using a bespoke archaeological database with specifically designed data types to access the differing data models. Although this approach to data storage would be the ideal, the investment in designing and supporting such a system is enormous, particularly when attempting to implement it within a large project. The approach described here took account of standard conversion formats to enable the integration of information between packages and the use of Object Linking and Embedding (OLE) and Open DataBase Connectivity (ODBC) to share data.

"Archaeology is above all a multi-disciplinary subject drawing on a wide range of skills and specialisms... From a computer scientist's perspective, archaeological applications provide some significant challenges, one of which is to develop information systems that can cope with this variety. In the processes of research, excavation, analysis and publication each of the many specialisms generates vast quantities of data, much of it of widely differing types, and the challenge is to provide ways in which this can be presented to and used by all." (Ryan, 1991: 1)

In order to achieve these aims, we felt that a radically different information system was required. One that was rigorous, robust, capable of responding to a dynamic data resource and with the ability to realise the temporal, spatial and aspatial relationships of the excavated record. Current limitations within computer science regarding the modelling of three dimensional information and temporality compound the problems. Another requirement, and complication, was to use software systems that are available to the majority of research and collection bodies, thus ensuring that the project information could be disseminated and analysed effectively after collection.

The conceptual data model

The first stage was to produce a conceptual data model to be approved by the project team and client. The conceptual solution to the problem was outlined covering broad issues and approaches and highlighting any envisaged problems. It had to conform to the conceptual data model provided by the client in order to successfully integrate all sub-contractor works into its overall program and, furthermore, it had to transcend the limitations of the client's model to achieve our own goals.

The spatial management model

To conform to the client's data model, all spatial information is maintained and managed within AutoCAD MAP software. MAP is not just an application, but offers a whole new way of working by providing concurrent design while fulfilling the prescribed requirements for the archaeological discipline by using a software system that is in wide use throughout the industry. The bolt-on application of MAP extends the functionality of AutoCAD by including a powerful topological database builder that can create and seed polygons and export them to a variety of different GIS packages. The ability to visualise raster imagery is also supported. The functionality of this software makes it an ideal environment in which to manage a spatial data set that is updated regularly. The topology builder allows the project

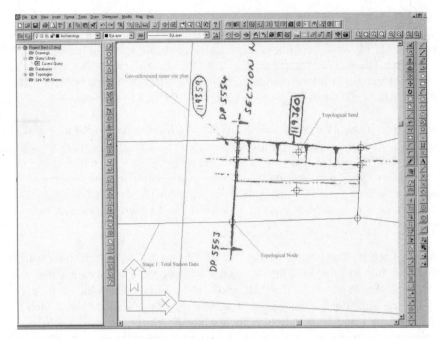

Figure 2. Stage 2 integration of plans by scanning and digitising.

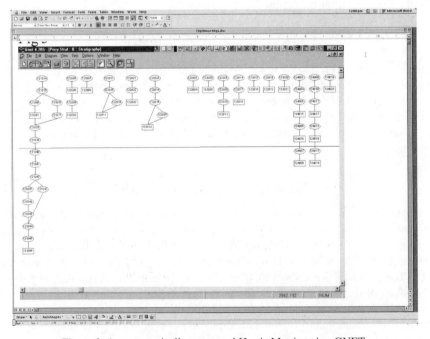

Figure 3. An automatically generated Harris Matrix using GNET.

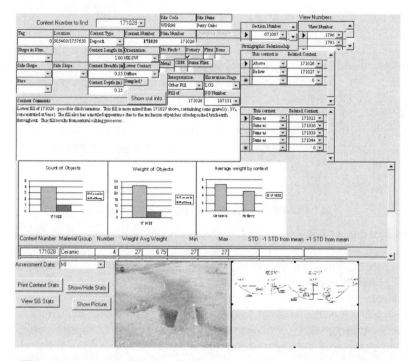

Figure 4. An example of automatically generated object statistics for a context.

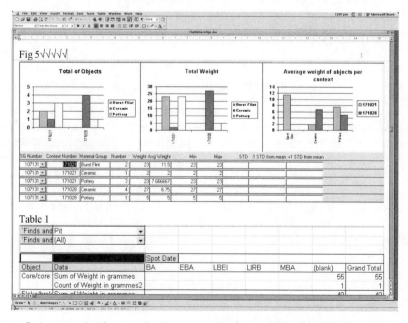

Figure 5. An example of automatically generated object statistics for a Stratigraphic Group.

team to export daily snapshots of the information to the site GIS and to incorporate and manage the three-dimensional VR model visualised within Internet Explorer.

To achieve this data model it was determined that a two-stage data collection procedure would be necessary. Stage 1 is a pre-excavation survey by Total Station, and Stage 2 consists of the direct integration of planimetric information into the pre-excavation model. All plans and sections contain geo-referencing information and each is scanned, digitised and associated with the correct contexts, Figure 2. A proportion of site photographs are taken digitally as they provide a faster mechanism for appraisal and integration, and a digital video camera is used to record interviews with excavators and other information more suited to multimedia.

The aspatial data management model

A single co-ordinated Relational Database Management System model has been devised using Microsoft Access to maintain the aspatial data set during the excavation process. The database has been designed to analyse the object, environmental and context records at the landscape, grouping and assemblage levels.

Referential integrity is essential to the effectiveness of a relational database and during the project design this consideration was fundamental to the development of the information and work flow-lines, Figure 8. Traditional excavation flow-lines do not always reflect this, for example, environmental and object processing and data entry can occur before the context record is entered into a database. Furthermore, dispersing data to specialists at the assessment stage can limit the analysis of information at the assemblage level, mainly due to the different levels of assessment and data structures. The single model proposed here enables the inter-rogation and analysis of information as a whole, thus realising the maximum potential of the aspatial data.

Data articulation and analysis

The on-site assessment of objects and environmental samples allows the dating of objects and deposits and an insight into the formation, economic and environmental processes repre-sented on the site. Furthermore, a running Harris Matrix is automatically generated and validated from the context and group records using GNET software (Ryan, 1988), Figure 3. The combination of these data sets allows phasing which can be fed back into excavation procedures.

The aspatial data set can be analysed within Access, for example Figures 4 and 5, Excel, Table 1, or in conjunction with GIS.

Spatial analysis and visualisation can occur within both AutoDESK World, Figure 6, and G-Sys GIS, Figure 7.

The VR model is built within the spatial management system to articulate the third dimen-sion. This has been a particularly useful tool for the excavation team as they can place themselves within the landscape during any particular period and view the reconstruction, allowing further debate and hypothesis testing.

'Finds and	Pit ▼							
'Finds and	(All) ▼							
		Spot Date						
Object	Data	BA	EBA	LBEI	LIRB	MBA	(blank)	Grand Total
Core/core	Sum of Weight in grammes						55	55
	Count of Weight in grammes2						1	1
Flake/brok	Sum of Weight in grammes						40	40
	Count of Weight in grammes2						12	12
Misc/Multi	Sum of Weight in grammes						17	17
	Count of Weight in grammes2						3	3
Retouched	Sum of Weight in grammes						42	42
	Count of Weight in grammes2						6	6
Scraper	Sum of Weight in grammes						49	49
	Count of Weight in grammes2						2	2
Unidentifie	Sum of Weight in grammes						1049	1049
	Count of Weight in grammes2						21	21
Utilised bla	Sum of Weight in grammes						8	8
	Count of Weight in grammes2						1	1
Vessel	Sum of Weight in grammes		62	8199	10	319		8590
	Count of Weight in grammes2		1	15	1	1		18
(blank)	Sum of Weight in grammes						1706	1706
	Count of Weight in grammes2						10	10
Quern	Sum of Weight in grammes	2087						2087
	Count of Weight in grammes2	1						1
Nodule	Sum of Weight in grammes						7	7
	Count of Weight in grammes2						1	1
Total Sum of Weight in grammes		2087	62	8199	10	319	2973	13650
Total Count of Weight in grammes2		1	1	15	1	1	57	76

Table 1. An example of a combined table using the finds and context tables.

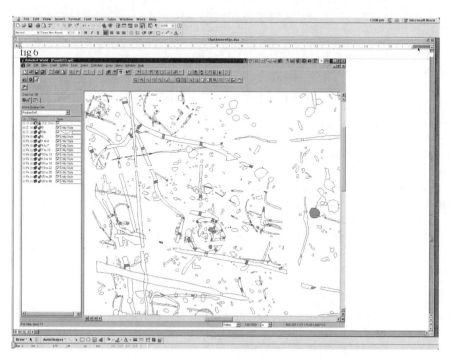

Figure 6. GIS analysis within AutoDESK World showing a thematic map of fired clay by weight.

Anthony Beck

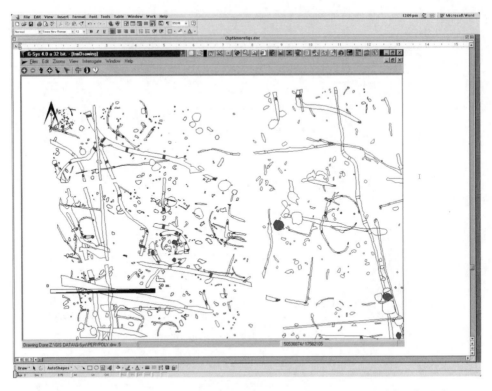

Figure 7. GIS analysis within G-Sys showing the distribution of cuts containing fired clay.

Implementation, the data flow-line and modular systems

Within many industries, many projects implementing GIS solutions have failed. In order to avoid this we decided to compare the approaches of successful and unsuccessful projects. Using Campbell's and Masser's work (1993) it was determined that the most important factors likely to lead to success were, firstly, user-directed implementation which involves the participation and commitment of all the stakeholders in the project, and, secondly, simple applications producing information which is fundamental to the work of potential users.

End-users were consulted at all stages of the project design and have been encouraged to give their own insights into the recording and analysis system. The process of excavation and analysis has been reduced to a flow-line for which modular system manuals have been produced, Figure 8. It is essential for us to understand where data leakage occurs within the system and how to re-evaluate the system approach to prevent leaks occurring. This flow-line is the framework on which the system manuals hang.

However, implementation does not end here and it has been recognised that the introduction of any new approach is a difficult process as there is friction to change at many levels and for many reasons (Campbell and Masser 1993). In order to mitigate against this friction, feedback is essential.

Figure 8. The information flow-line.

Information feedback

Core information is fed back to the field practitioners as part of the data validation procedure and to allow effective record maintenance, Figure 1. Context Group records are disseminated and regular site tours are held in order to encourage team inter-action and to increase current understanding. These feedback mechanisms are essential, especially during the early stages of the project to re-inforce confidence in the approach and to help unite the team as a working unit. Furthermore, occasional lectures, discussion groups and training trips have taken place to maintain a sense of training and continuing professional development. These feedback mechanisms result in the creation of the *Project Design Update Note*, a summary of current understanding in the Landscape Generic phase and how it has influenced strategy in Landscape Specific phase.

Other considerations including deposition, dissemination, data re-use and metadata

So, what is the future for this data set? It obviously has vast research potential, partly because such a co-ordinated approach to fieldwork is rare. The ADS would be the ideal location for subsequent data dissemination and re-use and contact with them has been ongoing. Although the project was established before the ADS had drafted its deposition policy, we are attempting to adhere to their Metadata standards. Other mediums of dissemination under discussion include the Internet and CD-ROM.

The project's approach has a great reliance on state-of-the-art technology that requires considerable skills to use. This is a potential problem for external specialists, some of whom may have individual software skills, but few, if any, will be familiar with all the necessary areas. Therefore, a means to make the data set more accessible to specialists, and other interested parties, is under discussion and will probably reflect the Web-CD approach adopted by Powlesland at West Heslerton (Powlesland, 1997). The archive is stored on CD-ROM but is accessed through an Internet browser using clickable HTML drawings and text, thus allowing access to the spatial, aspatial and interpretative components through one interface.

Conclusion

"The question-centred approach requires a certain courage. Being selective, it is also sacrificial: archaeological remains deemed irrelevant to the questions are ignored. But advantages flow from it. Questions can be framed to explore what people were doing in the landscape at large. History was not enacted just in the handful of places which happen to have found their way onto sites and monuments records. The question-driven project also knows what it wants to collect and why it is collecting it. Moreover, the result of the work is likely to be a coherent story accessible to the public at large." (Morris, 1997)

With reference to O'Connor's quote at the very beginning of this paper, I believe that we have addressed what this particular sub-discipline is about, at least currently. We are applying a bespoke approach to an age-old problem, which should allow research and scholarship to transcend some of their ingrained limitations. Some elements of the project's approach are radical, particularly within the commercial operating environment. The digital archive is based upon the integration of many advances achieved over the past decade, however, and upon completion of the fieldwork a critical re-appraisal of the field, recording and analysis systems used will occur in order to refine the approach.

The ability to 'intellectually' re-interpret approaches to fieldwork has allowed us to create a systematic approach to data collection that takes into account the benefits of modern, accessible information systems. It is able to express elements of the 'fuzzy' nature of the aspatial data set (Gillings and Wise, 1999), for example, by incorporating confidence values. The spatial data set can be used for GIS analysis, VR reconstruction and publication. The emphasis on referential integrity and data validity allows conformity in information production thus enabling successful data management and analysis. The ability to articulate the third dimension and develop theories about the archaeological record while in the field should allow multiple organic narratives to evolve during excavation. Furthermore, information pertaining to project auditing, finances and tracking has resulted in accurate project updates and forecasts to the client resulting in a well-managed project.

For this project at least, the portents of doom for excavation-based Archaeological Information Systems outlined by Biswell *et al* (1995) are unfounded. Here, we have demonstrated that *PPG16* can give opportunities to archaeologists to explore new areas of theory and practice. The evolution of this project can be viewed as a product of exemplary management resulting from the Total Quality Management techniques adopted by BAA. These regard all sub-contractors as team members striving towards the same goal so that archaeologists' roles are elevated from inconvenient nuisances into major project stakeholders. This approach has already demonstrated that we can expect more from the archaeological resource during excavation than traditional excavation frameworks currently offer.

Bibliography

Allen, K.M.S, Green, S.W., and Zubrow, E.B.W (eds), 1990. *Interpreting Space: GIS and archaeology.* London: Taylor and Francis.

Andrews G., Barrett J., and Lewis J.S.C., in prep. *Interpretation not record.*

Andrews G., and Barrett J., 1997. *Heathrow T5 Research Design.* BAA, (unpublished internal document).

Andrews G. and Barrett J., 1998. *Archaeological Fieldwork Phase 2 Project Design.* Framework Archaeology, (unpublished internal document).

Berry, J. K., 1987. *Introduction to Geographical Information Systems: Management, Mapping and Analysis for Geographical Information Systems (GIS).* Proceedings of a special workshop for South Florida Water Management District.

Biswell, S., Cropper, L., Evans, J., Gaffney, V., and Leach, P., 1995. 'GIS and excavation: a cautionary tale from Shepton Mallet, Somerset, England', in Lock and Stančič (eds), pp.269–86.

Burrough, P.A., 1986. *Principles of Geographical Information Systems for Land Resource Assessment.* Oxford: Clarendon Press.

Campbell, H, & Masser, I, 1993. *Implementing GIS: the organisational dimension.* London: Association of Geographic Information (conference proceedings).

Chadwick, A, 1998. Archaeology at the edge of chaos: further towards reflexive excavation methodologies, *Assemblage*, 3, http://www.shef.ac.uk/~assem/3/3chad.htm

Champion, T. C., 1991. Theoretical Archaeology in Britain, in Hodder, I., (ed) *Archaeological Theory in Europe: The last Three Decades.* London: Routledge, pp. 129–60.

English Heritage, 1991. *The Management of Archaeological Projects*, London: HBMC (2nd Edition).

Gillings, M, 1994. *GIS and Upper Tisza Project, final report to the Research Committee*, (unpublished private document).

Gillings M, and Wise A, (eds) 1999. *GIS Guide to Good Practice.* York: Archaeology Data Service.

Harris, T. M., and Lock, G. R., 1990. 'The diffusion of a new technology: a perspective on the adoption of geographical information systems within UK archaeology', in Allen *et al.* (eds), pp.33–53.

Hodder, I., 1993. Changing Configurations: The Relationships between Theory and Practice, in Hunter, J., and Ralston, I. (eds), pp.11–18.

Hodder, I., 1999. *The Archaeological Process: An Introduction.* Oxford: Blackwell.

Hunter, J., and Ralston, I., (eds), 1993. *Archaeological Resource Management in the UK: An Introduction*, Stroud: Sutton Publishing Limited.

Lock, G., and Stančič, Z. (eds), 1995. *Archaeology and Geographical Information Systems: a European Perspective*, London: Taylor and Francis.

Lyall, J. and Powlesland, D., 1996. The application of high resolution fluxgate gradiometry as an aid to excavation planning and strategy formulation, *Internet Archaeology*, 1 http://intarch.ac.uk/journal/issue1/lyall_index.html

Morris, R., 1997. Right and wrong ways to do archaeology. *British Archaeology,* no. 29.

Nickerson S., Nickerson Associates WebPages http://nickerson.icomos.org/

O'Connor T., 1998. Environmental Archaeology: A matter of definition. *Environmental Archaeology*, vol. 2, 1998, pp. 1–6.

Powlesland, D. 1997. Publishing in the round: a role for CD-ROM in the publication of archaeological field-work results, *Antiquity*, 71, 274, pp. 1062–6.

Richards, J.D. 1997. Preservation and re-use of digital data: the role of the Archaeology Data Service, *Antiquity* 71, 274, pp. 1057–9.

Ryan, N. 1988. Browsing through the stratigraphic record, in Rahtz, S.P.Q. (ed) *Computer Applications and Quantitative Methods in Archaeology 1988*, BAR International Series 446, Oxford, pp. 327–34.

Ryan, N, 1991. Beyond the relational database: managing the variety and complexity of archaeological data, in Lock, G. and Moffett, J. (eds) *Computer Applications and Quantitative Methods in Archaeology 1991*, BAR International Series 577, Oxford, pp. 1–6. http://www.cs.ukc.ac.uk/people/staff/nsr/arch/baas.html

Stine, R. S., and Decker, T. D., 1990. 'Archaeology, data integration and GIS', in Allen *et al*, (eds), pp.134–140.

CHAPTER 7

English Sites and Monuments Records –
Information, Communication, and Technology

Ben Robinson

Introduction

Locally maintained Sites and Monuments Records (SMRs) aim to provide a comprehensive and comprehensible catalogue of archaeological monuments, fieldwork, observations, and finds within their administrative areas. They underpin the national assessment and selection of monuments for legal protection, they form the basis for the work of archaeological advisors within the Local Planning process, they inform investigation and conservation management projects, and help to provide a local context for investigative results. They often provide a starting point for local studies work, and hold great potential as elements of an educational and research network of national and international significance.

At the time of writing there are about 80 SMRs in England, which together provide complete geographical coverage of the country. They are usually managed within one of the Local Government tiers (County Councils, Unitary Authorities, or District Councils) although SMRs are also maintained by National Parks, and by the National Trust. SMR services for one former Shire county that has been divided into six Unitary Authorities are provided on a contractual basis by a commercial operator. The management picture is further complicated by agreements for joint SMR services across Local Government boundaries, the presence of Urban Archaeological Databases (which are records specific to some historic towns, which may or may not be fully embedded within existing SMR services), and some apparent duplication in coverage (Baker 1999, 1; Figure labelled "Records Coverage in England").

Around 21 paid staff, some of whom benefit from assistant posts, are fully dedicated to running SMRs. For the remainder of SMRs, archaeological staff divide their time (to greater or lesser proportions) between SMR duties and wider 'curatorial' duties. For example, 22 archaeological advisors to Local Planning Authorities are also engaged in SMR work; a third of them spend a third or more of their time undertaking SMR duties (all figures drawn from *ibid.*, 12).

Physically, a 'typical' SMR "...currently consists of a computerised text database, supported by mapped depictions of monuments on a paper or film modern OS [Ordnance Survey] base map. The computer records are normally supported by secondary paper records, photographs, copies of historic maps and other material...)." (ibid., Appendix 1).

Many SMRs have film overlays for crop-marked archaeological features. The boundaries of legally protected monuments (Scheduled Ancient Monuments, etc.) are usually marked, areas of surviving earthwork monuments may be marked, along with historic standing buildings, areas of surface finds scatters, extents of excavated sites, and the find spots of significant artefacts. Many incorporate some associated environmental and conservation information, such as the boundaries of Sites of Special Scientific Interest, Conservation Areas and Listed Buildings, Parks and Gardens, etc. SMR holdings often include a library of reports or supplementary documentation and plans concerning the primary record entries, and a collection of slides and photographs. All but a very few SMRs now make use of a computerised database for primary text records (English Heritage 1997, 64; Baker 1999, 18). Around a third of SMRs have a Geographic Information System application which links a text record database with a digital map base (ibid., 18) on which layers of some of the spatial information noted above may have been captured. Virtually all SMRs are (to greater or lesser extents) hybrid manual-computer systems.

Before examining the role that ICT has played in the development of SMRs, it is necessary to review their history. Many SMRs were implemented before the advent of suitable, economic data processing systems, and certainly before the introduction of effective purpose–built heritage information applications. The information they contain has been collected from a wide variety of sources, under different theoretical regimes applied with greater or lesser degrees of academic rigour, and with various degrees of accuracy. Some of these sources are several hundred years old, dating to the dawn of academic interest in our past. Very many pre-date the production of accurate scale maps of the country and any reliable means of obtaining the locative information we demand today. The Sites and Monuments Record is not a child of the Information Age.

SMR Prehistory – Mapping Archaeology in England

The cataloguing of the country's historic remains has a long history. William Camden's *Britannia* of 1586 provided the first attempt at the systematic survey of Britain's antiquities. Subsequent editions, produced throughout the succeeding two centuries, incorporated illustrations of field monuments, and the work of other antiquaries (such as extracts from Aubrey's *Monumenta Britannica* in an edition of 1695) to provide a topographic and period-based study and inventory. The fieldwork of antiquaries such as William Stukeley (1687–1765), Sir Richard Colt Hoare (1754–1838) and William Cunnington (1754–1810), fuelled by interest generated by the aristocracy's 'grand tours', laid the foundations for a blooming of gentleman-antiquary fieldwork during the nineteenth century.

The nineteenth century saw the publication of regional antiquarian studies (for example, Colt Hoare 1810; Artis 1828) and the incorporation of antiquarian notes into wider topographical publications (for example, Miller & Skertchly 1878). The proceedings and transactions of local antiquarian societies and museum societies, along with local newspaper reports of discoveries, provided further repositories of archaeological information.

The Victoria History of the Counties of England, begun in 1899, undertook to provide a systematic topographic survey on a county by county, parish by parish basis, for the whole of England. It quickly became the most respected starting point for local history research. Authoritative commentaries on ecclesiastical history, manorial history, churches, settlement development, came to be complemented by improving consideration of local archaeological discoveries and monuments. Publication is now undertaken under the auspices of the Institute of Historical Research at the University of London. At the time of writing, fourteen complete county sets have been published; a similar number of county sets are in progress (http://ihr.sas.ac.uk/vch/). These volumes have provided important sources of information and cross-referencing for Sites and Monuments Records fortunate to benefit from their coverage.

British archaeology owes much to the work of the Ordnance Survey, our official mapping agency, both for its production of comprehensive and accurate map coverage of these islands, and for its involvement in the mapping of antiquities. William Roy (1726–90), the 'Surveyor-General of Coasts and Engineering for Military Surveys', is credited with much of the impetus for a national mapping programme (Crawford 1960, 36). A keen antiquary , Roy found time to survey and map notable monuments whilst charged with building a road network in Scotland. His work, 'The Military Antiquities of the Romans in Britain', published by the Society of Antiquaries after his death, was hugely influential within the emerging discipline of field archaeology. His work, along with that of a few others who produced county maps during the eighteenth century, drew attention to ancient monuments and significant components of the landscape, thereby creating a model which was taken up by the national mapping agency.

In 1791 the Board of Ordnance instigated a national mapping programme in order to assist the planning of the nation's defences. Antiquities were marked on the first one-inch-to-one-mile map sheets published from 1801 (*ibid.*, 39). The remit of the Ordnance Survey, which remained under military management until recent times, was necessarily biased towards military mapping during times of need, but otherwise reverted to civilian tasks. During these times the work of the organisation was moulded by the interests of influential personalities within and by lobbying antiquaries without. Major-General Henry James (Director during the second half of the nineteenth century), for example, used the excuse of experimentation in printing procedures to produce elaborate editions of many of the county volumes of the Domesday Book (http://www.ordsvy.gov.uk/). The Ordnance Survey acquiesced to requests for the collation of information on local antiquities during its large scale mapping programme (Crawford 1960, 39; O'Neil 1946, 65), drawing on local antiquarian advice. This ensured the prominence of such features, but mapping was prone to the incorporation of poorly interpreted information, the popular antiquarian mythology of the day, and regional bias (Crawford 1960, 39).

The growing popularity of cycling, rambling and motoring after the First World War, led to the publication of maps aimed at the leisure market. Historic sites and features, were important components of such maps. Under official acknowledgement of the complexity in the recognition, interpretation, and mapping of field monuments, and public criticism of the

Ordnance Survey's performance in this regard (Ordnance Survey 1963, 2), Director General Sir Charles Close appointed O.G.S. Crawford, "a forceful, but distinguished and likeable" (http://www.ordsvy.gov.uk/) archaeologist, to head the newly-formed Ordnance Survey Archaeology Division. Crawford vigorously set about defining the archaeological recording practices of the new Division within an organisation whose attitude to his activities has been variously described as "somewhat reluctant" (Jones 1984, 5) and "indifferent" (Hampton 1989, 14). Crawford's first publication for the Ordnance Survey, the *Map of Roman Britain* (1924), however, was an unexpected resounding success. Encouraged by this, the Ordnance Survey launched a publication programme of archaeological and historical maps, and persevered with its archaeological survey.

Crawford, however, was not solely concerned with drawing the touring public's attention to our island's antiquities. He was acutely aware of the advantages that landscape context provide in the interpretation of archaeological remains, and perceived the value of distribution maps in discerning cultural groupings and their influence (Crawford 1960, 40–42). The rigour in information gathering that such archaeological interpretation demanded, drove the Ordnance Survey's archaeological recording programme well beyond the basic requirements of general public interest mapping. This is evident in Crawford's pioneering work in aerial survey, much of which concerns remains which are not topographic features in a traditional mapping sense (Crawford 1924; Crawford 1929; Hampton 1989, 14).

The Ordnance Survey's revision of Britain's mapping system after the Second World War provided a mechanism for the reassessment of its archaeological record. Further impetus for the revision of archaeological information was provided by the increasing rate of development attrition suffered by archaeological remains. The Ordnance Survey, conscious of the detailed recording roles of the Ministry of Public Buildings and Works Ancient Monuments Inspectorate, and of the ancient monuments Royal Commissions of England, Wales, and Scotland, redefined its own role as creating "a quick basic record giving the most important facts about archaeological sites, and particularly their precise location" before they disappeared forever. The records created in this way were hoped to "go far to offset the threat to archaeological knowledge made by the activities of the modern world" (Ordnance Survey 1963, 2). Such 'rescue mapping' was assisted by examination of existing written sources, air photographs, and by field visits; but the public also was invited to submit information, as it had been from the Ordnance Survey's earliest days. It was a method which recognised the value of local input, and one very similar to Camden's use of regional correspondents during the late 16th and early 17th centuries (Crawford 1960, 23).

The Ordnance Survey archaeological records, which eventually comprised standardised record maps and related index cards, provided the basis for much threat-led archaeological work during the 1960s and 1970s. It was these records, laboriously copied, which provided the backbone of many of the newly created local Sites and Monuments Records (Benson 1974, 226; Clubb & Lang 1996, 53). During the 1970s, however, the Ordnance Survey began to question its role in recording archaeological remains, and it was eventually concluded that such tasks were better suited to the three Royal Commissions (Darvill & Fulton 1998, 60–63). The Ordnance Survey Archaeology Division was dissolved, and its archaeological records, including some 400,000 record cards, were transferred to the Royal Commission on the Historical Monuments of England (RCHME) in 1983 (Clubb & Lang 1996, 55; Darvill & Fulton 1998, 64).

The Royal Commission on Historical Monuments (England) had been established in 1908 in order to "...make an inventory of the ancient and historical monuments connected with or illustrative of the contemporary culture, civilisation and conditions of the life of the people... from the earliest times to... 1700..." (RCHME, 1926, xix). The County Inventories of the Royal Commissions were begun during the first decade of the twentieth century. The pre-Second World War volumes tended to focus more on architecture than on field monuments, but the post-war volumes attempted comprehensive archaeological coverage of the counties concerned. They provided the most authoritative survey of local archaeology, but were prone to becoming rapidly 'dated' in an era of increasing fieldwork. The growing mass of archaeological information to be distilled made for slow progress through England's counties and eventually the county and town surveys were abandoned for a thematic approach to survey and publication.

Meanwhile, RCHME had gained responsibility for the National Buildings Record, which combined with the National Library of Air Photographs and National Archaeological Record (the RCHME's existing records supplemented those inherited from the Ordnance Survey) to form the National Monuments Record. A computerisation programme for the monuments and buildings record components of the national record was implemented in 1984, this culminated in the establishment of the Oracle-based National Monuments Record MONARCH database in 1993 (Clubb & Lang 1996, 55).

RCHME was given the lead role responsibility for the oversight of SMR development in 1989 (RCHME *et. al.*, 1998, 7), a function it held until its merger with English Heritage in 1999. Within the new English Heritage, liaison and support for SMRs is provided through the SMR Liaison Officer at the National Monuments Record.

The Implementation of Local Sites and Monuments Records

It is widely recognised that the first Local Authority Sites and Monuments Record to be created in England was that for the Oxford Region, although many subsequent Local Authority SMRs incorporated archaeological record sets collated by individuals and local societies from earlier times. The Oxford SMR, conceived during the period 1965–67, was established at the Oxford City and County Museum to "bring together diverse sources of information about the physical remains of man and his activities in the Oxford region into one manageable index" which was to be "locally accessible and comprehensive" (Benson 1974, 226). The SMR primarily was established to provide information for those interested in the "problems of the history and archaeology" of the region. A remit to assist researchers sat well within the aims of a Museum Service. Most SMRs, however, were conceived and supported on the basis of their usefulness as tools to manage archaeological resources; both to inform responses to local development proposals and as part of a national 'network' to assist the selection of monuments for legal protection. Their development has been very closely linked to the work of archaeologists employed to advise Local Planning Authorities.

The loss of archaeological remains through the extensive development and re-development schemes of the post-war decades was highlighted in many depressing, infamous, and often well-publicised cases, throughout the country (Jones 1984). The erosion of specific categories of remains was examined in detailed surveys by bodies such as the RCHME and Council for

British Archaeology (for example, RCHME 1960; RCHME 1969; Heighway 1972).

The Government's investigation into the measures of protection for 'field monuments', the 'Walsh Report' of 1969, drew attention to the general failure of the current system to safeguard supposedly protected Ancient Monuments. It had also recommended that Local Planning Authorities should make use of archaeological record systems staffed by archaeo-logical officers (Walsh 1969) to provide local advice. Whilst most of the 'Walsh Report' recommendations were not readily taken up by central government (Jones 1984, 52, 143) this latter recommendation had some effect.

The Town and Country Planning Act of 1947 established the first comprehensive mecha-nism for development control through Local Authorities. This Act, its subsequent replacement Acts, supplementary Acts and guidance, provides for the protection of aspects of the historic environment through the planning process. The desirability of the preservation of an ancient monument, whether Scheduled or not, was established as a "material consider-ation" in the determination of a planning application in the mid 1970s (Pugh-Smith & Samuels 1996, 37). *Planning Policy Guidance: Archaeology and Planning* (PPG 16 – DoE 1990), set a framework for the treatment of archaeological remains in the planning process. The first archaeological post within Local Government had been created during the early 1960s in Lancashire (Jones 1984, 26). During the 1970s, however, 'County Archaeologist' posts became increasingly common; there were nineteen by 1976 most were initially based within or closely linked to planning departments (*ibid.*, 26–29). In 1991 the number of archaeological advisors to Local Authority Planning Authorities had risen to about 100 (English Heritage 1991, 5). There are now around 540 'curatorial' archaeological staff within English Local Government organisations and National Parks (Aitchison 1999, 12).

Most Local Authority archaeological officers quickly realised that a comprehensive record of archaeological remains over their administrative area was the primary tool both in the selection of 'rescue' campaigns, and to inform development advice . For the Local Planning Authorities, motivation for the sponsorship of Sites and Monuments Records was provided by the need for their Officers' advice to draw on an explicit and rational record of the local archaeological remains. Further inducement was often provided through financial assistance from central government for data capture, SMR development, and for supporting archaeo-logical posts, which were often initially jointly funded with a gradual withdrawal of central government funding (English Heritage 1991, 5).

Recognition of the planning significance of information provided by SMRs, and thus their relationship to the work of Local Planning Authorities, was confirmed in The Town and Country Planning General Development Order 1988. A 'site of archaeological interest' was defined as a Scheduled Ancient Monument or Area of Archaeological Importance defined under the Ancient Monuments and Archaeological Areas Act 1979, or "which is within a site registered in any record kept by a County Council and known as the County Sites and Monuments Record".

Further validation of SMRs' role as development advice tools was provided by PPG16, and in planning policy guidance regarding the historic environment generally (Department of the Environment & Department of National Heritage 1994, 26). The first of these documents also draws attention to the wider informational uses of an SMR (Department of the Environment 1990, Annex 1).

SMR information gathering drew heavily on the historic archaeological sources described above, and was accelerated by its devolution to a local level. SMRs' proximity to locally interested parties, the individuals and societies immersed in 'their' archaeology, and their proximity to the archaeology in question, facilitated rapid accessioning of monument information in many records (Darvill & Fulton 1998, 65–66). SMRs, and archaeology services generally, often made good use of labour provided by individuals engaged on central government employment schemes. The value of locally-based SMRs was recognised in a joint report by the Council for British Archaeology and RCHME in 1975 (CBA & RCHME 1975). At this time distinction was made between "intensive" and "non-intensive" records at national and local levels (Clubb & Lang 1996, 54). By 1978 RCHME had recommended that county SMRs should be "the major, detailed archive for their areas" (RCHME 1978). The Department of the Environment (1981, 2) also recognised SMRs' value as "essential and primary data bases for the production of preservation and excavations policies", and collectively they came to be regarded as "the best national archaeological database" (Wainwright 1989, 167).

Accordingly, SMRs though considered as "properly a Local Authority responsibility" (DoE 1981, 2), were to play a crucial national strategic role in the assessment and management of the archaeological resource – Scheduled Ancient Monument selection (*ibid.*, 2; Wainwright 1989, 167; English Heritage 1991, 4). For this purpose, in order to help ensure greater consistency in information structure across SMR provisions, a network of Regional Sites and Monuments Record Working Parties was promoted and information standards guidance was provided (see below). Copies of the newly computerised national Ancient Monuments Records were to be made available to SMRs when available, and the mutual advantages of information exchange with national records were stressed (DoE 1981, 2).

Potential for tension existed, however, between the development of Sites and Monuments Records as local information resources and as a 'cogs' in the machinery of national conservation strategy. A Local Authority which had implemented a Sites and Monuments Record, primarily for the purpose of planning advice and the management of the local archaeological resource, but which was not in receipt of significant central government grant-aid, might be inclined to review its role as part of a national archaeological service. Archaeological Officers would be forced to balance the resource implications of adopting best practice national standards to form part of a national 'network', with the necessity of efficiently implementing and maintaining a working local system.

Localised political and economic environments inevitably lead to variable consideration of heritage concerns across Local Authorities. The provision of archaeological services, though encouraged by central government, was not a statutory responsibility for Local Government. The profile that archaeological issues gained in any one area was determined as much by the nature and vociferousness of the local 'heritage' community as by the density and significance of the archaeology. The effectiveness of the new Archaeological Officers in developing archaeological services was to a large extent influenced by factors beyond their direct control, but also relied heavily on their ability to engage interest groups, and their efficacy in promoting the worth of archaeology to their senior officers and elected members. The resources and internal advice that Archaeological Officers had to draw on, the presence and strengths of allied conservation services (buildings, natural environment) and internal technical expertise and support, were further crucial determining factors in the development of Local Authority archaeology and Sites and Monuments Records.

Modern administrative units often carve up regions which have historic integrity and which may, therefore, serve as better units for archaeological survey purposes. The periodic re-organisation of these administrative units, such as the merging and splitting of historic counties during the mid-1970s and the creation of Unitary Authorities from 1995, required the reconsideration of SMR provisions. Such change may or may not result in better SMR management depending on the particular circumstances of each SMR. The cumulative effect, however, has been a growth in the number of SMRs.

In summary, the implementation and development of Sites and Monuments Records has taken place within a framework guaranteed to produce national variability. It is arguable whether the national agencies provided enough incentive, support, and guidance to adequately address this issue, or whether Local Authorities were always sufficiently conscious of their responsibility as guardians of their patch of the national historic environment. This variability has had a profound effect on the implementation of ICT provisions for SMRs, and has been a major issue for the national agencies to address.

Information Technology – Driving SMR Standards ?

The implementation of any recording system requires the systematic organisation of information and the application of classification, if information is to be retrieved efficiently and used with any integrity. Manual SMR systems, card or paper records related to maps, demand at the very least a reference number, a common nomenclature to describe the date of the remains in question, and standardised locative information (such as a map sheet and full grid reference). If an SMR were to permit simple searches for various types of archaeological information, perhaps using an optical coincidence card indexing system, rigour in the classification of the form of evidence would be required. At the outset it was realised that such classification would pose problems for a rapidly developing discipline which did not benefit from a mature common vocabulary. Nevertheless, hand lists of keywords to described monument and evidence types were produced (Benson 1974, 232; DoE 1981, 1).

Information has to become data when captured by a computer system. In order to process *data* and to retrieve *information*, ranges of acceptable data have to be defined, and relationships between data items made explicit. The greater the limitations of memory and processing power of the computer system, the greater the rigour that must be applied in information classification and synthesis.

The question of information standards for ancient monument records was thus thrown into sharp focus by the desire to computerise the Department of Environment's Inspectorate of Ancient Monuments inventory of Scheduled Ancient Monuments. Advisory Note 32 "Ancient Monuments Records Manual and County Sites and Monuments Records" set principles for the transfer of paper Scheduled Ancient Monuments records to an Ohio Scientific C3C microprocessor with a 26Mb hard disc (DoE 1981). The need to restrict data capture to the contents of well structured manual record forms (AM7 Ancient Monuments Record form; and AM12 Field Monument Warden Report Form) was immediately recognised. Even so, a new Ancient Monuments Record form (AM107) had to be designed to better cope with the demands of computerisation. At the time it was hoped that future developments would eventually permit the capture of a greater range of information (*ibid*, 1).

The Advisory Note encouraged the adoption of the Ancient Monuments Records Manual practices by county Sites and Monuments Records. It noted that few SMRs possessed detailed operational manuals, but hoped that where the Advisory Note principles could not be adopted immediately, SMRs could "take them into account in their own plans for future refinement and development" (*ibid.*, 2).

In addition to introducing the grammatical precision necessary for successful retrieval, such as consistent use of upper case text and standard delimiters, Advisory Note 32 and subsequent guidance issued in relation to Ancient Monument Records (DoE 1983) ushered in changes in recording philosophy. Each separate 'site' was to be assigned a unique identifying Primary Record Number to avoid potential confusion between the Scheduled Ancient Monuments' county numbers, which could be applied to more than one site. The adoption of glossaries of standard keywords for certain record fields was of prime importance if full use was to be made of search facilities. Periodic amendments of the glossaries were envisaged (DoE 1983, 1).

The definition of what constituted a single archaeological 'site', acknowledged as a somewhat subjective judgement (*ibid*), became an important issue. Contiguous or superimposed monuments (a barrow inside a hill fort was the example given) were to be broken down into the constituent single sites. Complex sites, those sites that could be adequately described only by using more than one keyword within the fields "Site Type", "Period-general", "Period-specific", and "Form", could be recorded using multiple field sets separated by semicolons within Section 13 of the record. An example given related to a medieval manor, part of which was ruinous, part of which remained standing. The section entry, it was suggested might read "Manor/Medieval/C15/Ruined building; Manor/Medieval/C15/Roofed ruin".

Another example related to occupation of the same site spanning two defined periods of time, and displaying evidence of several "Site Type", and "Form" definitions. The section entry "Hillfort/Prehistoric/Iron Age/Earthwork; Settlement/Roman/Romano-British/Finds" was considered acceptable, the entry "Hillfort/Prehistoric/Iron Age/Earthwork; Beacon/Post-Medieval/Elizabethan/Other structure" was not. The latter demanded two separate records.

The completion of the record, therefore, involved some interpretation of the relationship between monument components; was the same site continuously occupied? Did the nature of occupation change sufficiently to merit re-classification under a separate record entry? Where uncertainty persisted it was possible to define separate cross-referenced records or to link records under a group number. A field for supplementary free text descriptions could be used to expand upon the nature of the evidence. The actual application of this recording method, however, was dependent on any individual SMR archaeologist's preference for 'lumping' or 'splitting' monument information. Such decisions were not so crucial in previous manual recording systems.

Whilst the suggested record structure is logical, given the available computer databases at the time, it markedly differs from 'traditional' archaeological narrative. The necessity of a record distinction between ruined and roofed parts of medieval building complex, for example, is understandable in a conservation and management context, but the repetitive robotic nomenclature does little for the wider appreciation of the monument.

The original keyword glossaries, especially the site type field, were augmented according to regional or local need. The "East Anglian Region Sites and Monuments Record Wordlist" of c. 1983, for example, differed from the Department of the Environment wordlist of the time (1983, 15–19), which itself contained amendments to the National Monuments Record Thesaurus of the time. The national agencies continued to publish thesauri to guide consistency (RCHME & English Heritage 1989; RCHME & English Heritage 1992; RCHME 1998b). Latterly, The Forum on Information Standards in Heritage (England) – FISHEN – has undertaken important work on the creation of data standards and thesauri within the INSCRIPTION framework for a national heritage reference data set (Lee 1999, 8; http://www.mda.org.uk/fishen/). Important work in setting standards for digital archives resulting from specific archaeological activities has been undertaken by the Archaeological Data Service, based at the University of York (see below).

Recording England's Past – A Data Standard for the Extended National Archaeological Record (RCHME, 1993) provided the next major guidance on SMR data structure. The standard was drawn up in the context of the availability of relational databases, the integration of archaeological and architectural records within the new unified National Monuments Record, and the implementation of Urban Archaeological Databases (UADs). UADs are, in effect, specialised SMRs designed to deal with the particular problems of the conservation of urban archaeological remains within the larger historic towns (*ibid*, 2). The lack of guidance in the Data Standard regarding the recording of monument complexes, spatial information, and conservation or management information was acknowledged. So too was the effect that developing software might have on the nature of future data standards (*ibid*, 3–4).

The unified RCHME National Monuments Record database (MONARCH), implemented in accordance with the 1993 Data Standard, highlighted the *relational* rather than *hierarchical* associations between monuments and archives, field workers and 'events' (recording activities) (RCHME 1993, 2; Clubb & Lang 1996, 55). An 'event-led' structure had been adopted for the computerisation of the Greater London SMR in 1983 (Clubb & James 1985; Charlton 1999, 4). The definition of 'monuments' within urban deposits is very often a matter of interpreting and relating various recording episodes, and thus an 'event-led' rather than monument-led record was considered better suited to the requirements of this urban SMR. An 'event–based' model was also adopted by the predominantly rural Northamptonshire Sites and Monuments Record at its inception (Foard 1978; Foard 1996). Until recent times, however, these SMRs were exceptional in terms of the relationships between events and monuments.

The latest data standards guidance, *MIDAS – A Manual and Data Standard for Monument Inventories* (RCHME 1998a), builds on previous RCHME data standards, SMR data standards promoted by the International Documentation Committee of the International Council of Museums (CIDOC 1995), and the SPECTRUM standard of the Museums Documentation Association. MIDAS, in some respects, is less prescriptive than the early attempts at standardisation in that its aim is not to "control the *content* of an inventory, but to provide a common *framework* within which inventories should develop" (RCHME 1998a, 1). Importantly, it draws attention to the desirability of separating the *interpretation* of "Monument Character" from the findings of individual recording 'events', so that increasing iterations of events may be used to re-interpret the monument (*ibid.*, 44). It also, introduces the potential uses of 'metadata', information about information (Miller 1998, 5; http://www.ariadne.ac.uk/issue5/metadata-masses/) in order to help users of inventories decide whether an inventory is likely to be relevant to their needs (RCIIME 1998a, 38).

The promotion of information standards by the national agencies, led by the imperatives for computerisation during the 1980s and 1990s, has gone some way towards assisting cohesiveness in the development of Sites and Monuments Records, not least by encouraging the SMR community to participate in the formation of those standards (DoE 1981, 2; RCHME and ALGAO 1993, iv; Clubb & Lang 1996, 57; Foard 1996, 3; RCHME 1998a, 'Acknowledgements'; Ray 1998, 4; Bourn 1999a, 3–7). Nevertheless, the criticism that "traditionally, local SMRs have not concerned themselves greatly with data standards" (Clubb & Lang 1996, 57) can be levelled with some justification. Many of the practical and psychological barriers to the discretionary adoption of national standards by SMRs outlined above, still persist. For example, whilst there is a growing consensus that the 'event-monument' model is appropriate for SMRs (Foard & Catney 1999, 1; Bourn 1999b, 7) some dissent is still evident at gatherings of SMR archaeologists. This is apparently partly fuelled by the lack of its widespread practical application to monument recording and the anticipated workload in data re-casting (Catney 1999, 3). It is worth remembering the wide spectrum of information quality that many SMRs currently accommodate.

One of the quirkiest SMR entries I know of (the SMR in question will remain anonymous) contains only the following in its free text description field: "It is said locally that in about 1930 a Major Munday found 'caves' at this place, into which a boy was lowered to bring up 'vases' filled with grain.". A parish is named and a six-figure grid reference is given, but no cross-reference, or corroborating evidence is cited. It is difficult to shoehorn such a record into the current thesaurus terms or MIDAS standards (perhaps we should add 'dangling infants' to our developing terminology for remote sensing?). And yet, one feels that the information might as well reside on the SMR, in hopeful anticipation that further supporting information will be forthcoming, or that formal archaeological survey will eventually detect something which explains the anecdote. After all, it is information that is unlikely to be recorded elsewhere.

At the other end of the scale of 'fuzzy data' tolerance, I recall an archaeologist responsible for planning advice declaring that the free text description field of his SMR was nothing but an annoying distraction and an unacceptable waste of memory. It should be lost, he argued, during the imminent data migration and replaced by a rationalised, totally keyword-based, record. Such purgation of SMRs is of course unnecessary and dangerous. This part of the record often contains important information and interpretation, not least the qualification for the keyword choices made under the indexed fields, which may not be recorded by any other means.

The hardware and software used by Sites and Monuments Records has been very largely determined by the systems preferred or tolerated by their respective managing authorities (Fernie 1997, 2; Foard 1997, 3; Gilman 1997, 4; Condron et al 1999, 62). Along with the influence of individual authority's Information Technology policies, archaeologists have been forced to consider the ready availability of IT support and expense of implementation in their decision to adopt particular systems. Monument record software for SMRs was produced by English Heritage (notably, a Superfile-based system) and RCHME developed an SMR version of the Oracle-based MONARCH database (Clubb & Lang 1996, 54). These various systems came to be adopted by many SMRs. Many others, however, have employed systems developed 'in-house'. Amongst these, Dbase-, Foxpro-, and Access-based applications have proved popular in recent years (Condron et al 1999, 62–63). A recent survey of SMRs' use of Geographic Information Systems and Computer Aided Design packages for mapping, revealed similar variation in software choice as is apparent in non-spatial database systems. MapInfo, ArcInfo/ArcView, Wingz have proved popular, although at least nine other products were in use amongst the 44 respondents at the time of survey (Fernie 1997, 2).

At the time of writing English Heritage is actively promoting an SMR package developed in conjunction with the Association of Local Government Archaeological Officers by ExeGesIS SDM Ltd. It is based on Access 2.0 and MapInfo. The ExeGesIS product was launched in March 1998 and by June 1999 25 SMRs had purchased the system (Fernie 1999a, 12), enough to warrant the establishment of a user group (Bourn 1999b, 12). The system is MIDAS compatible (its implementation requires the adoption of the 'events – monuments' model) and it incorporates the latest digital Thesaurus of Monument Types. The complete system (excluding hardware and 'internal' costs, but including standard software licenses) costs around £5000 to install (*SMR Software Partnership Pricing Guideline*). Aspects of the ExeGesIS package are still under development, and it has suffered some of the teething problems typical of software launched into a real working environment for the first time. Its price and reliance on MapInfo (or ArcView) and Access, whose use is not supported by all Local Authorities, might present disincentives for adoption for some. Nevertheless, the development of the ExeGesIS package, its promotion, and significant take up by the SMR community marks a considerable achievement, and a realistic opportunity to lever in greater structural conformity. The recent development of a common SMR desk manual (Fernie & Gilman 1999) is a further important initiative in guiding SMR conformity and setting aspirations for those SMRs which find themselves at the lower end of the evolutionary procession.

The fact that most SMRs have achieved computerisation of the majority of their primary text records, will greatly assist the task of migrating to new systems such as ExeGesIS. All migration contains an overhead in terms of policing automated re-casting and undertaking manual editing, but achieving information standards conformity across the SMR community within new systems should be a lesser mountain to climb than that faced during its initial digitisation. It is perhaps time, however, to underpin progress towards conformity with the long-suggested statutory status (Department of National Heritage & Welsh Office 1996, 46) and a museum-like registration process, for which adherence to accepted information models could form an important part.

Keeping up with the pace – Training and User Demand

The increasing use of ICT by SMRs, has raised skills issues for SMR archaeologists, who must balance the benefits of installing new systems against the 'learning curve' and general distraction to routine SMR tasks, inherent in their implementation. Learning ICT skills must sit alongside the development of the non-ICT skills necessary to run a publicly available heritage information service (such as maintaining currency in general archaeological and historical knowledge, obtaining detailed knowledge of archaeological reference sources and investigative techniques, comprehensive knowledge of local archaeology, customer care, the planning system, etc.). Training may mitigate this tension, but its efficacy is to a large extent dependent upon the aptitude of the trainee, and the sophistication of the application in question. About 70% of SMRs benefit from the availability of some form of relevant corporate ICT training (Baker 1999, 13), but there is a general perception that there is a dearth of SMR-specific training (Lang 1997, 8). This conforms to the general desire for more ICT training across the archaeological profession in this country (Condron et al 1999, 72) and indeed an identified ICT skills gap amongst archaeologists further afield (Eiteljorg, 1999, 6).

The frustrations that some SMR archaeologists feel in the distraction of new technology seldom have been committed to print. The issues have been raised forcefully by one SMR officer, however, who wonders whether the profession is becoming too "bogged down in technology" and forgetting what its there for (Smith 1997, 8). She also draws attention to the important consideration that some ICT knowledge is necessary just to communicate effectively with ICT support staff.

Television bombards us with computer re-animated dinosaurs and instantaneous walk-through reconstructions of monuments, and youngsters guide physically impressive treasure hunters through 'ancient tombs' via games consoles. We are becoming a more ICT literate society, and an expectation for ICT excellence, or at least usability and attractiveness, filters through even to the SMR world. This creates further pressure to keep pace with IT developments, particularly with those which assist our presentation to the outside world.

On a recent visit to my SMR a local Councillor was amazed at the GIS application's ability to find a named postal address, produce a map centred on the address, and provide a summary of the archaeology in its immediate environs. A somewhat younger A level student, however, whilst content with the distribution map of Bronze Age metalwork finds that the GIS produced for their project, was disappointed that such information could not be generated via the Internet.

Traditionally, the primary user groups of SMRs have been the archaeologists concerned with their management and those drawing on them for planning advice. As a consequence, SMRs have tended to be somewhat introspective in terms of the development of user-resources. The lack of a detailed analysis of SMR use and users was identified as a concern by the Inspectorate of Ancient Monuments of the Department of the Environment in 1984 (RCHME and ALGAO, 1993, 2). Since that time, however, remarkably few surveys of SMR use have been undertaken. Whilst the detailed analysis of use was beyond the 1999 'Baker' survey, the report nevertheless indicated that research and educational use is a seriously under-developed aspect of SMR function (Baker 1999, 1; 23–24). Only 57% of the responding SMRs had set aside a table or desk for use by external enquirers, and direct access to the SMR database was available in only 9% of cases (Baker 1999, 14). Most SMRs were evidently quite willing to offer some support for external user enquiries (*ibid.*, 14), but found it necessary to interpose SMR staff between the information and the enquirer. This manual 'shopkeeper' approach clearly limits access to the records, and serves as a disincentive to their leisurely exploration. But is the information that SMRs contain actually relevant to research and educational needs?

Cheetam (1985, 50) provides a ghastly impression of the perceived irrelevance of SMRs of the time to the academic community. One eminent landscape archaeologist recently has written of the publication of one of his detailed surveys: 'It thus seemed to the writer that, instead of consigning the newly discovered plan to the dustbin…or depositing it in local or national Sites and Monuments Records with much the same result, it was perhaps worth publishing in these proceedings.' (Taylor 1999, 81). In my experience, however, SMR information has been well appreciated by local historians, further and higher education students, and by those engaged in higher forms of academic work.

A more representative picture of the research relevance of SMRs, and how they might better respond to academic and educational need, has yet to be obtained, but it is clear that ICT has a large part to play in the development of this area (Robinson 1999a, 7–8; http://ads.ahds.ac.uk/newsletter/; Robinson 1999b, 10). It is particularly relevant and welcome that the wider dissemination of SMR information appears to sit comfortably within the central government's agenda for the development of ICT resources for 'life-long learning' (Heritage Lottery Fund 1999; New Opportunities Fund 1999). The injection of substantial amounts of project funding would permit the development of an array of exciting user-interfaces to SMR information.

SMRs – A National Network?

English Heritage's published strategy for English archaeology anticipated that the 1990s would see the "linking (of SMRs) under the aegis of the National Archaeological Record to form a true national archaeological record" (English Heritage 1991, 48). It will be apparent from the discussion above that this ambition has not been achieved (RCHME *et. al.*,1998, 7). The fantastic development of the Internet, however, has opened possibilities for networking SMRs which did not exist a decade ago.

The creation of an Internet discussion group, 'SMR Forum', which is jointly managed by the Archaeology Data Service at York and the National Monuments Record at English Heritage (Fernie 1999b, 11) is one manifestation of the 'networking' that communications technology can bring. For the first time SMR archaeologists, often working in physical isolation, are able to communicate with a large part of their community in a rapid and dynamic way. The forum has become the primary method for consultation on new documentation, and for sharing problems and solutions. Much useful discussion has taken place in the first few months of the forum's existence. FISHEN operates a similar Internet forum.

The most important demonstration of the potential for SMR networking via the Internet, however, has been provided by the Archaeology Data Service. This service, which forms part of the Arts and Humanties Data Service funded by the Joint Information Systems Committee and the Arts and Humanities Research Board, "collects, describes, catalogues, preserves and provides user support for digital resources created during archaeological research" (Archaeology Data Service 1999b, 8; http://ads.ahds.ac.uk). As the remit implies, ADS digital holdings and its links to digital holdings elsewhere, comprise a wide range of archaeological resources; from indexes to radiocarbon dates (Archaeology Data Service 1999a, 5) to comprehensive digital excavation archives (Archaeology Data Service 1999b, 7). At the time of writing data available through ADS already includes, the National Monuments Record Excavation Index for England, National Monuments Record of Scotland, West of Scotland Sites and Monuments Record, Greater London Sites and Monuments Record, and the Shetland Sites and Monuments Record (http://ads.ahds.ac.uk/catalogue/) all of which is available through 'ArchSearch'. The development of this holdings search technology has important consequences for the meaning of data conformity, and the necessity of absolute conformity in SMR format.

The Elastic SMR – Diversification and Broadening Remits

The original remit of SMRs as simple inventories of 'monuments' and archaeological obser-vations has been stretched somewhat by the broadening remit of archaeology itself over the last twenty-five years. Archaeological research and management now legitimately incorpo-rates remains of the more recent past and consequently a greatly extended monument set (see for example the 'Defence of Britain Project', Lowry 1995). Similarly, specialist sub-fields in survey and analysis (many branches of palaeo-environmental research, geophysical survey, etc.) which were minor considerations at the inception of most SMRs have developed to form important components of archaeological practice. Furthermore, archaeology takes an increasingly holistic view of landscape development (for example, Cornwall Archaeological Unit, 1998) and there have been some recent calls for the strengthening of links between SMRs and other environmental databases (RCHME *et. al.*, 1998, 10–11; Baker 1999, 4). Indeed the identification of SMRs as components of Local Environmental Information Management Systems or as Historic Environmental Information Resources (*ibid.*, 33), implies ambitions beyond the bounds of traditional archaeological subjects.

The question of whether the structure of SMRs, has kept pace with such developments is an important one. The large array of thematic heritage databases being maintained by various organisations (Brown 1999, 8) indicates that the present SMR 'network' cannot accommo-date the particular recording requirements of many specialist areas. The issue is demonstrated by the Department for Culture, Media and Sport's Portable Antiquities recording scheme.

Many SMRs have long recorded 'stray finds' of artefacts to complement the view of ancient land use provide by fixed monuments. Provision for describing archaeological evidence as such appears in both early and revised SMR information standard guidance (Department of Environment 1983, 21; RCHME and ALGAO, 1993, 97) but the standard-ised detailed description of such artefact finds does not sit very comfortably within these or the MIDAS standard (RCHME 1998a, 82). The Portable Antiquities scheme uses a custom-designed database (Department for Culture, Media and Sport 1999, 25) application of its own, from which information must be transferred to individual SMRs.

If we add the breadth of information generated by certain specialist heritage databases to the curation of local digital archives and the development of education and research inter-faces, along with the day-to-day tasks of information and enquirer management, we require SMR services which demand staffing provisions well beyond those recently recommended (Baker 1999, 4; Fernie & Gilman 1999, 66). At a national level the Historic Environment Information Resources Network (HEIRNET – http://www.britarch.ac.uk/HEIRNET/) and the Archaeology Data Service attempt to map and knit together the widening range of historic environment and archaeological digital resources. It is debatable whether these initiatives can or should be replicated at a local level by individual SMR services.

Conclusions

Over 650,000 retrievable archaeological records were held in English SMRs in 1995 and it is estimated that there will be nearly 1,000,000 by 2005 (Darvill & Fulton 1998, 65). It is impossible to contemplate the meaningful management of this information without ICT. The implementation of computer systems and the accessioning of a huge amount of archaeological information over the last thirty years have been considerable achievements (Clubb & Lang 1996, 53; Darvill & Fulton 1998, 65; Catney 1999, 1) but the perception that SMRs' collective "contents remain an uneven and inadequate representation of the surviving remains of England's archaeological past." (Wainwright 1989, 167) remains true.

Many of the ICT developments necessary to help SMRs fulfil their true potential are of recent origin and have yet to make a widespread impact. Nevertheless, enough has been glimpsed to suggest possibilities for future development. SMRs now stand on the threshold of the second phase of their evolution. The challenge of this phase is to see that they develop to accommodate defined user needs and extend to meet the range of modern archaeological concerns without losing their relevance or integrity. ICT developments offer the potential to integrate their local ownership, which has done so much to ensure their credibility in the planning process, with national networking to ensure their accessibility and full appreciation as a research resource.

Bibliography

Aitchison, K., 1999. *Profiling the Profession. A survey of archaeological jobs in the UK*, Council for British Archaeology, English Heritage, Institute of Field Archaeologists.

Archaeology Data Service, 1999a. *Archaeology Data Service News*, Issue 5, University of York/Arts and Humanities Data Service.

Archaeology Data Service, 1999b. *Archaeology Data Service News*, Issue 6, University of York/Arts and Humanities Data Service.

Artis, E T., 1828. *The Durobrivae of Antoninus*.

Baker, D., 1999. *An Assessment of English Sites and Monuments Records*, Historic Environment Conservation report 97/20.

Benson, D., 1974. 'A Sites and Monuments Record for the Oxford Region', *Oxoniensia* 37, pp. 226–237.

Bourn, R., 1999a. 'Events and Monuments: a discussion paper', in *SMR News*, Issue 8, RCHME.

Bourn, R., 1999b. 'Sites and Monuments Record Database: ExeGesIS Users Group' in *SMR News*, Issue 8, RCHME.

Brown, D., 1999. 'Other heritage data partners', in *SMR News*, Issue 8, English Heritage National Monuments Record.

Catney, S., 1999. 'So What is an event?', *SMR News*, Issue 7, RCHME.

Charlton, P., 1999. 'An example of events in practice', in *SMR News* Issue 7, RCHME.

Cheetam, P N., 1985. 'The archaeological database applied: North Yorkshire County Council Sites and Monuments Record at the University of Bradford', in Webb (ed.), pp. 49–56.

CIDOC, 1995. *Draft International Core Standard for Archaeological Sites and Monuments Records*, International Council of Museums (ICOM) and International Committee for Documentation/Comite International pour la Documentation (CIDOC).

Cleere, H., (ed) 1989. *Archaeological Heritage Management in the Modern World*, London: Council for British Archaeology.

Clubb, N. & James, P. 1985. 'A computer record for Greater London's Heritage', *London Archaeologist 5*, pp. 38–39.

Clubb, N. & Lang, A., 1996. 'A strategic appraisal of information systems for archaeology and architecture in England – past, present and future' in Kamermans, H. and Fennema, K. (eds), *Interfacing the past: computer applications and quantitative methods in archaeology', CAA 95* (Analecta Praehistorica Leidensia 28), pp. 52–72.

Condron, F. Richards, J. Robinson, D., Wise, A., 1999. *Strategies for Digital Data. Findings and Recommendations from Digital Data in Archaeology: A Survey of User Needs*, Archaeology Data Service, University of York.

Colt Hoare, R., 1810. *The Ancient History of Wiltshire. Part 1.*

Cornwall Archaeological Unit, 1998. *Cornwall's Historic Landscape. Presenting a method of Historic Landscape Character Assessment.* Cornwall Archaeological Unit.

Council for British Archaeology & Royal Commission on Historical Monuments (England) 1975. *Report of the Working Party on Archaeological Records*. London.

Crawford, O G S., 1924. *Air Survey and Archaeology*, Ordnance Survey Professional Papers N.S.:7) Southampton.

Crawford, O G S., 1929. *Air Photography for Archaeologists*, Ordnance Survey Professional Papers, N.S.: 12).

Crawford, O G S., 1960. *Archaeology in the Field*, London.

Darvill, T. & Fulton, A K., 1998. *The Monuments at Risk Survey of England*, Bournemouth University and English Heritage.

Department of National Heritage and The Welsh Office, 1996. *Protecting Our Heritage: A Consultation Document on the Built Heritage of England and Wales*, DNH and the Welsh Office DNH J0098NJ.

Department of Culture, Media and Sport, Buildings, Monuments and Sites Division 1999. *Portable Antiquities Annual Report 1997–98.*

DOE Inspectorate of Ancient Monuments, 1981. *Advisory Note 32: Ancient Monuments Records Manual and County Sites and Monuments Records.*

DOE Inspectorate of Ancient Monuments, 1983. *Guide to the Compilation of DoE Record Forms for Scheduled Monuments.*

Department of the Environment, 1990. *Planning Policy Guidance: Archaeology and Planning.*

Department of the Environment and Department of National Heritage, 1994. *Planning Policy Guidance: Planning and the Historic Environment.*

Eiteljorg, H., 1999. 'Training – a necessity too long overlooked', *Archaeology Data Service News*, Issue 6, University of York.

English Heritage, 1991. *Exploring Our Past. Strategies for the Archaeology of England.* London.

English Heritage, 1993. *Conservation Issues in Local Plans.* London.

English Heritage, 1997. *Archaeology Division Research Agenda* (draft). London.

Fernie, K., 1997. 'Current implementation of Spatial Data Systems in SMRs', *SMR News*, Issue 4, RCHME.

Fernie, K., 1999a. 'NMR sponsors advanced training course', *SMR News*, Issue 8, English Heritage.

Fernie, K., 1999b. 'SMR forum: a new e-mail discussion group for SMR professionals', SMR News, Issue 8, English Heritage.

Fernie, K., & Gilman (eds) 1999. *Documenting the Historic Environment. Recording Guidelines for Sites and Monuments Records in England*, unpublished circulation draft for SMR Users Group.

Foard, G., 1978. *The Northamptonshire Sites and Monuments Record. Part 1: Archaeology. A Guide to the Structure, purpose and use of the archaeological record*, Northamptonshire County Council.

Foard, G., 1996. 'What is a *Site Event?*' in *SMR News*, Issue 3, RCHME.

Foard, G., 1997. 'MapInfo in Northamptonshire', *SMR News*, Issue 4, RCHME.

Foard, G. & Catney, S., 1999. 'Message from the Chairs', *SMR News*, Issue 7, RCHME.

Gilman, P., 1997. 'ArcInfo and ArcView in Essex County Council Archaeology Section', *SMR News*, Issue 4, RCHME.

Hampton, J., 1989. 'The Air Photography Unit of The Royal Commission on the Historical Monuments of England 1965–1985' in Kennedy, D. (ed). *Into the Sun. Essays in Air Photography in Archaeology in Honour of Derrick Riley*, Sheffield.

Heritage Lottery Fund, 1999. *Unlocking Britain's Past. A strategic framework for support from the Heritage Lottery Fund for Sites & Monuments Records.*

Heighway, C., 1972. *The Erosion of History. Archaeology and Planning in Towns*, Council for British
  Archaeology.
Jones, B., 1984. *Past Imperfect: The Story of Rescue Archaeology*, London.
Lang, N., 1997. Reply to Linda Smith in *SMR News*, Issue 4, RCHME, National Monuments Record.
Larsen, C U., (ed) 1992. *Sites and Monuments. National Archaeological Records*, Copenhagen: National
  Museum of Denmark.
Lee, E., 1999. 'FISHEN' in *SMR News*, Issue 8, English Heritage National Monuments Record.
Lowry, B., (ed) 1995. *20th Century Defences in Britain. An Introductory Guide. Handbook of The Defence of
  Britain Project,* Council for British Archaeology.
Miller, P., 1998. 'Metadata for the masses', in *SMR News*, Issue 5, English Heritage National Monuments Record
Miller, S H. & Skertchly, S B J., 1878. *The Fenland Past and Present.* London
New Opportunities Fund, 1999. *Information for Applicants Funding the Digitisation of Learning Materials.*
O'Neil, B H. St J., 1946. 'The Congress of Archaeological Societies', *Antiquaries Journal* 26, pp. 61–66.
Ordnance Survey, 1924. *Map of Roman Britain,* Southampton.
Ordnance Survey, 1963. *Field Archaeology. Some notes for beginners issued by the Ordnance Survey,* Ordnance
  Survey Professional Papers, New Series, No. 13. London:HMSO.
Pugh-Smith, J. & Samuels, J., 1996. *Archaeology in Law*, London.
Ray, K., 1998. 'Modelling the Resource: Monuments, Events, Archaeological elements and GIS' in *SMR News*,
  Issue 5, RCHME.
Robinson, 1999a. 'The Future Direction of Sites and Monuments Records: from planning to research' in
  Archaeology Data Service 1999a.
Robinson, 1999b. 'The future directions of Sites and Monuments Records: from planning to research', in Fernie
  (ed) 1999. *SMR News*, Issue 8, English Heritage National Monuments Record.
RCHME, 1926. *An inventory of the Historical Monuments in Huntingdonshire.* London: HMSO.
RCHME, 1960. *A Matter of Time. An archaeological survey of the river gravels of England prepared by the
  Royal Commission on Historical Monuments (England.* London: HMSO
RCHME, 1969. *Peterborough New Town: A Survey of Antiquities,* HMSO.
RCHME, 1978. *Survey of Surveys.* London.
RCHME, 1998a. MIDAS – A Manual and Data Standard for Monument Inventories.
RCHME, 1998b. *Thesaurus of Monument Types (2nd Edition).*
RCHME & English Heritage 1989. *Revised Thesaurus of Architectural Terms.*
RCHME & English Heritage 1992. *Thesaurus of Archaeological Site Types* (2nd edition).
RCHME & ALGAO, 1993. *Recording England's Past: A Data Standard for the Extended National
  Archaeological Record.*
RCHME, ALGAO, & English Heritage, 1998. *Unlocking the Past for the New Millennium*: A New Statement of
  Co-operation on Sites and Monuments Records Between the Royal Commission on the Historical Monuments
  of England, English Heritage and the Association of Local Government Archaeological Officers.
Smith, L., 1997. 'When is an SMR Officer, not an SMR Officer?', *SMR News,* Issue 4, RCHME.
Taylor, C C., 1999. 'The Bulwark, Earith, Cambridgeshire', *Proceedings of the Cambridge Antiquarian society*
  Volume LXXXVII, pp. 81–86.
Wainwright, G J., 1989. 'Management of the English landscape', in Cleere, H. (ed) 1989.
Walsh, Sir David., 1969. *Walsh Report: Report of the Committee of Enquiry into the arrangements for the
  protection of field monuments, 1966–68,* HMSO.
Webb, E., (ed) 1985. *Computer Applications in Archaeology 1985*. University of London Institute of Archaeology.

CHAPTER 8

A view from above:
can computers help aerial survey?

Rog Palmer

When the Editors asked me to contribute to this volume, the brief I wrote down was: 'Use of computers – has it changed what we do, what we can do, what we ought to do?' Coming at a time when my main working computer was dead (there must be a moral there somewhere..?) preparing the paper seemed an ideal opportunity to sit and think and to sound out colleagues about the 'what we ought to do' aspects. To put this into context requires a brief review of where we are now, for which my examples come mainly from England.

As a photo interpreter, it is logical for me to begin with the collections of air photos, then move through mapping to analysis, and to end with flying. This is also the route taken by most archaeologists who work with air photographs. Following this sequence, with examples, seemed an appropriate way of showing how past and present practices have, or have not, made use of computers. In general I think the net result will be to show an under-exploitation of technology, particularly in archaeological research, although this may be better than indiscriminate use of unsuitable applications simply because it can be done.

Without our collections there would be very little archaeological merit, beyond discovery, to aerial survey. In Britain and much of Europe, archaeological aerial photography and photo interpretation is principally concerned with identifying and recording old holes in the ground, formerly ditches and pits, that are now filled, levelled, and are not so efficiently detectable by any other means. One point that should be common knowledge by now is that these levelled archaeological features are not always visible from the air and so to build up a reliable picture we need to accumulate photographs taken over many years and probably at different seasons. That single sentence determines the way we need to work: the libraries hold this accumulation of photographs which we examine and interpret to compile maps. These maps are the only sensible way to pool the photographed information and it is they that give us our 'reliable picture'. The information on the maps allows us to measure, compare, analyse, and so try to understand the roles and uses of this past civil engineering that may now be recorded on aerial photographs. Those same maps will indicate gaps in our present knowledge towards which future survey can be directed.

Archives – the past and present

The recently published *Directory of Aerial Photographic Collections in the United Kingdom* (second edition: NAPLIB, 1999) lists an estimated 1,100 publicly accessible collections which range in size from a few hundred pictures to the millions held by major survey companies and national libraries. Despite the fact that the majority of these have not been taken for archaeological purposes many do show unidentified features. There is no shortage of photographs to examine, and new photography, especially if it is archaeologically directed, is almost certain to record further relevant information (see analysis by Whimster, 1983; 100–105). Topographical extent and user-experience teaches which of the 1,100 collections do not need searching for any specific research. For example, much of my work is in the county of Cambridgeshire and I know that most of the information (*most*, but not all) should be sought in four places: Cambridge University Collection (CUCAP), the County Record Office (CRO), the National Monuments Record: Photographs (NMRAP), and on the shelves behind me which hold my own photos. To search these four collections takes, at present, four separate and different enquiries.

A typical cover search (based on an actual mapping assessment undertaken in September 1998) will show the routines necessary to collate information from CUCAP's card index that has developed from its 1945 origins and the computer-generated list that NMRAP provide. I should explain at this point that my purpose is to identify photographs which record a specific area. These I will examine, interpret and map. It is of little interest at this stage to know that someone once identified features within my area as, for example, a causewayed enclosure, henge monument, or Roman fort – I need to map all visible archaeological and relevant natural features and draw my own conclusions. Thus I search entirely on a National Grid (NGR) basis, usually by drawing a box on a 1:50,000 map and noting the relevant co-ordinates. Our specimen area is some 40 hectares – not a large area, but is in the Welland Valley, so likely to have a lot of purpose-taken oblique cover. I also like to look outside the study area to see if features may continue (undetected) into it, so the search of the 40 hectares actually extends into 6 km squares.

A search of my own photographs is easy and has nothing to do with computers (although I do maintain a basic index on the machine). My few hundred photos are kept in NGR order and I flick through them, pulling out any of the area which, in this case, total seven. I decide against a visit to the CRO because I know that the Cambridge office has little cover of the Welland Valley and that the most useful is duplicated at NMRAP. The CRO index is efficient but antiquated, comprising a large and heavy book of flight traces from which print numbers are identified, so as to be written on to paper request forms which the helpful staff use to pull prints. Despite the apparent lack of sophistication, requests for photos at CRO are dealt with quickly by friendly humans.

CUCAP is a 15 minute bike ride from where I work. I do not use their extensive place-name/subject index, but instead search the smaller NGR index which holds copies of the archaeologically relevant cards. My search produces only 16 oblique photographs at three locations and I write a list showing NGR, photo number and date of photography. Vertical photographs are not always listed on the NGR cards and are identified by first searching a 'general cover' map at 1:250,000 scale. The small scale, and cumulative compilation on these maps makes it difficult in 'busy' areas to identify relevant sortie numbers. However, three sorties cover my area and details of these have to be found by searching through ring-bound annual indexes which hold flight traces at a range of scales (usually either 1:50,000, 1:63,360 (from the pre-metric age), or 1:25,000) from which I identify photograph numbers, date and contact scale. These are added to my written list. The search of this relatively small area may take between 30 and 45 minutes. The listed prints can now be pulled from their boxes which are kept in date ordered filing cabinets. The 40 hectare cover is straightforward to extract, but recent examination of a 5 x 5 km area required converting my NGR list to a photo-number list before I could efficiently pull the prints. Easy with a computer list; tedious, and prone to error, on paper.

CUCAP remains a pre-computer archive. Their recent vertical photographs are indexed direct from the in-flight GPS (Global Positioning System) but are available for public search as computer-generated translucent prints which can be overlain on 1:50,000 base maps. Plans exist for computerisation of the index (Wilson and Palmer 1998, 47) although clear direction seems lacking.

Before my trip to CUCAP I will have completed and faxed (or e-mailed) a request for a similar search to NMRAP. This entailed filling in my name and address and identifying the search area – in this case by drawing a box with SW and NE NGRs added. All photographs at NMRAP are indexed by location, date, format and copyright on a PHOTONET database which can be searched for a point, area or line to produce a list of photographs. My request will ask for all oblique photographs and all verticals of scale greater than 1:12,000. Search of my 40 hectare area produced a list of 145 oblique photographs and 20 sorties (98 prints) of verticals. Priority searches are despatched within two working days and cost £35. Listed photos can be edited (perhaps to eliminate all verticals taken at un-informative times of year) and a telephoned request will get the prints pulled in five days, which usually gives me time to work through Cambridge material first. Each customer enquiry is logged on a database allowing related enquiries to be answered rapidly and easing the production of annual reports. The following figures give an idea of the use made of a national archive. In the year 1998–99 NMRAP had 3,349 enquiries, not all archaeological, relating to aerial photographs. These requests included 210 by commercial archaeological organisations and consultants, 514 by environmental consultants (whose work may include archaeological concerns), plus additional internal enquiries. The enquiries resulted in 751 pre-booked visits to examine a total of 69,000 vertical and oblique photographs. In addition, an unknown number of oblique prints are examined from the open-access shelves, (I am grateful to Fiona Matthews, NMRAP, for providing the statistics for this summary).

These two collections represent the extremes of those in daily use by archaeologists in England. Neither is impossible to search, although using the CUCAP index to study a large area of the country necessitates several days preparation. For my work in Wessex (begun in 1976 – not only well before the days of PCs, but before CUCAP had copied their NGR index) it was an essential but time-consuming task to make my own card index by searching on a parish listing and converting that to Ordnance Survey quarter sheets (5 x 5 km square). By the time I was involved with the Fenland Survey (from 1987) and other research in west Cambridgeshire I was able to maintain a dBase index by inputting from the NGR cards to make a list that I could sort topographically and, to allow easy pulling of prints, by photo number. The efficiency of NMRAP is perhaps a result of meeting the increasing public and specialist consultation of aerial photographs at a date that coincided with their inheritance of the RAF post-war verticals previously held by the Department of the Environment. Archive-wise, CUCAP has grown little beyond being St Joseph's personal research department and current thoughts about the structure of its proposed computer index seems to give little consideration to how it is presently used by customers and to the desirability to adopt a system that will be compatible with others, such as PHOTONET, that are currently in use. The University, in its current moves to wind up CUCAP, seem unaware of the financial potentials of this major and historic collection of photographs. Judging by the success of NMRAP's collection management, an efficiently designed and user-relevant computer index would contribute significantly towards creating a self-financing department.

Another successfully indexed collection is that maintained by the National Monuments Record of Scotland. NMRS chose Genamap GIS to index their archive of aerial photographs and has developed an interactive system, ICARUS, which also acts as an interface to enable queries to be made and linked to other NMRS databases. Thus it is easy, for example, to identify photographs of a specified type and date range that cover a site that was shown on the OS first edition, or has recently been field surveyed (Moloney 1997). Development of integrated search facilities such as this are likely to be of benefit to many current and future archaeological investigations.

Archives – the future?

National collections held in government care are developing web access. RCAHMS already has open access to a selected level of NMRS data (http://www.rcahms.gov.uk/canmore.html) and I think that EH are preparing test samples which are intended to include NMRAP infor-mation. It is safe to anticipate that in a few years it ought to be possible for registered users to access these addresses, define a search area, and be presented with a list of photographs. From there it is a short step to expect to be able to request low-resolution images that will allow searchers to decide which photographs they do not want to see (on the basis of cloud cover, poor archaeological detail, and useless control information) and file an edited list with a request to pull the prints for examination. Such an index already exists to provide access to satellite images held by the US Geological Survey (http://edcwww.cr.usgs.gov/Webglis/glisbin/search.pl?DISP) so is obviously not a major management problem. A logical next step would be to expect that a single web address will combine information held at several libraries or even that each of the national collections will also include their chunk of CUCAP index. To my knowledge, this amalgamation does not feature in anyone's plans.

Once we have digital access to our libraries it is likely that we may be encouraged to buy material as high resolution scans rather than paper prints (indeed, publishers already prefer that medium). Sale of material is one thing but frequent consultation is another, and most archaeological users want to examine, not buy, many photographs. I'd like to assume that our national archives will take advantage of modern communication so that in a few years I will be able to access their collections to obtain short-term loans of high-resolution copies of selected photographs without leaving my office. As even now it is extremely easy to make a digital copy of just about anything, accession to this futuristic library immediately raises problems of copyright and copying. I would expect my digital loan to come with a set of conditions, agreed, perhaps, at registration, which I hope would allow me to make selected prints for my own use rather than being on-screen read-only copy. Current technology allows electronic tagging so that it would be a trivial matter for the future library to keep track of access to and copying of any such loans. Therefore any deviation from the agreed conditions could be noted, billed as necessary, or for the very naughty, result in a ban on further access. Such a change in policy does not only affect our libraries. It is essential that any change in access, such as would result from meeting requests for digital products, can be efficiently handled by a sufficiently sized in-house scanning unit.

In the less distant future it is of importance to work in Europe to establish effective curation of the RAF Second World War verticals that are currently at Keele University. Storage conditions are inappropriate for this historic international archive and I am informed that indexing is little better than an incomplete card index and the memory of the current curator. The RAF wartime cover of Europe is partial but does contain some archaeological information, as was spectacularly demonstrated by the work of Bradford and Williams-Hunt in Italy (Bradford 1947; 1949; Bradford and Williams-Hunt 1946). Recently discovered Luftwaffe photographs are said to include block cover of a considerable part of Central Europe (Chris Going, *pers comm*) and as such should at least be examined, at best copies purchased, by archaeological photo interpreters from the countries concerned. Obviously, a first step in this process is to compile an easily-accessible index and this may be one aspect for consideration at meetings and workshops that are proposed as a first step in establishing a Europe-wide set of standards to cover all aspects of aerial work.

Mapping – the past and present

Use of the computer to aid accurate mapping was introduced to the archaeological world by Irwin Scollar at the CBA symposium on aerial reconnaissance in 1974 (Scollar, 1975). Since 1960, Scollar had been taking oblique photographs of archaeological features in the Rhine valley area and had written a computer program (and engineered a hardware system on which to run it) to meet the increasing needs of rescue workers to place a small trench accurately to investigate a known archaeological feature. His program, based on photogrammetric principles, was able to calculate three-dimensional ground co-ordinates for a given point on a photograph. Calculation of several points could provide an outline for a simply shaped feature, such as a Roman camp (*ibid* Fig 3): more complicated shapes could require a lot of individual calculations. Scollar's lecture and publication provided inspiration for my own program which used plane transformation equations to produce scaled graphical output from digitised input (Palmer, 1977). This necessary first stage of my research program allowed rapid and relatively easy compilation of maps from hundreds of individually transformed interpretations and so provided data for my study of sites and landscapes within a 4,000 sq km area.

It is necessary here to interrupt the flow of computer mapping to note the processes involved in photo interpretation and mapping as these are relevant to what follows and to future developments. Photographs identified by library searches are sorted to find those which best show the archaeological features and have sufficient control points (ie modern features which can be matched on photograph and map) to allow mapping. For a small area, a single print may be found that fulfils these conditions and a transparent overlay is mounted on this. Control points and interpreted archaeological features are marked on the overlay which, to produce vector output, is traced using a digitiser and that tracing is then transformed to plan. Once the interpretation has been made in the way described, it is usually faster, and certainly more accurate, to produce the mapped version by using computer transformation. Output can be printed to scale and traced on to a map or map overlay or can be combined digitally, matched with a modern base map, and finished using programs such as CorelDRAW or AutoCAD. The drawback of this method is that each tracing can introduce errors. However, this is the way that most computer-assisted mapping has been done in Britain.

The flow chart, Figure 1, assumes that Scollar's program was the founder of those that followed, although sideways relationships are uncertain. After pursuing the possibilities of using a 'micro computer' (the forerunner of the ubiquitous PC) for running a graphical output program (Palmer, 1980) and with changes to the University mainframe, my OBLIQUE faded into the past although it was installed on a number of other machines in England. It was, in fact, extremely user-unfriendly although it served my own purposes more than adequately. A one-off system was devised for RCHME (Burnside *et al,* 1983) which took input via a mono-comparator to produce graphical output, but the main thrust of software development was undertaken by John Haigh, a mathematician at Bradford University (Haigh *et al,* 1983). Haigh's AERIAL programs, initially written for PC-DOS and easy to use, are in widespread use in Britain, with some copies in Europe and an outpost in New Zealand. Initially they calculated plane transformation only, but the latest (and possibly final) version of the vector-output program allows optional use of terrain modelling when necessary (Haigh 1993) and has been converted to run in a Windows environment.

Returning to my 40 hectare example; from the couple of hundred photographs that had been taken of the area I had selected 28 for primary interpretation. Overlays of these were digitised using AERIAL 4.2 with colour conventions to distinguish ditch, possible ditch, medieval cultivation, palaeo-channel and recent features. These 28 files were combined in AERIAL, converted to DXF format, and input in AutoCAD LT where they automatically located as layers above an OS digital data base that had been supplied by my client. In AutoCAD I was able to edit duplicated features, smooth out shaky digitising, add minor detail from other photographs, and adjust line widths for printed output. Interpretation had been carried out at a 1:2,500 scale and a digital copy was supplied to the client along with a printed reduction bound into my report.

With use of Windows came accessible power to manipulate images on a PC, and John Haigh continued development to produce his AERIAL 5 series that transform scanned images to raster files that match maps (Haigh, 1996). A little before this, Jürg Leckebusch had adapted programs developed by Irmela Herzog (one of Irwin Scollar's outstanding research assistants) to make a package, RECTIFY, which included a GIS and database (Leckebusch, 1993). Unfortunately Zurich prices were well beyond archaeological organisations.

Since 1975, Scollar and his team at Bonn had continued to investigate methods of computer transformation and image processing (numerous papers, summarised in Scollar *et al,* 1990) and after his retirement he used that knowledge to compile a low-cost software

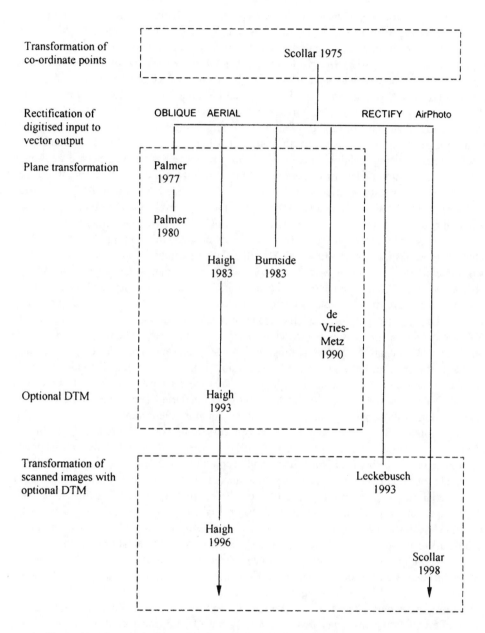

Figure 1. A flow chart of the development of computer programs that convert oblique sources to plan form. Irwin Scollar's early programs and OBLIQUE were written in Fortran and run on IBM mainframes. Scollar later used a purpose-built mini-computer at Bonn. From 1983 the main programs used for this work were all PC-based. For publications, see references. Source: author.

suite, AirPhoto, for Windows (Scollar, 1998a; b). In principle, AirPhoto is similar to AERIAL 5, both programs enable a certain amount of image processing (such as sharpening, contrast adjustment, and so on) and are able to transform images, but in practice there are important differences. AERIAL was developed mainly to meet UK requirements and fulfils the need to geo-locate transformed output with precision on DXF base maps such as the OS provide. Transformation matches the UK National Grid and offers a simple numerical grid (based on a Gauss-Krüger projection) for use elsewhere in the world. AirPhoto currently offers the user a choice from 27 different national grid systems and is better tuned for work on the range of European map projections. It also includes the facility to cross national borders without losing locational precision. Bonn experience has enabled Scollar to allow a choice of algorithms and transformations, including a recently added three-point + DTM method. In keeping with the times, AirPhoto can be downloaded from the web for a free trial. Regular updates are similarly available to registered users. Development of both programs is continuing and the authors are usually willing to consider specific requirements.

These image transformation programs have already changed the working methods of photo interpreters as has the use of AutoCAD Map and GIS which can import raster images. As a photo interpreter, however, it worries me somewhat that a scanned and transformed image may be thought of as an adequate and acceptable replacement for considered interpretation. Certainly these programs enable accurate measurements to be made from the processed images – but measurements of what? It could be argued (but I hope it isn't!) that such elementary correction is adequate to allow trench location for small scale evaluations. Maybe, in the case where one exceptionally clear photograph shows uncontroversial archaeological features and has sufficient control for accurate transformation. But where the need is to identify types of feature, such as on a gravel terrace where the photographs show a palimpsest of archaeological ditches, periglacial cracks, recently removed boundaries, and patches of deeper soil, interpretation of those photographs is a necessary step. Or where the photographs are being used to compile information about an area it is necessary to extract the relevant information and prepare a map which shows only that. It is also necessary to remind readers of the potential storage problems involved when using and keeping bitmap files.

Two approaches are currently being tested to make use of transformed bitmap data. Within EH's Aerial Survey, and in at least two of the English County Councils (Essex and Northamptonshire: see Markham, 1998) the corrected raster images are being used as the basis for a vector layer over which an on-screen interpretation is traced. Use of zoom allows fine detail to be followed accurately, although stereoscopic examination, except of prints next to the computer, is not within the scope of currently affordable systems. I am told this method is adequate for production of 1:10,000 mapping such as the above are compiling for the English National Mapping Programme.

Still in its very early stages is my own idea for transforming scanned data, Figure 2. My photo interpretation remains as always, carefully traced on a transparent overlay on which control points are also marked. After checking that those control points accurately transform the photograph I use the same control to transform a scanned overlay and so produce, with no further tracing, a raster plan to match a map background. If raster format is acceptable, the transformed image could be layered directly above base maps in AutoCAD Map or GIS, but vector is currently preferred. The problem then arises of automatically converting that raster information to vector so that, a) it can be added to an OS base map, mixed with other similar output, and edited as necessary, and b) file size remains manageable. Various bitmap to vector conversion routines are available, and I am currently investigating Corel OCR-TRACE 8, Adobe Streamline and Able Software R2V in the hope of finding one that will trace with sufficient accuracy and simplicity to reproduce my original lines with a minimum of further manipulation.

Using this process on a recent mapping job required scanning three separate overlays and super-imposing one on the others (no problem as AirPhoto allows mosaics to be compiled). The resulting raster file was converted using Corel OCR-TRACE (version 6) to produce a vector file in which I had combined outline and centre line traces. This was necessary to include some of the finer details but resulted in a vast file as that version of OCR-TRACE had no smoothing capabilities and each line was converted as a series of steps. This file was then imported over a digital OS base in AutoCAD Map where it had to be hand located and stretched to the correct scale by matching grid co-ordinates – not an ideal method. The combined file was edited to remove duplicated features but not smoothed or otherwise edited. My client accepted this as a reasonable working map which has since provided useful and accurate guidance in the field (Francis Pryor, *pers com*). The three files, where they overlapped, matched extremely well but it is not known whether this was due to the relatively level fen-edge environment or the avoidance of multiple tracings.

Let's return to the concept of digital mapping. To me this means that computer assistance has been used at *all* stages of the mapping – so we may have files that have been created from digitised input through AERIAL 4, edited to match a digital background map in, for example, AutoCAD, and which can be digitally printed and may be accessible using other software. One of the useful facilities in the computer rectification software is their calculation of error, or mis-match, values for control points which give the user an idea of their accuracy. These values are repeatable and may be attached to each file. Thus 'pure' digital mapping can be produced to stated accuracy limits. In addition is the purely visual checking that can be made (but not easily documented) of features between control points on a transformed image. In an effort to meet the digital age there has been a worrying move to produce what I will call 'pseudo-digital' mapping at 1:10,000 scale. This has been created by digitising mapping previously made by a hotchpotch of methods (from sketching to computer assisted) and, although now digital, fails to meet the standards expected, but never defined, of mapping which has that term attached. I suggest that potential users of any 1:10,000 digital mapping check on its origins if the intention is to use it for much more than an indication of presence or absence. At larger scales this ought not to be necessary as the majority of computer-assisted work produced at, say, a 1:2,500-level will usually include a statement of accuracy.

Mapping – the future?

In Britain, where the majority of archaeological mapping has taken place, we are reasonably content with things as they stand although we need to remain aware of new developments and be willing to spend the time checking them out. Some of my recent demonstrations of Scollar's AirPhoto seemed to be met with a definite lack of enthusiasm to move from the known to the new. If we lose our sense of enquiry, why bother to do anything?

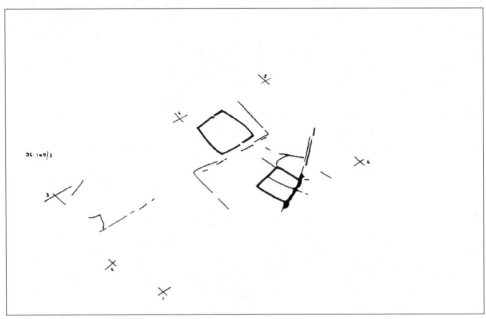

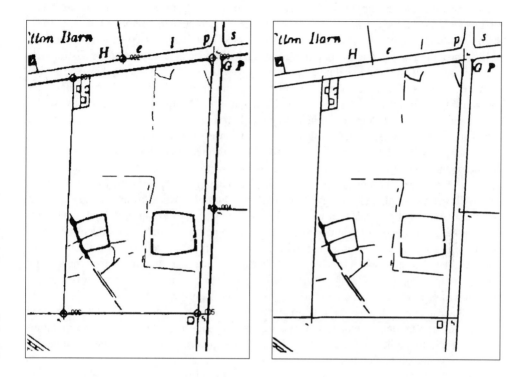

Figure 2. A future means of mapping?

Top left: An oblique aerial photograph centred on a field showing two enclosures
and associated features.

Bottom left: A copy of the transparent interpretative overlay showing the main ditched
archaeological features and six control points. The overlay was scanned and transformed
using AirPhoto to produce a raster image matched to an OS 1:10,560 base map.

The figure (*above left*) is enlarged to 1:5000 and has been printed to include the
computer-set control points. If raster images are not too excessive for storage
this form of output may be suitable for SMR data (the area shown is a 28KB file).

However, it may be desirable to convert the transformed output to vector (*above right*)
to allow easier manipulation and smaller (21KB) files. This test extract was made using
Corel OCR-TRACE 8 to follow the outlines of the bitmap image. Certain levels of adjustment
are possible but it is difficult to retain precise detail and accurate line widths of the original.
Source: author.

At least in Britain we appreciate the usefulness of mapping from aerial photographs as a first stage in landscape (or site) study. In other parts of Europe, aerial photographs tend to be seen as an end product in themselves or may be used as a guide for geophysics or surface collection with any 'mapping' continuing the great European tradition that the distribution map will solve all archaeological problems! This follow-up work on the ground is to be envied as, with the mass of material accumulated in Britain it is rarely possible unless development threatens a site. But it may also be wise in Europe to plan ahead and devise ways to use the information on aerial photographs when the limit of ground resources is passed. Interpretation and mapping is one way of making that information accessible to archaeologists.

In Vienna, Michael Doneus has been creating high-precision photogrammetric surveys (Doneus and Neubauer, 1998) on which information from obliques can be added. This process tends to be very slow and restricts its use to mapping for specific projects. Following the AARG-run (Aerial Archaeology Research Group) training week in summer 1998, a lead in area mapping is being taken at the Institute of Prehistory at Poznan in Poland, which has hardware and software for running AERIAL and, importantly, staff and students keen to pursue this as a means towards research. Similarly, a research project recently begun in south-western Romania includes photo interpretation, mapping and analysis as part of its aerial survey although funding is still being sought to provide computer hardware and software to support this element of the programme (Hanson, 1999). With increasing archae-ological aerial survey in Europe, it is important that the desk-bound aspects are not ignored and that interpretation and mapping begins to combine and make sense of the accumulating scraps of photographed evidence. It is logical to expect that mapping will be digitally produced, stored and manipulated.

Even with the help of computers, we are still reliant on the human interpreter to decide what data are archaeological. The full potential of image processing remains to be examined although Danny Donoghue at Durham has been investigating aspects of this for some years with types of imagery that, mostly, are not within the usual budget range of most archaeo-logical projects. In the conventional aerial archaeological world, Donoghue's methods are unusually high technology and have been recently applied to survey at West Heslerton (Powlesland *et al*, 1997; Caldwell, 1997). As part of that work, 12 channels of multi-spectral data were collected for processing and analysis on PC. Geo-corrected images of each channel were draped over a DEM and visually checked to identify those most relevant to the recording of archaeological features at the time of survey. One advantage of using digital multi-spectral data is the ease with which channels can be combined for examination, and the publication noted when this was done and which channels or combinations proved most informative. Many previously unrecognised features were noted (Powlesland *et al*, 1997, 4.2) although this is likely to result from any new cover of the area. Continued investigation of this kind should be encouraged although it is essential to balance the high cost of obtaining and processing these data against the returns. It is also necessary to remain aware of the unpredictable nature of the phenomena we seek to record and the degrees to which many variables may play on the non-visible as well as the visual evidence.

Image processing and the enhancement that it can bring leads tentatively to the possibility of being able to train computers to automatically identify, for example, crop-marked features. Many photographs of archaeological features, especially those published, are relatively clear yet even those are likely to include indistinct parts or places where a crop-marked ditch may gradually fade, perhaps to re-appear elsewhere on a similar alignment. Even with enhancement it is unlikely that the computer will ever match the abilities of the skilled human interpreter and the decision-making that goes into deciding whether a faint line really exists, or whether the gap noted above may be real, may pass through a poorly responsive patch, or may suggest where the ditch has been ploughed away. So I think such a form of mechanical help is not likely in the near future. Neither is it a very practical means of dealing with the hundreds of photographs that may usually be examined in the course of mapping a small area. But, as is suggested below, computer training may prove viable to help our analytical work.

Analysis – the past and present

The aerial world has readily grasped the use of computers to assist mapping but when we turn to examine the analytical work that is necessary to move from the photographs and maps towards understanding the past we find that surprisingly little (with or without a computer) has been done. This lack of past demonstration is, I think, why there is little current research that uses aerial photographs as primary data. From the early days of aerial photography, easily recognised types of feature were classified directly from the photographs and frequently fitted types already identified from field investigation of earthworks. This visual classification is continued in the forthcoming publication of RCHME/EH's survey of causewayed enclosures (Barber *et al*, forthcoming) and shows just how much can be achieved by this basic process and by repeated aerial survey. The 17 excavated sites listed by Isobel Smith (1971) were almost doubled by the addition of sites of similar morphology recorded only on aerial photographs (Palmer, 1976). Twenty years later that total has again been doubled by RCHME's new survey.

Increased aerial survey recorded a much broader range of forms than had been recognised on the ground and showed that in parts of the country it was possible to combine the photographed evidence to map joined up landscapes and so produce a prehistoric and Roman equivalent of the modern map. Classification of these landscapes often did little more than pick out the most easily identified and recurrent shapes, as in Brian Perry's work on enclosures in Hampshire (Perry, 1970). Elsewhere can be seen the use of maps showing unclassified landscapes as a background on which to display surface finds (Phillips, 1970). In Wessex, Collin Bowen strove masterfully to decipher complete landscapes (1975; 1990) by visual inspection, survey and thinking – the method known in RCHME as analytical field survey.

In the 1970s university computer services offered analytical software in the form, usually, of SPSS (Statistical Package for the Social Sciences) and enabled relatively easy access to other purpose-written programs. In Britain Christopher Smith published the results of numerical taxonomy and cluster analysis on stone homesteads in North Wales (Smith, 1974). At that date, similar computer sorting was usually of artefact types and this was an early attempt to apply it to structures. Use of the computer allowed Smith to compare 21 attributes rather than the half dozen or less that previous workers had manipulated. Similar work was being carried out in Africa in the 1970s, where Peta Jones was attempting to analyse features identified on aerial photographs. Jones also identified 21 attributes, of which 7 were directly of the site itself, 2 concerned relationship with surrounding features, and 6 were locational. Unfortunately the statistical package she was using allowed only two attributes to be compared at one time and her results were more informative of locational variance than of differences in site morphology (Jones, 1978).

At about the same time we moved from classification directly from the photographic prints to analysis of features that had been mapped from photographs. This allowed greater precision of measurement and more accurate comparison and sorting of shapes and sizes. For my own attempts at analysis of Wessex features I had intended to use SPSS. From my mapped results I had chosen 34 attributes, including 9 major and 5 minor site characteristics and 16 concerning association and distance of each site to other features, and applied these to a test sample of 437 sites (Palmer, 1983). In those days (technologically way back in prehistory) work was not done, as now directly at the keyboard and, before using SPSS, it was necessary to measure areas and distances and then code these by hand on forms. The next stage was to prepare punched cards for submission to the computer, although by the time I had coded my forms I was happy to accept the visible patterns on these and relied on human analysis. Although I did define a number of 'basic' and 'complex' forms these did not stand up to cross-examination, and certainly did not provide a 'date-by-shape' sequence for which I had hoped (Wilson, 1987; 17–23). More useful was the indication that distance and relationship to other features was significant – although this is perhaps unsurprising in view of the weight these were given in my division of attributes.

Research at about the same time was directed mainly towards classification of site morphology – where 'site' usually equated with what were hoped to be settlement enclosures (eg Macinnes, 1982; Whimster, 1989; Bewley, 1994). Interestingly Derrick Riley reversed that process by first analysing field types and tagging enclosures on to those (Riley, 1980), all, however, were done without use of the computer. Bewley's work in Cumbria, carried out some 10 years before its publication, provided the foundation on which RCHME's MORPH classification was based. MORPH was designed initially to enable systematic description of features and so provide EH's Monument Protection Programme with data recorded only on aerial photographs – although its originators hoped that it would have wider application (Edis, *et al*, 1989). Input to the program certainly broke features into a large number of component parts and allowed intra-site data to be compiled and compared making it possible, for example, to list all enclosures of a certain form within a defined size range (eg Fenner, 1995; Fig 9). MORPH did not easily assimilate inter-site relationships although, of course, this was not necessary for MPP. Other than to complete uniformly the records of ongoing external NMP projects in three counties, MORPH is being replaced to enable data from all sources in the National Monuments Record to be compatible. There has been no published testing of its broader application and it is perhaps a telling comment on its usefulness that no mention of its application to archaeological analysis is made in the recent publication of NMP work in Lincolnshire (Jones, 1998; Winton, 1998). Although MORPH, or morphological analysis, made much of that work possible, a reader's impression is likely to be that its main use in that volume has been to generate distribution maps which are based on the one attribute, date, that has to be guessed by the photo interpreter! (Bewley, 1998; see similar use in Fenner, 1995; 95–99).

While not solely concerned with information from aerial photographs, Collin Bowen's publication of the Bokerley Dyke environs (1990) stands as an exemplary archaeological survey and shows how much can be achieved by patient investigation of the ground, the air photographs, and the mapped combination of the two. It has to be asked whether analysis of any more formal kind, by brain or by computer, would add any understanding to that small patch of Wessex. More recent aerial survey and research on the Yorkshire Wolds has not strayed beyond elementary division of enclosures by shape and measurement (Stoertz, 1997) although showing an impressive level of descriptive analysis that is possible by looking at the maps and thinking. This raises the question, not for the first time, of whether it is possible to develop meaningful classifications of what may be called everyday settlement features. We have little trouble with the 'ritual' sites, our henges, causewayed enclosures, temples and the like are relatively easy to classify with confidence, and we can similarly sort domestic forms by their main morphological characteristics. Whether these forms ever had significance in the past, in which case our sorting is potentially useful, depends on such unknowns as whether there ever were distinct phases of fashionable shapes for homesteads and the like. Finding out is a problem for the future.

Philosophy aside, one further way of attempting to classify sites has come from recent work by Sam Redfern who, with his Windows-based Aerial Archaeology System, has developed an approach to automated morphological-topographical classification (Redfern, 1997; 1998). Redfern has worked directly from photographs, training the computer to identify and extract simple shapes which it can automatically measure and classify according to pre-defined shape parameters. At the same time, use of stereoscopic pairs of photographs has allowed the computer to generate topographical information which can be added to each site's attributes. Redfern's published work deals with classification of circle-like sites because these are relatively easy to train a computer to recognise, but application of the classification to small areas of Ireland show that it is able to identify and sort differences in form and location which provides the archaeologist with material for discussion (*ibid*; 32–37).

Analysis – the future?

Without research input from universities I think it fair to guess that there will be little advance in understanding the information recorded from the air (see also the summary of 'further needs' by Duncan 1997; 30–32). In Britain such research flourished (if less than half a dozen students equals a flourish) around 1980 since when no hard thinking has, to my knowledge, been applied to problems presented by aerial information. The most recent and most complex classificatory system, MORPH, was more for management and administration than to aid thinking and it is likely that any succeeding government-derived classifications will serve a similar brief. Putting our past in neatly defined boxes may, or may not, be a useful aid to its management and protection, but we can only begin our attempts to understand that past by devising problem-based strategies.

What part might computers play in these strategies? Not much I think because of the way that we work, or certainly that we work at present. All the 'classification' that I have seen has been primarily visual. I, and others, have mapped our landscapes, which we can reproduce at, say, 1:25,000 so as to look at fairly large areas of land without covering the whole wall with maps. This is important because the rest of the wall is where we stick the larger-scale cut-outs of our 'sites' which we move around and arrange in groups according to shape, area, and certain other characteristics that are probably indefinable because although we are aware of them we are not quite certain what they are, let alone how to code them for a computer. "But," you might say, "computers can measure area and sort things into shape-defined groups." Quite honestly, so what, if that information gets us no closer to archaeological understanding? Recently I heard of an amusing argument for why CUCAP need to get on with its computer indexing because, "…at present no research student could query it to ask for a list of all square enclosures on the 200m contour…". I would very much hope that no serious research student would ever see the *archaeological* need to ask such a query, but it does indicate the effect that GIS-driven research can have on common sense. To get the most from computers we need to think of appropriate questions relevant to our study, not to the manipulation of computers.

Our earlier efforts at morphological analysis were hopeful because of its apparent successes at sorting out artefacts. But although artefacts may be grouped according to a large number of their attributes, we know that flints, for example, were used mainly to cut, scrape, poke or bash, that pots were likely to be containers, and that elaborate examples of either may have had a status above pure functionality. When we try to use attribute analysis to help examine our landscapes mapped from air photographs we soon meet problems. Our 'facts' can be neatly defined, mainly as ditches, banks and pits, but it is the patterns, combinations and associations of these which need to be comprehended in order to begin to guess their past uses. The probability that each of these holes in the ground was likely to have played many roles in the past does little to help our understanding as at any one time a ditch, or parts of it, may have been equally important to a local community as a toilet, rubbish tip, 'wishing well', and boundary. Excavation is necessary to help identify the first three, but we may guess at the third when studying our mapping. I've attempted to show the complexity of what we are needing to understand and, perhaps, to let those who are better versed in manipulating data, edge towards ways of defining bits of the landscape to help our explanations of its past exploitation. A way forward might come from definition of combinations of features, as most recently has been put to us by Francis Pryor whose farming life allowed him to identify sets of bronze age ditched-features that reflected those currently in use for aspects of sheep management (Pryor 1996; 1998, especially Chapter 7). To me, Pryor's discovery provided a tremendous insight and if we are able to identify other facets of the working landscape we may eventually be able to link these together to illustrate how past communities managed their livelihood, something I regard as far more important than the current trend for guessing their 'symbolic' habits.

Here, returning to the supposed theme of this paper, is where computers may be able to help. Automatic pattern recognition is simpler for humans than computers and the range of shapes met in a normal archaeological landscape, to say nothing of superimposition or sub-division, offers a tremendous challenge to persuade the computer to unravel. However, if we are able to define parameters for each 'function' it is not beyond the realms of possibility that we may be able to train a computer to recognise similar patterns in a mapped landscape. This is a relatively simple approach which puts limits on how far we need to break up those landscapes into component parts. At present I think that less is better: twenty years ago I would have said just the opposite. A recent review of past attempts to classify (Duncan 1997) was able to show just how little success we had achieved, or how little demonstrable success, for it is one thing to propose groups of sites but to test those hypotheses requires field work and, to date, very little has been directed towards the broad study of landscapes. Excavators continue to favour the pleasures of detailed chronology and relish their ability to divide our past into diminutive units. Aerial archaeologists mostly remain desk, or cockpit, bound and so rarely get the opportunity to test their own suggestions – certainly not on the lavish scale that is required if we are to make any headway towards understanding landscapes rather than (possibly uncharacteristic) sites. The sheer volume of evidence provided by aerial survey requires a new approach to archaeological field investigation if we are ever to hope to study those sites before they are ploughed away.

Airborne – the past and present

The main impact computers have had on the airborne elements of aerial survey is in the use of GPS (Global Positioning System) as a navigation aid and to assist flight recording. Their impact is less recognised in photography itself, where they smoothly manage the formerly time-consuming effort of exposure metering with separate handheld instruments. Since GPS makes air navigation so much easier now, flying time to and from sites can be reduced to some extent and pilots can assign more of their time to screen the airspace for other planes, reducing the collision danger and making flying safer.

In-cockpit display shows the co-ordinates (initially as latitude and longitude but usually calibrated to NGR over Britain) of the aircraft position and the instrument can be set to record this automatically at specified time intervals to document a complete track and/or can be activated manually to note the position of sites photographed. This is now in common use by oblique photographers in Britain and the more affluent parts of Europe. Each flight can be downloaded as a series of co-ordinates and as vector information which can be displayed over a map background. Use of GPS is cost-efficient by saving time in the air formerly used to pin down on a paper map the position at which one has taken photographs. Using GPS, these positions are saved now by storing special co-ordinates by the press of a button (see Figure 3). Back on the ground, GPS eases on the problem of accurately locating the targets on finished prints as cataloguing will be done using a download of that flight as a guide. From a researcher's point of view, the continuous tracking also provides a record of ground that has been overflown, hopefully adequately observed, on which nothing has been recorded. In addition empirical data on survey intensity and history can be established for a region.

Otto Braasch, who acts as pilot and surveyor, also uses a Skyforce navigation system Colour Tracker. This cockpit-mounted instrument is a digital moving map in colour on which symbols can be placed to indicate sites which have been detected or are to be visited. The unit, driven by GPS, can show a track and time to fly from the current position to that selected, and can even control the autopilot steer to it (Braasch 1997; 36). The improved version Observer, displays different thematic maps and text, plus symbol information from individual data bases and thus can hold air survey history reaching back many years. In addition two scanned photographs or plans of each site can be stored and displayed to assist in identifying archaeological features and so help airborne decision making.

Rog Palmer

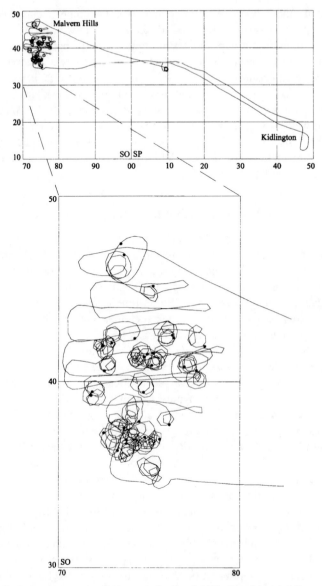

Figure 3. A GPS derived trace of a flight made by English Heritage's Aerial Survey southern team on 29 April 1999 from Oxford (Kidlington) to the Malvern Hills. The trace shows a pattern of east-west aligned searches, which allows effective observation of an area. Targets identified are orbited and photographs taken where indicated by the large spots. The GPS used was a GARMIN SRVY II CLASS III and the downloaded file was printed using AutoCAD Map. In the GPS software each photograph point (input during flight) is numbered and relates to an NGR list which also shows the form (earthwork, crop mark, etc) through which each site was visible. Information provided by Damian Grady: illustration copyright © English Heritage.

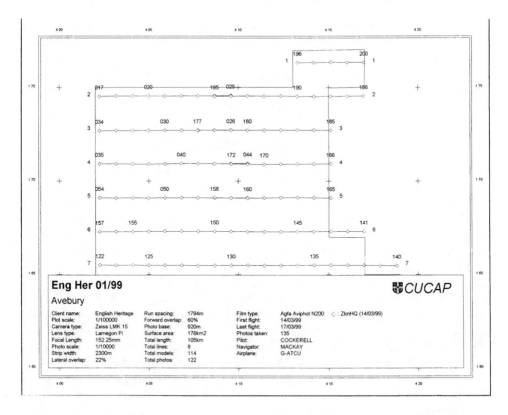

Figure 4. A computer-generated flight trace from a GPS-controlled vertical survey of the Avebury area flown by CUCAP in March 1999. Flight planning, airborne control and this figure were all done using Track'air Tracker. The precision flying made possible by use of this equipment is obvious by, for example, the accurate linking of flights made on different dates. Information and illustration provided by Tim Cockerell: illustration copyright © CUCAP.

Vertical surveys can also make efficient use of GPS in the planning stages, during flight, and to produce final sortie details. CUCAP, for example, use a Track'air Tracker, which is able to plan the survey by showing flight lines and numbers of photographs to be taken once a target's location, extent, and scale has been input. Tracker offers options such as least number of prints, or with flight lines along specified axes. The appropriate plan is named and filed and loaded into the flying GPS instrument which shows a little moving aircraft that the pilot has to track along the pre-determined flight lines. Flying control at this accurate level can be used to link different flights and allows precise continuation of surveys made on different dates (see Figure 4). Back on the ground, a downloaded file shows the actual flown track and is the basis of the printed flight traces which allow users to locate photographs.

Use of computer meteorological sites is also replacing faxed weather reports. These enable a pilot to see actual weather patterns from satellite data and so decide if an area to be visited is likely to be clear or cloud covered. There is a range of images and data that can be accessed, including half-hourly updates of images taken from fixed satellites (for a selection of these along with links to other sites, go to: http://www.adams66.freeserve.co.uk/sat.htm). Despite this use of technology, other factors combine to produce good or bad conditions for aerial photography and sometimes the only satisfactory answer can come from a telephone call to the control tower at an airfield in the survey area.

Airborne – the future?

The greatest need has absolutely nothing to do with computers but is to convince the aerial photographers that photographs with inadequate control information, although adequate to allow visual classification, or even to indicate which field contains an archaeological site, offer little more than frustration to the archaeologist who needs to interpret and map from them. If mapping is a way towards beginning to understand what has been photographed then it is essential that new photography allows this mapping to be carried out. Michael Doneus has shown that a competent photo interpreter is able to identify features that could not have been seen from the height of the aircraft (Doneus 1997; 25–27). Despite frequent encouragement to urge oblique photographers to fly higher and let interpreters find things on their photographs, their need to discover for themselves keeps them close to the ground and our requests for control points go unheeded. It is partly as a response to this that I have been examining the potential for vertical photography, to be searched on the ground, rather than base our record on observation and decision in the air recorded on oblique photographs. And now we can return to computers since a logical step from suggesting that vertical photographs provide better data than targeted obliques is to program a drone to do the airborne work!

It is more probable, however, that archaeological reconnaissance will continue to rely on oblique photographs taken to record observations made during flight. At present many observers in Britain fly with 1:50,000 maps that show rough indications of features previously recorded. This is usually sufficient to indicate whether a site is new or adds significantly to previous knowledge, in which case photographs will be taken. Technology is beginning to rear its head in this direction by allowing a GIS-derived map to be flown. This can show the modern background plus detailed mapping of known archaeological features and can layer previous flights if relevant. The cockpit-mounted display, Observer, manufactured by Skyforce, may suit the solo observer (see above), while a laptop system, linking MAPINFO and Garmin GPS, is being developed at Northants County Council and will allow 'back seat driving' (Markham 1998; 19). Both systems are able to display a moving-map while airborne. Use of visual aids of this kind raise the question of just how much time should be spent in the air to decide whether to photograph or not. One thing that the constant GPS traces show (Figure 3) is just how much time and fuel can be spent circling a site while trying to decide and then waiting for its best view to come round again. Once in the air, film is the cheapest part of the survey process and, as a photo interpreter, I would prefer pictures to be taken of anything, suspect, good, bad, or indifferent, so that people on the ground, with more time and more comparative material, are able to work with the maximum amount of cover.

Use of multi-spectral and non-visual sensors offers considerable archaeological potential. This has been successfully demonstrated in less accessible areas of the world (eg Adams 1980; Parry 1992) but is usually shunned in Britain and those parts of Europe where there are few restrictions on flying and archaeological reconnaissance and where we are used to conventional high-resolution photographs. John Hampton's early test of multi-spectral photography (Hampton 1974) included two observations: that it was not possible to predict when and where any one of the tested film-filter combinations would perform better than others, and that panchromatic film with a yellow filter was consistently good. Admittedly film technology has improved since the early 1970s and we are now able to record good detail using medium-format colour negative film and employ the additional red sensitivity of Kodak Technical Pan monochrome stock. Just as conventional film has changed so has multi-spectral imagery been enhanced by digital technology and the recent work at West Heslerton shows promise for future testing. CUCAP have the equipment to acquire IRLS (infra-red line scan) data, but this source still remains to be properly evaluated as to its archaeological potential. While archaeological aerial survey continues to be run as a low-budget sibling of 'real archaeology' many of the current and imminent forms of data gathering will remain beyond reach and probably also will remain unevaluated. To make the most of new technology, both in image acquisition and its processing requires that aerial survey drops its apparent pride in doing things on the cheap and campaigns to be given an adequate budget to test and exploit all means of gathering aerial evidence of our rapidly diminishing past.

As with multi-spectral data, examination of satellite imagery has proved valuable in the identification of archaeological features in parts of the world not usually covered by conventional photography or inaccessible to the airborne observer. Martin Fowler has kept archaeologists informed of improvements in the resolution of satellite imagery and has made use of it to study parts of Wessex (Fowler 1994 to present; http://ourworld.compuserve.com/homepages/mjff/). Some of the best material currently available, with a claimed ground resolution of 1.4m, is almost as good as conventional 1:10,000 vertical photography, and can very clearly record archaeological features via crop marks or as earthworks, Figure 5. Its potential is currently being assessed as an unofficial part of the new research project in Romania and, as a low-cost and easily-obtained medium it would make a worthwhile investment as archive material in any country just beginning its aerial survey. Scanned satellite imagery, regardless of its archaeological content, could be placed as a GIS layer from which information on past land use may easily be extracted.

Concluding thoughts

Have I strayed too far from my brief? Probably – but without being given an outline of the current situation it would be meaningless to describe how and where computers help our work. I hope that the narrative approach has provided context to what aerial survey may be trying to achieve at present and has hinted at possible future developments.

Because its use is now so commonplace, I have made no mention of the ease of communication that email has made possible. Within my own workspace, for example, it has allowed rapid response with Irwin Scollar when testing beta versions of AirPhoto, and

Figure 5. Part of a Russian KVR-1000 satellite image which shows the archaeological potential of
these high-definition sources. The area is some 5 Km south of Stonehenge where earthwork round
barrows, crop-marked enclosure ditches, and crop- and soil-marked lynchets of 'Celtic' fields are
clearly visible. The figure was scanned at 300 dpi from a 16 x 20 inch print and is reproduced here
at close to its original size. Claimed resolution is 1.4m and the level of detail recorded is close to
that on many 1:10,000 vertical photographs. The image was taken early one morning in June
1993 and is printed with shadows towards the viewer and east(±) to the top of the picture.
Image supplied by Nigel Press Associates Ltd © SOVINFORMSPUTNIK 1993.

close involvement with research in Romania, Poland and New Zealand. There is also the
benefit to others of the web pages that deal specifically with archaeology from the air (eg.
http://rs6000.univie.ac.at/AARG/ and http://www.univie.ac.at/Luftbildarchiv/). There is
no mention either of digital cameras for the simple reason that those currently available do
not match the resolution of conventional film. I am told that Vintern, a company that
makes cameras for military reconnaissance, have recently declassified digital cameras that
do exceed the resolution of film – but I do not know how astronomical their price nor
whether they are likely to be operable in a normal small cockpit environment. It is
currently easier to take photographs on film and convert these to digital form as and when
required.

We have seen the use and potential of computer indexes for our collections and the possibilities, that may be only a few years away, of effective on-line access to the photographs. Computer transformation has proved to be an essential tool for mapping: there is no other means that would allow us to begin to deal with the millions of photographs that show archaeological features. And I hope that mapping itself has been shown to be the principal medium by which we can analyse and so begin to approach an understanding of those old holes in the ground and their uses to past communities. Once mapped, once digital, the information is in the right form to be integrated with other data – and we have seen that such a system is being developed at NMRS. Others need to follow that lead. The ability of computer software to integrate different data provides perhaps the most powerful tool at our future disposal, but it remains for we humans to pose the right questions. Selective automated pattern recognition may be one way towards this end and is one way in which computers could be applied to help identify facets of past landscapes.

But it is our thinking that requires some direction. At present we seem to be wallowing around in the mud – sorry, the crop – and need to do some radical thinking about how we may approach examination of those pasts which aerial survey allows us to record. It is easy to feel swamped by the sheer mass of information and, at times, there seems to be no possibility of decipherment. But once we have been able to define our questioning then we will be better placed to assess the future contribution of computers.

Acknowledgements

I thank those colleagues listed below for information, be this as specifically requested or in passing, which helped in the writing of this paper: Bob Bewley, Otto Braasch, Tim Cockerell, Chris Cox, Martin Fowler, Damian Grady, Françoise Hivernel, Pete Horne, Phil Markham, Fiona Matthews, Sam Redfern, Irwin Scollar, Davy Strachan, Katy Whitaker. However, I must stress that the opinions expressed above are my own.

Bibliography

Adams, R.E.W., 1980. Swamps, canals and the location of ancient Maya cities. *Antiquity* 54, pp. 206–214.

Barber, M., Dyer, C. & Oswald, O., forthcoming. *The Genesis of Monuments: Neolithic causewayed enclosures*. EH, Swindon.

Bewley, R.H., 1994. *Prehistoric and Romano–British Settlement in the Solway Plain, Cumbria*. Oxford: Oxbow.

Bewley, R.H., 1998. England's National Mapping Programme: a Lincolnshire perspective. In R.H. Bewley, (ed) *Lincolnshire's Archaeology from the Air. Occasional Papers in Lincolnshire History and Archaeology* 11, pp. 9 17.

Bowen, H.C., 1975. Air photography and the development of the landscape in central parts of southern England. In D.R. Wilson (ed) *Aerial Reconnaissance for Archaeology. Council for British Archaeology Research Report* 12, pp. 103–118.

Bowen, H.C., 1990. *The Archaeology of Bokerley Dyke*. RCHME, London.

Braasch, O., 1997. Bemerkungen zur archäologischen Flugprospektion in West und Ost. In J. Oexle, (ed). *From the air – pictures of our common past in Europe (Aus der Luft – Bilder unserer Geschichte: Luftbildarchaologie in Zentraleuropa)*. Landesamt für Archaeologie mit Landesmuseum für Vorgeschichte, Dresden, pp. 29–38.

Bradford, J., 1947. Etruria from the air. *Antiquity* 21, pp. 74–83.

Bradford, J., 1949. 'Buried landscapes' in southern Italy. *Antiquity* 23, pp. 58–72.

Bradford, J. and Williams-Hunt, P.R., 1946. Siticulosa Apulia. *Antiquity* 20, pp. 191–200.

Burnside, C.D., *et al*. 1983. A digital single photograph technique for archaeological mapping, *Photogrammetric Record* 11, pp. 59–68.

Caldwell, A., 1997. Report of the second meeting of the Remote Sensing Society Archaeology Special Interest Group held at Durham University on Saturday 14th September 1996. *ArchSIG Newsletter* 1, pp. 15.

de Vries-Metz, W.H., 1990. The use of a simple PC when mapping archaeological traces on (extremely) oblique aerial photographs. In C Leva (ed), A*erial photography and geophysical prospection in archaeology: proceedings of the second international symposium, Brussels 8-xi-1986*. CIRA-ICL, Brussels, pp. 87–102.

Doneus, M., 1997. On the archaeological use of vertical photographs. *AARGnews* 15, pp. 23–27.

Doneus, M. And Neubauer, W., 1998. 2D combination of prospection data. *Archaeological Prospection* 5, pp. 29–56.

Duncan, S., 1997. Who's afraid of morphological analysis? *AARGnews* 14, pp. 27–32.

Edis, J., MacLeod, D. and Bewley, R., 1989. An archaeologist's guide to classification of cropmarks and soilmarks. *Antiquity* 63, pp. 112–126.

Fenner, V.E.P., 1995. The Thames Valley project. In J. Kunow (ed), *Luftbildarchäologie in Ost- und Mitteleuropa/ Aerial Archaeology in Eastern and Central Europe. Forschungen zur Archäologie im Land Brandenburg* 3, pp. 93–102.

Fowler, M.J.F., 1994 to present. Articles following the development of accessible satellite imagery and its relevance to archaeological survey appear in almost every edition of *AARGnews* 9–18.

Haigh, J.G.B., Kisch, B.K. and Jones, M.U., 1983. Computer plot and excavated reality. In G.S. Maxwell (ed) *The Impact of Aerial Reconnaissance on Archaeology, Council for British Archaeology Research Report* 49, pp. 85–91.

Haigh, J.G.B., 1993. A new issue of AERIAL – Version 4.20. *AARGnews* 7, pp. 22–25.

Haigh, J.G.B., 1996. Another member of the AERIAL software family. *AARGnews* 12, pp. 26–33.

Hampton, J.N., 1974. An experiment in multispectral air photography for archaeological research. *Photogrammetric Record* 8 (43), pp. 37–64.

Hanson, W.S., 1999. Go East Young Man: a new reconnaissance programme in Romania. *AARGnews* 18, pp. 15–17.

Jones, D., 1998. Romano-British settlements on the Lincolnshire Wolds. In R.H. Bewley (ed) *Lincolnshire's Archaeology from the Air. Occasional Papers in Lincolnshire History and Archaeology* 11, pp. 69–80.

Jones, P., 1978. An approach to stone settlement typology of the late iron age: stone walling on the Klip River 27° 10' S, 29° 10' E. *African Studies* 37, pp. 83–97.

Leckebusch, J., 1993. RECTIFY: a program package for the rectification and interpretation of aerial archaeo-logical photos. *AARGnews* 7, pp.26.

Macinnes, L., 1982. Pattern and purpose: the settlement evidence. In D.W. Harding (ed) *Later prehistoric settle-ment in south–east Scotland, Edinburgh University Occasional Paper* 8, pp. 57–73.

Markham, P., 1998. Air photography and GIS; the Northants approach. *AARGnews* 16, pp. 17–20.

Moloney, R., 1997. 'Flying too close to the sun?' Air photography and GIS. *AARGnews* 15, pp. 13–14.

NAPLIB, 1999. *Directory of Aerial Photographic Collections in the United Kingdom (Second Edition).* NAPLIB, Dereham.

Palmer, R., 1976. Interrupted ditch enclosures in Britain: the use of aerial photography for comparative studies. *Proceedings of the Prehistoric Society* 42, pp. 161–186.

Palmer, R., 1977. A computer method for transcribing information graphically from oblique aerial photographs to maps. *Journal of Archaeological Science* 4, pp. 283–290.

Palmer, R., 1980. A proposed microcomputer system for the transformation of air photograph interpretations. In J. Stewart (ed) *Microcomputers in Archaeology. Museum Documentation Association Occasional Paper* 4, pp. 41–42.

Palmer, R., 1983. Analysis of settlement features in the landscape of prehistoric Wessex. In G.S. Maxwell (ed) *The Impact of Aerial Reconnaissance on Archaeology. Council for British Archaeology Research Report* 49, pp. 41–53.

Parry, J.T., 1992. The investigative role of Landsat-TM in the examination of Pre- and Proto-historic water management sites in Northeast Thailand. *Geocarto International* 7:4, pp. 5–24.

Perry, B.T., 1970. Iron age enclosures and settlements on the Hampshire chalklands. *Archaeological Journal* 126 (1969), pp. 29–43.

Phillips, C.W. (ed), 1970. *The Fenland in Roman Times*. Royal Geographical Society Research Series 5.

Powlesland, D., Lyall, J. & Donoghue, D., 1997. Enhancing the record through remote sensing: the application and integration of multi-sensor, non-invasive remote sensing techniques for the enhancement of the Sites and Monuments Record, Heslerton Parish Project, N. Yorkshire, England. *Internet Archaeology* 2. http://intarch.ac.uk/journal/issue2/powlesland/index.html

Pryor, F., 1996. Sheep, stockyards and field systems: Bronze Age livestock populations in the Fenlands of eastern England. *Antiquity* 70, pp. 313–324.

Pryor, F., 1998. *Farmers in prehistoric Britain*. Tempus, Stroud.

Redfern, S., 1997. Computer assisted classification from aerial photographs. *AARGnews* 14, pp. 33–38.

Redfern, S., 1998. An approach to automated morphological-topographical classification. *AARGnews* 17, pp. 31–37.

Riley, D.N., 1980. *Early Landscape from the Air*. Collis, Sheffield.

Scollar, I., 1975. Transformation of extreme oblique aerial photographs to maps or plans by conventional means or by computer. In D.R. Wilson (ed) *Aerial Reconnaissance for Archaeology. Council for British Archaeology Research Report* 12, pp. 52–59.

Scollar, I., 1998a. AirPhoto – a WinNT/Win95 program for geometric processing of archaeological air photos. *AARGnews* 16, pp. 37–38.

Scollar, I., 1998b. AirPhoto – a WinNT/Win95 program for geometric processing of archaeological air photos. *Archaeological Computing Newsletter* 51, pp. 23–25.

Scollar, I, Tabbagh, A, Hesse, A & Herzog, I, 1990. *Archaeological Prospecting and Remote Sensing*. Cambridge: Cambridge Univeristy Press.

Smith, C.A., 1974. A morphological analysis of late prehistoric and Romano-British settlements in north west Wales. *Proceedings of the Prehistoric Society* 40, pp. 157–169.

Smith, I.F., 1971. Causewayed enclosures. In D.D.A. Simpson (ed) *Economy and settlement in neolithic and early bronze age Britain and Europe*. Leicester: Leicester University Press, pp. 89–112.

Stoertz, C., 1997. *Ancient landscapes of the Yorkshire Wolds*. RCHME, Swindon

Whimster, R., 1983. Aerial Reconnaissance from Cambridge: a retrospective view 1945–89. In G.S. Maxwell (ed) *The Impact of Aerial Reconnaissance on Archaeology. Council for British Archaeology Research Report* 49, pp. 92–105.

Whimster, R., 1989. *The Emerging Past: air photography and the buried landscape*. RCHME, London.

Wilson, D.R., 1987. Reading the palimpsest: landscape studies and air-photography. *Landscape History* 9, pp. 5–26.

Wilson, D. and Palmer, R., 1998. AARG Conversation No 3: David Wilson and Rog Palmer: 29 July 1998. *AARGnews* 17, pp. 39–47.

Winton, H., 1998. The cropmark evidence for prehistoric and Roman settlement in west Lincolnshire. In R.H. Bewley (ed). *Lincolnshire's Archaeology from the Air. Occasional Papers in Lincolnshire History and Archaeology* 11, pp. 47–68.

CHAPTER 9

Is there such a thing as "Computer Archaeology"?

André Tschan and Patrick Daly

Introduction

A "computer archaeologist", as the title would imply, should be out in the field with his or her trusty trowel digging up old hardware and software relicts from long-gone milestones in Information Technology (IT). Obviously, this is a colloquial caricature[1] as must be clear to the layman and scholar alike, however, while this potential misnomer may eventually be resolved within semantics, the lack of an appropriate and recognised naming convention serves as a general indicator for an overall trend within archaeology.

Despite the impact Information Technology has had in archaeology (Huggett 1993: 7, Perkins 1992: 1), particularly over the last decade (Ryan 1988: 1–27, Scollar 1999: 5–10), there seems to be only a limited *strategic* and *formal* incorporation of IT or Information Systems (IS) in ever-increasing and notoriously data-rich archaeological endeavors[2]. It is our belief that the absence of a directed focus on strategically implementing IT within archaeology poses a dilemma for the discipline as a whole as well as for any archaeologists that possess a high degree of technical competence or expertise in Information Technology.

The following, therefore, addresses the relationship between computer technology and academic/professional (*e.g.*, commercial units, museums, heritage industries, local authorities, *etc.*) archaeology given a predominantly North American and European context. Specific attention is paid to the roles of IT within archaeology focusing on its relationship with the theory and substance of the discipline, the training required, and the employment opportunities available. Our aim is to identify the level of recognition for "computer archaeology" throughout the discipline and the degree to which it is a self-contained and formal entity[3] with its own operational infra-structure and active research agenda. Based on an historical assessment and survey of the *status quo*, this is an attempt to define the requirements and structure needed for the successful development and implementation of "computer archaeology" for today's archaeological profession.

Should there be a relationship between archaeology and IT?

It must be clear to anyone who is currently involved in any archaeological endeavour that there has been a marked increase over the past several decades in the overall quantity and quality of data (Gaines 1984: 64, Kvamme 1989: 139–140). The reasons for this development are manifold and need no further description beyond the fact that there have been improvements in the detailed recovery of archaeological remains, advances in analytical methodologies pertaining to material culture, intensified commercial and heritage activities, and significant new research areas (*e.g.,* landscape archaeology, regional studies, *etc.*) (Cooper, 1985: 79, Stewart 1999: 21). This wealth of data poses a challenge inasmuch as any retrieved information demands a means for effective assessment and preservation for posterity. Consequently, because of its potential to contain and handle large amounts of data consisting of many different types of archaeological information, IT must be considered a promising addition to the standard tools available to archaeologists (Reilly and Rahtz 1992: 21).

Information Technology can be applied at any stage of a research or commercial archaeology project[4] (Martlew 1984: 7, Richards 1985b: 2, and for case studies see Scholtz and Million (Cultural Resource Management) 1981: 15–26, and Valenti (academia) 1998: 13). In addition, archaeological computing offers tools specifically designed to enhance the methodological analysis of cultural and environmental evidence. In other words, next to capturing, manipulating and creating archives for future generations there is a whole host of computer technologies that facilitate or allow detailed interpretations and reconstruction of the archaeological record (Marciniak and Raczkowski 1992: 50).

Nonetheless, the question of whether or not there should be an explicitly structured relationship between archaeology and IT is by no means answered conclusively. The fact that archaeology is a productive primary data source for computer-based analysis (Huggett 1986: 21), in conjunction with the aforementioned build-up of information on the archaeological record and ever-more affordable and powerful equipment, makes some IT tools increasingly enticing to researchers and professionals alike. This potentially acts as the main impetus to abandon some "traditional" practices and opt for "digital" archaeological methods[5]. However, some experiences indicate that a non-holistic embrace of IT implementations in the field can detract from achieving optimal results[6].

At the same time, internal and external forces acting on the discipline may also play an influential role (Martlew 1988: 499, Ross 1991b: 11)[7]. This is especially the case when IT becomes a preferred solution or a direct response to limited project resources, departmental peer pressure, changing theoretical foci in archaeology, or commercial industries that demand ever-increasing performance coupled with greater product quality and enhanced efficiency in project management (Gaines 1984: 65, Lock and Spicer, 1985: 103, Palmer 1989: 1). Hence, within this context, computer technology increasingly represents a highly valuable or even necessary resource for archaeologists. It also suggests that a more intrinsic and potentially inevitable relationship between archaeology and IT will depend on an appropriate setting and strategic formal framework[8].

A survey of IT in academic archaeology

To address our questions concerning the role of IT within academic archaeology in a tangible manner, we decided to engage in a survey of universities in the United States[9]. The main aim was to provide a general and "empirical" overview of these institutions, specifically focusing upon the structure and extent to which archaeological computing is implemented as part of an overall departmental research/training agenda.

Our selection of North American institutions was initially the consequence of having gained educational and operational experiences within this particular academic culture. At the same time, we considered that this deliberate focus would provide the best chance to investigate a large as well as comparable number of archaeological faculties. Finally, at many US universities, there is an additional set of dynamics relating to archaeology because it is typically a sub-discipline within an anthropology department[10]. Thus, both the availability and amount of computing resources as well as the pool of faculty members and post-graduates who may use IT in teaching and research expands significantly across the sub-disciplinary boundaries. This can bring greater access to resources and a wider research or training agenda "into the mix".

The eventual representative sample used in this survey is based on a ranking of 'top tier' American institutions as compiled by an independent university evaluation organisation (USB Research Informatics 1999). This allowed us to investigate those universities that, in addition to being driven by a strong research directive, had the likelihood of a good IT infrastructure, a recognised and sizeable number of faculty members, and a combination of general, highly specialised and professional teaching/training (post-graduate study) programs.

Survey fields

We opted to use the Internet[11] (the Net) as the main source for our survey since it was the most efficient tool for acquiring the core data set that we deemed essential for our assessment. However, in order to validate any information obtained from the World Wide Web (WWW) pages, we also sent out a detailed hardcopy survey (comprised of our selection of database fields) addressed to departments for which we already had information. Thus, based on the initial results from the Net and the returns for our questionnaire, we are satisfied with the overall accuracy of the results presented here.

The database itself consisted of a series of general areas, subsequently broken down into detailed constituent parts, in order to hold the records for our survey. The detailed information from the various selected Internet sources and the hardcopy returns were then entered according to the following set of conceptual headings and respective data fields (Table 1):

Academic institutions

Of the WWW sites approached, we found that for 60, of an original total of 74 universities, there was a listing for anthropology departments with research and training programs. The rest were either technical institutions or places where archaeological endeavours are under-

Table 1. The survey database.

ACADEMIC INSTITUTIONS
  University / Department

COMPUTER ACTIVITY
  Mention of computers or dedicated departmental computing facilities

TYPES OF IT IMPLEMENTATION
  Computerized Mapping / Data Management / GIS / Modeling / Simulations / Multimedia /
  Virtual Reality / WWW Applications / Other

FACULTY
  Number of faculty – quantitative methods (QM) / Number of faculty - IT research

TRAINING AND EDUCATION 1
  Number of courses – quantitative methods (QM) / Number of courses – IT research

TRAINING AND EDUCATION 2
  Number of Masters theses listed / Number of Masters theses with IT focus
  Number of Ph.D. theses / Number of Ph.D. theses with IT focus

Table 2. The survey results

	VALUE	%
COMPUTER ACTIVITY		
Number of departments surveyed for computer activity	38	
Mention of computers or dedicated department facilities	8	21.0
TYPES OF IT IMPLEMENTATION		
Mention of specific IT implementation type	19	
Computerized Mapping	3	15.8
Data Management	3	15.8
GIS	5	26.3
Modeling/Simulation	1	5.3
Multimedia	1	5.3
Virtual Reality	2	10.5
WWW Applications	2	10.5
Other	2	10.5
FACULTY		
Number of faculty	1120	
Number of faculty – QM	32	2.9
Number of faculty - IT research	21	1.9
TRAINING AND EDUCATION 1		
Number of courses	1624	
Number of courses – QM	37	2.3
Number of courses – IT research	15	0.9
TRAINING AND EDUCATION 2		
Number of Masters theses listed	799	
Number of Masters theses with IT focus	10	1.3
Number of Ph.D. theses	470	
Number of Ph.D. theses with IT focus	3	0.6

taken without the recognition of an actual departmental structure. Out of the 60, some 38 had sufficient information available on the Net to allow us to complete our investigation and achieve our desired goal for data collection and analysis.

Computer activity

The first question that we wanted to address was whether or not there was explicit mention of computer activity in department overviews. Obviously, this is a somewhat broad description that covers anything ranging from IT availability to dedicated computer facilities as well as special training courses and degree programs involving IT in archaeology. Yet, even based on such an overly generous category definition, we found that only 21 percent of all departmental descriptions did (prominently or otherwise) announce computers and/or IT resources (Table 2).

Types of IT implementation

The next step was to generate a more comprehensive breakdown of departmental computer use. For this purpose we gathered information based on the aforementioned computer activity analysis, the research profiles of faculty members and any project-specific WWW pages that related to the department or indicated some form of IT involvement. The survey records for academic institutions that listed specific computer tool implementations were then further separated into the most popular types of IT application areas (Table 2).

Faculty

As will be discussed further, it is our assertion that there has to be at least one member of faculty that is committed to the implementation and development of IT for a department to engage in a vigorous and productive archaeological computing program. In order to evaluate the current potential for such persons already having established their place, we went through every faculty member's research/interest profile.

Information was collected regarding any mention of Information Technology and quantitative methods[12]. Quantitative methods (QM) are a fairly standard field of research that usually refers to handling advanced mathematical and statistical procedures involving large sets of data and, in many cases, the use of computers is part of this process. It is therefore reasonable to suspect that archaeological computing could have been lumped into this QM category, where it might reside at present despite being more than just an additional area of methodology. However, even with this enlarged focus, less than 5% of faculty members expressed interest in IT and/or quantitative methods[13] (Table 2).

Training and education 1

In order to identify IT as part of the respective instruction set applying to the training and teaching of undergraduates and graduate students, we also examined the courses offered by the surveyed departments. However, the statistical results obtained should be viewed only as a possible trend because the course listings were unavailable for some departments.

All courses, irrespective of whether they were undergraduate or graduate, that involved some element of IT or QM were aggregated and tallied. A separate count was kept for both, but in some instances the same teaching or research program contained Information Technology and Quantitative Methods. Nonetheless, the actual final results show that slightly more than 2 percent of all courses incorporate QM while less than 1 percent explicitly focus on or include IT (Table 2).

Training and education 2

Finally, we investigated the number of completed theses that have been submitted for graduate degrees (Masters and Ph.D.). Our criteria emphasised those works that had clear IT research, implementation, or development agendas. Based on the accessible data (Table 2), 1.3 percent of all Masters submissions had a directed archaeological computing content. An even lower 0.6 percent of Ph.D.'s involved some form of active IT research.

Despite the limited number of theses accounted for in this analysis it is clear that these figures are significant especially since many professional archaeology posts (academic and commercial) get filled from this pool of people. In other words, beyond job postings specifically seeking "computer archaeologists", this negligible IT representation regarding graduate research implies a very low probability for a department or unit inadvertently, or by reasonable chance, acquiring a trained archaeologist that also has specific technical skills and experience in archaeological computing.

What is "computer archaeology" and what are "computer archaeologists"?

At this point it is necessary to separate the terms "computer archaeology" and "computer archaeologists" since we believe that each pertains to a different conceptual idea. This is not only for the purpose of a possible titular definition but also to clarify the underlying structural composition of IT in archaeology. Much like in a game of chess, "computer archaeology" might represent the game itself while "computer archaeologists" would act as the playing pieces. Based on his or her role characteristics (in line with the level of computing expertise) the "computer archaeologist" will therefore be subject to a set of functional parameters for specific assignments. In other words, the differing levels of skill attained by IT trained archaeologists also defines the tasks that she or he can handle successfully and the specialist role each may play as a member of an archaeology department or commercial enterprise[14].

This analogy would also imply that "computer archaeology", by virtue of such an all-encompassing definition, will incorporate any archaeological computing technology available to "computer archaeologists" while clearly delineating according to the function and the degree of complexity for such tools. However, the critical point is that in chess conceptual elements are required for the game to actually become a whole. Consequently, "computer archaeology", like chess should be subject to *an accepted formalised structure* as part of an operational definition within archaeology. The setting (the "board") and the pool of human resources (the "figures"), depend on such an acknowledged set of implementation guidelines for IT in archaeology (the "rules") as well as application-specific design strategies (the "how to play" manual).

We argue, therefore, that archaeological computing, regardless of the setting and the people involved, becomes a piecemeal or purely task-oriented endeavour when there is no inextricably linked conceptual and operational framework in place. This means that any currently recognised absence of a formalised structure (acting as an all-encompassing foundation), by default, also excludes the possibility of a singularly unifying and universally recognised identity and titular description for archaeological computing. Thus, by this argumentation it is safe to suggest that, at present, there is *no* such thing as "computer archaeology" and we emphatically support this notion. Clearly, this situation requires a remedy that can establish the necessary widespread profile and comprehensive recognition of IT in archaeology and we advocate a holistic integration of archaeological computing as an academic sub-discipline within an "industry-wide" departmental structure.

"Computer archaeology"

Based on the preceding survey data indicating a marked absence of any IT implementation framework, it can be argued that throughout American archaeological departments there is no clear evidence for "computer archaeology". Nonetheless, this conclusion can not deny the fact that, according to the collected results, there is a highly recognisable engagement in archaeological computing using a plethora of different means for data capture, data management, analysis and output. However, for this work it is important to know that the Information Systems approach that we advocate incorporates not just a specifically designed hardware and software infrastructure[15], but it also, and most crucially, establishes some actual and distinct role definitions regarding human resources in "computer archaeology".

This clearly indicates the need for a conceptual and operational concentration of IT resources in archaeology by creating a self-contained framework that can accurately differentiate the palette of methods and computer tools used in archaeological computing. Without such a setting IT requirements are potentially difficult to evaluate not only with respect to the appropriate level of skills needed to perform a specific job but also with regards to finding an appropriate pool of people from which to attract and recruit a skilled workforce. At the same time, many archaeological ventures involving disparate or random computer use may, paradoxically, be the result of one of IT's main strengths and benefits: namely being inherently varied, flexible, neutral, and non-specific for any particular time and space when applied to investigations of the past. Essentially a highly desirable virtue, it is exactly these intrinsic IT characteristics, allowing for a vast application development freedom, that could also be the biggest drawback in more widely recognising the often sophisticated nature of archaeological computing as a distinct and self-contained entity in its own right. Thus, without actually creating or enforcing this framework for "computer archaeology", the trend will undoubtedly continue where IT is approached using a purely operational agenda, based on many separate institutional or commercial application settings[16]

"Computer archaeologists"

As Huggett (1989: 3) indicates, the appropriation of IT in archaeology is generally an attempt to improve the efficiency and quality of data; involving the capture, manipulation or storage as part of a research or commercial environment. Hence, Information Technology, despite differences in function among all the available hardware and software, shares on a fundamental level this conceptual "sense of purpose". Furthermore, for "computer archaeology" to become a reality as its own recognised and accepted field within the general discipline, requires, in addition to the formal structure suggested above, a great many skilled archaeologists that can actually employ and create applications using computer tools.

However, while a broad level of knowledge about the past and/or a high degree of proficiency in the field may be generally desirable, an archaeologist will most likely obtain an in-depth specialisation with regards to a cultural group, a specific time period, a geographical region or some detailed aspect of material culture. This suggests that any computer skills potentially fall into the category of "additional" technical aptitude acquired parallel to one's overall career development. Consequently, the archaeologist is required to become an expert in a particular area of archaeology while any IT knowledge might then be applied to this specific focus. At present, therefore, it is up to the individual to decide whether any extra computer skills may or may not be actively pursued. Clearly, any such decision will be made in line with the actual usefulness to his or her field of expert knowledge, the research or operational agenda in place, the level of already achieved technical abilities or, simply, one's personal interest. This does not represent the ideal situation envisioned by us and described by Moffett's most fundamental recommendation, where:

"A Computer Archaeologist must have a strong archaeological background combined with anequally solid computing background." (1991a: 31).

Consequently, the degree of IT competence or specialised expertise[17] will vary considerably throughout the discipline as a result of the career choices made by individual archaeologists. Hence, a more accurate role definition for "computer archaeologists", one that results from assessing individual levels of aptitude within a structured organisational setting, is necessary. Once a conceptual and operational "computer archaeology" umbrella is established, all forms of archaeological computing can be embraced and this formal framework will then allow exact identifications regarding any skill-based positions as part of this functional structure. As a result, there will be a clear separation into distinct areas of overall "computer archaeologist" expert knowledge with discrete areas of specialisation (*e.g.,* CAD, databases, GIS *etc.*).

An implementation framework for "computer archaeology"

The previous sections on IT in archaeology contain the basic conceptual outline for what we believe is currently one of the most progressive and substantive aids for archaeological investigations. However, some aspects that we have already addressed warrant some additional exploration inasmuch as we strongly advocate a strategic IT framework for archaeology based on an Information Systems approach to ensure a holistic integration of computer tools together with the people that can use them[18].

Information Technology should be approached as early as the archaeological project design. It can be essential, depending on the scope of a study or commercial endeavour, that the right computing technology is in place prior to commencing an excavation or survey (Cleere 1984: 15). Hence, subject to the specific archaeological research agenda, the raw data can be recorded using a strategic and predefined computerised collection process (*e.g.*, selecting file formats that guarantee the overall portability for subsequent analysis or information dissemination) resulting in a core digital resource from which any further work can be derived. Furthermore, any engagement in archaeological computing should also involve an application of archaeological theory to a quantifiable source, which in turn possibly allows a more "contextual" interpretation and reconstruction of the archaeological record. Yet, this does not mean that mere proficiency in data entry, data query programming or desktop-publishing will by default result in a successful or "objective" interpretation of the archaeological record (Lock and Wilcock 1987: 12, Henderson 1991: 201, Scollar 1999: 8)[19]. For this purpose, far more advanced Information Systems approaches, beyond specific one-off IT usage, are required.

As a basic example this scenario describes IT with regards to the overall potential when applied as an integral element of an archaeological project. However, it really only exemplifies the differences between our explicit preference for an IS approach and single task-oriented operational hardware/software applications. There are additional distinctions necessary which specifically address the human resources and the levels of expertise that are required as part of our recommended IT implementation framework for "computer archaeology". In other words, the people applying computer tools in archaeology need to be addressed further since they are currently subject to no universally accepted identity (as a consequence of the specialised parts they might play within a project setting)[20]. With this in mind, we present the following models, Figures 1 and 3, for academic and public/private archaeology respectively.

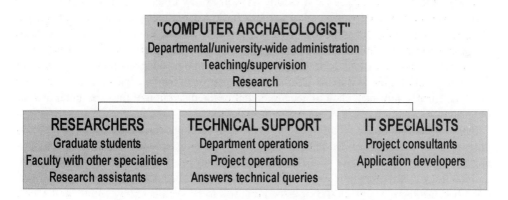

Figure 1. An IT implementation model for academic archaeology

The "computer archaeologist"

Undoubtedly the suggested integration of IT within archaeological projects, involving either single specialised analytical computer tools or, what we strongly recommend, an holistic implementation strategy, requires an expert level of skill. It is this expertise that should conceptually identify participation in "computer archaeology". However, the aforementioned absence of a formalised structure for IT in archaeology stifles support for any unifying defin-ition that would be applicable to anyone with the capacity to design and implement a computer infrastructure as part of an archaeological investigation.

"Computer archaeology" requires a substantial versatility in understanding archaeological remains/processes from a theoretical and physical perspective. This is in conjunction with having a comprehensive grasp of the means best suited for the capture, management and dissemination of data. In other words, anyone using a word-processor or a spreadsheet is required to know the functional parameters of a specific program. A "computer archaeolo-gist", on the other hand, could be oblivious to the detailed usage of any particular hardware and software while she or he clearly needs to comprehend the conceptual role of the selected tool within the wider context of an archaeological setting[21] (Moffett 1991a: 31). Consequently, a "computer archaeologist", by achieving a broad understanding of IT in archaeology, acts as an active resource for a project by choosing the appropriate computer tools and the required workforce[22]. Once selected it is the task of trained workers to then apply their respective archaeological computing talent as part of a specific investigation. This approach bears close resemblance to IT implementations for corporate businesses and it is suggested that "computer archaeology" may operate most effectively when using such a proven and successful structural design.

At the same time, it is the capacity to integrate IT as a central part of an archaeological investigation that defines a level of expertise appropriate for describing someone as a "computer archaeologist". Together with a business model approach for IT in archaeology, this establishes a role definition for an archaeological computing expert equal to that of a group head. The "computer archaeologist" needs to be the spokesperson or resource for all computer and IT related issues at a faculty as well as any other administrative level[23]. In other words, because general IT concerns transcend the department, a "computer archaeolo-gist" must additionally act as the liaison to the university administration whenever a situation demands such involvement[24]. Most importantly, the "computer archaeologist" takes control and makes general decisions concerning, among other things, the procurement of computer facilities, what IT courses may be offered and the degree of active engagements in research projects. Clearly, any such choices need to be left to the discretion of the "computer archae-ologist" in recognition of his or her realm of expertise.

Being a member of the faculty also brings with it teaching responsibilities. As with any other member of staff (regardless of their speciality or sub-discipline affiliation), a "computer archaeologist" will also have to be prepared to lecture on introductory archaeology and anthropology topics often unrelated to IT and archaeological computing. This is a significant point because there is a general course load that has to be shouldered by faculty and people will seldom gain employment if they can not partake in instructing these standard classes. Any person hired as a "computer archaeologist" will have to achieve the necessary education to handle such responsibilities. Such additional requirements will come on top of arranging and teaching a series of specific (theoretical and practical) courses regarding IT in archaeology[25], Figure 2. Moreover, these archaeological computing classes need to be designed for under-graduates and post-graduate students in accordance with their respective abilities and career prospects[26]. The "computer archaeologist" must be capable of handling advanced courses/seminars concerning IT related methodologies for archaeological research[27].

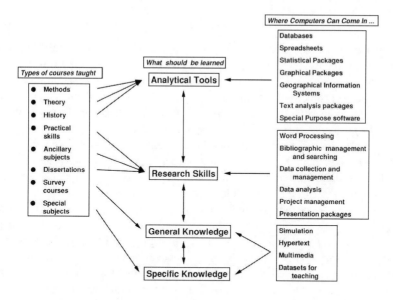

Figure 2. A potential course outline for students in archaeological computing
(based on Perkins 1992: 2)

Furthermore, to ensure that anyone under the direct supervision of a "computer archaeol-ogist" has access to ample and appropriate case study opportunities, it would be necessary to arrange active project participation[28]. However, this paramount demand to find such suitable assignments for the purpose of completing a study or a degree program must be preceded by a solid archaeological research agenda as designed by both the student and the supervisor.

A final area of responsibility for a "computer archaeologist" includes a personal engage-ment in research projects that are designed to foster the overall development of IT for archaeology/anthropology/social sciences. The emphasis for this lies in making a contribu-tion to a wider academic, and public, community of which archaeology is a single member among a great many. Hence, this is the first step towards reversing what is currently a rather negative exchange balance between archaeology (anthropology) and other disciplines. The discipline should have a greater input in designing the set of tools that it wants to employ whereby any promotion of "computer archaeology" would counteract a trend where methods and tools are constantly siphoned off from other fields. It has been claimed that not many useful discipline-transcending contributions have been offered by archaeology to the general world of science[29].

In order to achieve such a goal there has to be a considerable leap forward regarding both a successful IT implementation framework and a fuller recognition of archaeological computing. For this purpose, "computer archaeologists" should also become involved, either directly or as consultants, with research that is being conducted by other members of faculty, demanding a continuous involvement process regarding the design and application of archaeological computing from initial grant proposals to final archive developments and publication[30].

Researchers

The "computer archaeologist" represents the dedicated IT faculty member and she or he will serve as the core around which any successful archaeological computing program is established and in line with our proposed business model approach, there are additional categories of people that answer directly to her or him. Composed of post-graduate students and other types of staff, researchers will be the major source of IT-related production within those archaeology departments that adopt this implementation framework. Members of this category depend on specific training in both IT and archaeology/anthropology[31]. However, becoming highly skilled in the application of Information Technology is a "hands on" process and any academic program or extra-curricular opportunities must accommodate for this[32] by increasing the currently available course offerings[33].

Furthermore, many post-graduate students (in America at least) are funded to either work as teaching or research assistants. It might be highly beneficial to establish department-funded schemes that are dedicated specifically to consulting for IT in archaeology. This will entail recipients of such monies to work a set number of hours a week providing archaeological computing support to students and faculty in the form of a "help desk" for research-related inquiries. Not only will this take a considerable workload off the "computer archaeologist", who as a faculty member is burdened with many other responsibilities, but it also provides readily available IT support by people that understand the unique characteristics and nature of archaeological or anthropological data.

Overall, for the category of researchers, Information Technology is essentially a tool to be used for instruction and as need arises, involving those routine as well as complex project-specific tasks that nowadays, more often than not, should be handled by virtue of some form of Information Technology. The acquisition of this IT knowledge, essential for developing computer-based applications for archaeology, requires training and education which is subject to considerable investments in both time and effort. It is through perseverance and experience that there is advancement and one's acquired conceptual and operational archaeological computing skills will achieve an eventual recognition of expertise. Hence it is from this pool of "computer-literate" researchers that the next generation of "computer archaeologists", technicians and IT specialists will most likely come. This category represents the main staging platform as part of the business model IT implementation framework for "computer archaeology".

Technicians

It is impossible to discuss our IT in archaeology implementation framework without also considering technical support. Hence, if a department wants to establish a conducive setting that allows significant research with regards to archaeological computing then it will also need to address the two main distinct areas involving technicians.

Firstly, technical support for a departmental infrastructure or daily operational tasks is a close reflection of the general advice and help that most universities currently offer to departments and faculties. This type of technician is, therefore, predominantly involved in the maintenance of computer facilities and applies his or her expertise in hardware/software to overall matters of equipment installation, upgrades and fixes, while also managing any local area networks (LAN) for the department. In essence, this position, as an integral part of the proposed IT implementation framework, is designed to ensure that the facilities are fully operational so that new research may be undertaken or archaeological computing that is already in progress can be continued unhindered. Short of this technical support for a department-mental IT infrastructure, there will be too much time wasted when highly skilled "computer archaeologists", researchers or IT specialists get involved in taking care of potentially mundane computing problems.

A second type of technician operates within the tight confines of an IT setting for archae-ological investigations. This is a highly project-specific job that requires expertise in the operation and maintenance of select hardware/software and equipment. Contrary to an overall departmental infrastructure setting, a permanent archaeological computing environ-ment, this level of technical support is called upon only in circumstances that demand his or her active operational project involvement/intervention; a role potentially easily misinter-preted or confused with that of an IT specialist[34].

IT specialists

IT specialists create specific applications with regard to the capture, management or dissem-ination of archaeological data. She or he will very rarely act in the capacity of a "computer archaeologist", researcher or technician because the actual computing focus is prescribed by task-specificity and by the set of highly specialised hardware/software tools that require a recognised high level of expertise in their usage. In other words, regardless of whether somebody possesses the capacity to integrate IT in archaeology using a holistic Information Systems approach, the actual archaeological computing requirements when engaged in a project only demand the ability to accomplish a specified number of chores and "to do the job" as is expected. Within the context of an overall project design and in line with our model for an IT implementation framework for archaeology, an Information Technology specialist can be much likened to that of an independent consultant.

Public/private archaeology

Clearly, academic archaeology represents only one element of the wider archaeological community. In fact, the majority of archaeological work (*e.g.*, survey, excavation, cataloguing, archiving, presentation, *etc.*) is undertaken by the commercial archaeology and heritage (public/private) sectors. Thus, considering the often enormous quantity of informa-tion that is collected and processed, in addition to stringent time constraints and other professional pressures, the usefulness of Information Technology in these areas becomes obvious. Yet, as with academic archaeology, a strategic IT implementation framework would be required to fully harness any archaeological computing potential (Figure 3).

The academic model presented above is designed so that the structural elements are as flexible as possible, thus making it applicable to many different archaeological circum-stances. However, there are some fundamental differences regarding the role requirements for public/private archaeology, especially concerning the "computer archaeologist".

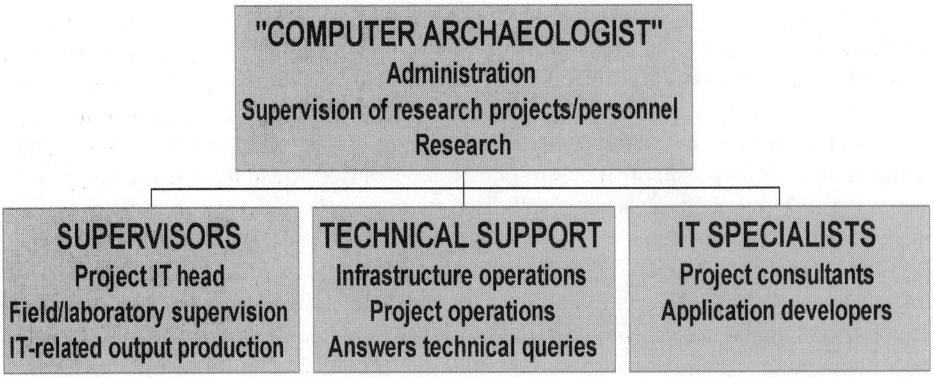

```
                    ┌─────────────────────────────────────────┐
                    │           "COMPUTER ARCHAEOLOGIST"       │
                    │              Administration              │
                    │   Supervision of research projects/personnel │
                    │                 Research                 │
                    └─────────────────────────────────────────┘
```

SUPERVISORS	TECHNICAL SUPPORT	IT SPECIALISTS
Project IT head	Infrastructure operations	Project consultants
Field/laboratory supervision	Project operations	Application developers
IT-related output production	Answers technical queries	

Figure 3. An IT implementation model for public/private archaeology.

For the "computer archaeologist", the main administrative concerns will be the same in an academic setting as in public/private archaeology. She or he will have to oversee all major decisions regarding Information Technology from initial equipment procurement, set-up of facilities, hiring of qualified personnel and actual IT application development and strategies. However, whereas in academia a "computer archaeologists" would be responsible for supervising students and teaching, supervision in public/private archaeology focuses primarily on the incorporation of IT during project design and the management of the required pool of people in charge, i.e. supervisors.

In addition, the IT needs within the commercial and heritage industries call for technology that is easy to standardise and reproduce, involving tools that are efficient and capable of handling large amounts of information; including data recorded using conventional methods (*e.g.*, file archives, drafted plans, aerial photographs, *etc.*). Hence, the main research agenda of the "computer archaeologist" should reflect these needs by emphasising the design of methodologies and applications for wider use in data collection, analysis, storage, and presentation to the public. The biggest difference between the two IT implementation models presented here, however, relates to researchers and supervisors in their capacity as the primary sub-category respectively. In academia, researchers represent mainly graduate students who are engaged in some form of IT research and application development as part of a degree program. They therefore focus more on specific problems and the tools best suited for arriving at a desired solution or result. At the same time, due to the time constraints for degree completion, students can not be expected to achieve the variety of experiences that allow for higher levels of implementation efficiency. The supervisors, on the other hand, are mainly responsible for overseeing the actual use of IT through all project stages. This involves initial project assessment, conceptual IT designs, data management, supervision of field and laboratory personnel, and output production suitable for presentation or publication. They answer directly to the "computer archaeologist" in addition to the main project director(s).

Finally, the other two main categories in this proposed IT implementation model (technicians and IT specialists) are essentially subject to the same role definition in academia as in public/private archaeology and therefore change neither function nor purpose.

Discipline and industry employment opportunities

The first and foremost question that comes to mind regarding any employment potential relates to whether there is actually a genuine need or demand for "computer archaeologists" in archaeology. At present, nearly every "computer archaeologist" working in the discipline will already be the product of a non-formalised or self-designed "computer archaeology" education[35] (Martlew 1988: 499, Moffett 1991a: 31). This means that any acquired IT skills may disproportionately stress computing over the general theory and substance of the discipline. The major predicament, therefore, relates to whether or not archaeology as a whole can absorb Information Technology specialists, "computer archaeologists", who, more often than not, are looked upon as mere technicians[36], seemingly short of the "established" archaeological proficiency that is required in gaining rewarding employment in education/training.

This view also implies that any demand for "super archaeologists", skilled in computer applications and recognised speciality areas of archaeology will always be greater than the severely limited or barely existing human resources at present offer. Yet change, i.e., a set of appropriate training/education programs, that would boost these low numbers could come about if the discipline as a whole responds constructively to the assessment made by Carman *et al*:

"Archaeology is being forced by external change to alter both the structures which comprise the profession and the functions which its professional practitioners undertake. This in turn affects the nature of archaeological employment and the skills needed to run organisations and projects." (1995: 4–5)

This suggests also that experts in IT in archaeology need to prepare accordingly. In other words, acquiring the "necessary" specialised archaeological skills enhances the overall chances in getting work within academic/commercial archaeology, but at the same time the job for which she or he gets hired may not actually entail any archaeological computing. Thus, it might be up to archaeology as a whole to recognise "computer archaeology" as a distinct entity and the discipline should support its "home-grown" talent by adopting a formal IT strategy.

It may be worth reiterating that any recognition of "computer archaeology" *per se* depends on the advocated sub-disciplinary or commercial department context. For it is this formal setting with its specific functional parameters and personnel requirements that will allow individual advancement according to a progressive scale based on archaeological computing expertise, that goes far beyond the currently non-existent or scarce employment opportunities for "computer archaeologists"[37].

A recommendation for the future?

We would be very surprised if current and successful large grant applications for archaeological research involving the major US and European funding bodies did not have at least *some* mention of IT applications. At the same time, any suggested inclusion of Information Technology-oriented tools for investigations of the past should provide a wider breadth regarding sources of funding[38]. Thus, in order to get financial support for a research project, chances may increase when advocating some usage of archaeological computing tools and methods. Yet, to secure further project monies from the same body will sooner or later depend on the results obtained from the actual integration of IT in archaeology.

Our intuition is that there will be a foreseeable future when the discipline as a whole will be expected to apply a standardised set of archaeological computing tools and methodologies as a matter of routine. The consequence of not incorporating or engaging in such practice may therefore result in a loss of funding or support, particularly when monies are subject to a competitive tendering process. This affects commercial archaeological endeavours where bids are subject to the demands of individuals or industries situated outside of archaeology and where other applicants for the same project exhibit a more dedicated inclusion of archaeological computing and IT.

Conclusion

A major objective of this work was to evaluate the status quo regarding Information Technology in archaeology. We believe that our survey of American universities substantiated what everyone currently involved in archaeological computing undoubtedly already knows, that the situation is far from ideal. While there is a small number of well-organised and structured European "computer archaeology" programs[39] and possibly the odd equivalent elsewhere, most departments will, when pushed, struggle to conceptually and operationally handle anything beyond the most basic archaeological computing needs. Overall, a recent example of the fact that any recognition within the general archaeological community for IT in archaeology is sorely lagging behind is based on the "new" predicate given by Hodder (1999: 117–128) to often well-proven archaeological computing technologies[40].

Nonetheless, as an important aspect of our everyday life and as part of the "modern" world that surrounds us, IT has become a basic "ubiquitous" fact in archaeology (Wilcock 1981: 9, Huggett *et al.* 1998: 1). We are, therefore, getting ever closer to the point where an overall "computerisation" of archaeology will be recognised and subsequently treated as an integral part. There can be no real desire or justifiable reason to be left in a technological wake even though, at present, it *may* just be possible to cut corners by farming out IT needs, placing responsibility upon people that lack the skills/training to do the job, or by simply ignoring the situation wholesale. However, over the next decade many archaeology departments and public/private enterprises will have to face the reality that they could be wholly unprepared to successfully incorporate IT into their research and organisational strategies.

There is probably no aspect of archaeology that currently is not already permeated by IT or could benefit from it. At the same time, careful planning is required in order to cultivate a strong IT element within archaeology. Neglecting to adhere at every stage to such a critical plan will surely hinder the potential for continued research, subject to the highest attainable standards, into the current millennium. We argue that the fundamental structure with regard to a successful integration of IT in archaeology involves a strategic implementation framework[41] in line with a full sub-disciplinary or industry-wide departmental status for archaeological computing. Information Technology in archaeology is subject to a rather urgent agenda and this development of "computer archaeology" must not be placed on the shelf or put off until later.

Acknowledgements

Ian Johnson (University of Sidney), Gary Lock (University of Oxford) and Paul Miles (Oxford Archaeological Unit) deserve our gratitude for taking time out of their busy schedules to tell us "what's really going on" in archaeology. Special thanks go to Robert Bewley, Jayne Gidlow, and Wlodzimierz Raczkowski. Additional thanks go to everyone at WAC 4, CAA 99 or any other place we pinned you down. Such personal discussions involved Tyler Bell, Stuart Cakebread, J. Flasch, Francesco Menotti and John Wilcock. Last but not least, we salute Colleen for putting up with us while being the best companion one could wish for.

Notes

1. See Moffett (1989: 11) for a highly descriptive and insightful account.
2. With respect to the heritage industry in archaeology, Lang (1999: 233) identifies to-date a general: "...lack of strategic direction and a general failure to harness information to maximum effect." Evans (1985: 14) attributes an overall mismanagement of (financial and human) resources as a primary crippling factor and reason why not more "effective Information Systems" are instigated or a "core of trained individuals" exists for archaeological computing. Hence, despite undertaking their IS strategy survey as late as 1997, the Royal Commission on the Historical Monuments in England (RCHME) (Watkins 1999: 195–199) clearly is an early proponent in the trend for strategic management of IT resources.
3. An argument, not entirely accepted by us, seems to suggest that "computer archaeology" could bypass formal departmental structures and, in line with a particular theoretical approach, may opt for a less rigid application format (Hodder 1999: 179). However, advocating such "less fixed" approaches regarding IT in archaeology should cause raised eyebrows since the very nature of the proposal will surely continue any current piecemeal usage of computers; and therefore support the potential absence of a wider recognition for archaeological computing throughout the discipline. Hence, the: "...serious problem of credibility and thus education" would be perpetuated (Callow 1988: 469).
4. Although, Lock (1985: 35) points out: "When and why the initial decision is made to use a computer can drastically affect the outcome of the exercise."
5. This may be especially the case when either hardware or software packages offer promises of greater efficiency or even entirely new possibilities relating to data capture and storage, analysis or interpretation as well as archive development and information distribution. The computer is a "power-tool" in comparison to other means used to investigate the past (Wilcock 1973: 18).
6. Surely the example presented by McVicar and Stoddard (1986: 225–227) in their summary of the Gubbio field project highlights this particular problem regarding archaeological computing when: "It became clear that, regardless of the theoretical advantages of on-site computers, our supervisors and excavators could not use micros as 'thinking tools' in the same way as they could use 'paper and pencil'; to ignore this human factor would have endangered the excavation itself."
7. For example, Lang (1999: 227–234) describes comprehensively how heritage information is affected through political, social and technological changes in the public sector.
8. Cooper (1985: 84–85) identifies that: "...the problems of implementing computer systems are far more organisational than technical." And: "The main points to come out of the literature are the need for long-term strategic planning for the introduction of computers rather than short-term tactical decisions [our emphasis], and the need for the strategy to be based upon a full understanding of the technology itself, of the goals of business, and most importantly of the structure of the information resource itself and the way it is used to achieve these goals."
9. This seemed most appropriate since it is our suspicion that academic institutions will be the primary supplier of trained IT personnel for the commercial and heritage industries, in addition to anyone remaining in academia.
10. Archaeology represents only a single part of a vastly larger and all-encompassing structure that contains additional research areas or faculties such as social and cultural anthropology, physical anthropology and linguistics.
11. There are some caveats that apply when using the Internet as an information source. On one level, this includes the absence of any conforming standards for World Wide Web pages, thus often resulting in differences regarding the quality, quantity and comprehensiveness of content (van Leusen et al. 1996: 508). Furthermore, any unavailability of

departmental information on the Net does not automatically preclude that there is also an absence of a fully integrated computer engagement with an active IT research program and dedicated computer facilities – it could simply mean that there are no Web pages available.

12. Any QM or IT interest expressed by a faculty member may represent only one of many research foci.

13. This outcome should be approached with some caution since archaeological computer usage may be more widespread, but it falls short of a specific announcement of interest by members of faculty.

14. This is in complete contrast to Cooper and Richards (1985: 10) who, in the name of the Institute for Field Archaeologists (IFA), argue that: "…the application of computers is…an essential prerequisite of professional competence in many areas", and: "Computer literacy is not seen as a specialist skill, in the same way that a field archaeologist may be a finds specialist or an aerial photographer, or an underwater archaeologist..."

15. For comprehensive explanations regarding systems analysis and development see Flude (1984: 31–44), system software life cycles see Ross (1991a: 43), an actual IS strategy implementation see Murray (1995: 83–87) and a highly commendable description regarding IT integration in archaeology from a management's perspective see Cooper and Dinn (1995: 89–94).

16. Evans (1985: 13) clearly laments this absence of any shared objective or common range of [end-] user definitions despite most archaeologists working with the same information and materials. This point is echoed by Flude (1985: 18) who points out that: "There is little co-operation in the equipment and software that is being used", and therefore: "…when a unit wants to get computer equipment they are as likely to set up a different computer system on their own as adopt one of the existing systems." More fundamentally, Cooper (1985: 89) stresses that: "…computers in archaeology should be based on an explicit and long-term strategy, rather than implicit and random developments."

17. The terms "competence" and "expertise" are clearly delineated based on a similar separation between "computer literacy" and "computer expert" as suggested by Richards (1985a: 121–125). Thus, the former identifies the ability to essentially handle operational assignments while the latter is indicative of a high level of proficiency in IT design, implementation, maintenance and analysis as part of an archaeological project.

18. Cooper and Dinn (1995: 89) emphasise that: "For many management theorists, technology has a crucial influence on organisational design and is one of the most important factors to be taken into account in the structuring and effective management of an organisation." This means that: "…technological change is likely to influence archaeological organisations and their structures, and the roles of archaeological professionals, very widely."

19. Although, it must be pointed out that our proposed archaeological computing or IT implementation framework is a theoretical construct and as such it can not incorporate "field tested" results that could lead to smaller pragmatic or major fundamental changes. Similarly, because of potential resource shortages, we can foresee a realistic situation where many of the tasks outlined are done by the same individual within his or her organisational setting.

20. A case in hand when using IT is the potential to create illusions that fool our perception rather than foster a more advanced way of thinking (Reilly and Rahtz 1992: 21). At the same time Henderson (1991: 201) reminds us that computers are used as tools in archaeology and not "machines that give additional rigour to data or hypotheses".

21. We accept essential skills for a "computer archaeologist", as identified by Richards (1985b: 3); to be the "good understanding of systems analysis" and the "comprehensive, up-to-date knowledge of the elements of a computer system". On the other hand, any ability to "design and implement a major computer program" as well as "fluency in at least two programming languages" seems to us desirable but a less practical set of pre-requisites as compared to the former two and others explained later.

22. Ideally based on one's high degree of IT knowledge and an overall (theoretical and practical) implementation expertise. Hence, the "computer archaeologist" should "act as an interface" between his or her hired hands and the Information Technology that is in place (Lock 1984: 3)

23. This requires additional preparatory training for a "computer archaeologist" if Cooper's (1995: 73–74) claim still holds true: "Whilst archaeological projects and other activities such as cultural resource management have increased in complexity both in terms of their size and in terms of more ambitious goals and programmes, the development of the management techniques to drive them has not occurred at the same rate…". For: "Project management techniques can be applied not only to projects external to organisations…but also activities which occur within organisations such as the installation of new computer systems."

24. Most major universities have institution-wide committees, which among other things, decide on the allocation of resources or provide special grants/funding for IT researches. Having a knowledgeable dedicated specialist working with or as part of such a committee can therefore only improve any IT related support that the department receives from the university.

25. This is a clear problem area as Martlew (1988: 499–501) points out: "The rewards of research – conferences, publications and promotion – do not extend to teaching. Consequently there is little incentive for lecturers to spend time developing innovative courses in archaeological computing, to the detriment of their research and ultimately their promotion prospects."

26. Particularly when considering that "most archaeology undergraduates will not become professional archaeologists" while opting for private sector employment opportunities where acquired IT skills are generally useful (Dobson 1990: 17).

27. Richards (1985a: 124, 1985b: 3) recommends that: "…courses must be taught by archaeologists or those familiar with archaeology" where: "…examples must be in an archaeological context." For an overall (although dated) survey of archaeological computing in academia see Martlew (1988: 499–504).

28. Students should work on projects (e.g., as IT officers) where they are in charge of the implementation and management of an archaeological computing infrastructure. At the same time, students should be using these projects for their thesis aimed at advancing IT research within archaeology/anthropology. This ensures that they acquire a wide range of archaeological and IT skills (Richards 1985b: 4) including database applications, CAD, GIS, multimedia or VR to name a few.

29. Wilcock (1981: 14) states that: "The computer scientists have moved at least half-way toward the archaeologists, and it remains for the archaeologists to reciprocate". This is in clear opposition to Richards (1985b: 3) who suggests that archaeology should: "…borrow the services of the appropriate [IT] specialist as and when we require them".

30. This co-operative spirit may also foster a more generally accepted practice regarding information dissemination and archive design by advocating the Internet, multimedia tools or CD-ROM technology; and establishing a wider adherence to the "publish or be damned" (eighth) commandment for archaeological computing (Rahtz 1993: 2).

31. Richards (1985b: 3) implies that: "archaeologists must be trained in computers" and he thereby somehow already presupposes a previously acquired full training as an archaeologist. We, on the other hand, advocate a combined program for IT and archaeology; one that emphasises each of the two speciality areas according to the respective archaeological computing topic being taught. This is also very different from the concept of a "post-graduate conversion course" where students take up to a year off from their normal program and sign up for a specific IT training course only to then return to their respective fields of research including archaeology (Rush 1985: 5).

32. There should not just be research/training in the application of IT in archaeology. Any successful program might also involve computer-related courses for museum/exhibition work, cataloguing/analysing material culture, text transcription, faunal analysis or discipline-specific hardware/software developments.

33. For example, a post-graduate degree in IT in archaeology would have to entail the necessary anthropology/archaeology classes combined with specialist IT training, ideally made available within the department itself or alternatively accessed through other disciplines where the required infrastructure is in place (e.g., computer science, geography, geology, etc.).

34. Considering that an IT specialist fulfils a single-purpose role within an overall research project could suggest the same operational status as that of a (project support) technician. However, it is the (holistic) understanding of a computer tool regarding its purpose and use within the wider context of an archaeological investigation in conjunction with the required application skills that sets IT specialists apart from technicians performing routine (maintenance and support) tasks.

35. The paramount danger is that without a structural setting to identify and assess the degree of qualification, Voorrips' (1984: 48) vision of archaeologists practising their digital "magic" can come true; involving bad systems analysis, bad programming or bad operator task management; the obvious outcome of which has to be "bad archaeology."

36. The issue over the role and nature of "computer archaeologists" and their actual existence or status as technicians was put forth as a topic for further debate (Baker et al. 1985: 1). But as Moffett (1991b: 9) points out nobody seized the opportunity to discuss this matter at all, and hence to this day it still seems to be an unresolved matter.

37. At the same time, it needs to be pointed out that any expertise regarding IT in archaeology, due to the computing skills involved, will also act as a potential "back door" with regards to employment opportunities within, for example, other academic fields or the private industry. Greene (1988: 21) stresses that only a minority of graduates actually opt for careers in archaeology anyway and that most will enter other areas of employment. However, there is no (automatic) guarantee for getting such gainful work because of the highly topical nature of archaeological computing as well as the lack of IT-based certification and the likely absence of an industry-specific work experience portfolio (CV).

38. Surely there will be an increasing number of research and government funds that can be approached similar to the Computers in Teaching Initiative (CTI), the Information Technology Training Initiative (ITTI) or the Teaching and Learning Technology Programme (TLTP), which explicitly sought the application and integration of IT solutions (Perkins 1992: 1, Campbell 1993: 12)

39. For example, the M.Sc. program offered by the Department of Archaeology at the University of Southampton (the first opportunity for an archaeological computing degree as posted in Vol. 18 of the Archaeological Computing Newsletter (ACN) in 1989), satisfies many of the key structural and functional requirements suggested in our advocated (business model) IT implementation framework.

40. For some computer applications (e.g., statistics, databases, graphics and image processing, GIS, remote sensing, simulation and artificial intelligence) have a track record of at least 15 years and many (including the Internet at 35 years) far longer than that (Scollar 1982: 189–198, Huggett et al. 1998: 1, Scollar 1999: 5–12,).

41. It is unfortunate that Clubb (1999: 219), demonstratively one of the most ardent advocates of strategic planning for IS and IT implementation in archaeology (Clubb 1991a: 81–84, Clubb 1991b: 85–92, Clubb and Startin 1995: 67–73), in his commendable and comprehensive review on the topic seems to fall foul right at the end when he calls for "national" frameworks. For we believe that any such initiative in line with Cooper's (1985: 85–86) strong calling for technological uniformity will undoubtedly spark vigorous debates over "standardisation" issues as seen since the inception of the CAA conference. Consequently, it will therefore not result in the required fruitful discussion on actual structural elements regarding the technology, methodology and the role of the various human resources involved in a strategy for implementing IT in archaeology.

Bibliography

Baker, K., Huggett, J., Reilly, P., Smith, D. & Spicer, D., (eds) 1985. Editorial, *Archaeological Computing Newsletter*, Vol. 2., pp. 1.

Callow, P., 1988. Across the generations: a long-term computing project. In Rahtz, S.P.Q., (ed) *Computer and Quantitative Methods in Archaeology 1988*. Oxford: BAR International Series S446(ii), pp. 453–470.

Campbell, E., 1993. Multimedia for Teaching Archaeology Undergraduates: The TLTP Project. *Archaeological Computing Newsletter*, Vol. 36, pp. 12–16.

Carman, J., Cooper, M.A., Firth, A. & Wheatley, D., 1995. *Introduction: Archaeological management*. In Cooper, M.A., Firth, A., Carman, J. & Wheatley, D., (eds) *Managing Archaeology*. Theoretical Archaeology Group (TAG). London: Routledge, pp. 1–16.

Cleere, H., 1984. 'Only Connect'. In Martlew R., (ed) *Information Systems in Archaeology*. New Standard Archaeology. Gloucester: Alan Sutton Publishing, pp. 9–20.

Clubb, N., 1991a. Procuring medium-large systems. In Lockyear, K. & Rahtz, S., (eds) *Computer Applications and Quantitative Methods in Archaeology 1990*. BAR International Series 565. Oxford: Tempus Reparatum, pp. 81–84.

Clubb, N., 1991b. The operational requirement for the record of scheduled monuments. In Lockyear, K. & Rahtz, S., (eds) *Computer Applications and Quantitative Methods in Archaeology 1990*. BAR International Series 565. Oxford: Tempus Reparatum, pp. 85–92.

Clubb, N.D., 1999. Have we failed to Provide a Strategic Vision for Information Systems in Archaeology? In Dingwall, L., Exon, S., Gaffney, V., Laflin, S. & van Leusen, M., (eds) *Archaeology in the Age of the Internet. Computer Applications and Quantitative Methods in Archaeology CAA 97*. BAR International Series 750, pp. 219–226.

Clubb, N., & Startin, B., 1995. Information systems strategies in national organisations and the identification, legal protection and management of the most important sites in England. In Wilcock, J. & Lockyear, K., (eds) *Computer Applications and Quantitative Methods in Archaeology 1993*. BAR International Series 598, pp. 67–73.

Cooper, M.A., 1985. Computers in British Archaeology: the need for a national strategy. In Cooper, M.A. & Richards, J.D., (eds) *Current Issues in Archaeological Computing*. BAR International Series 271, pp. 79–91.

Cooper, M.A., 1995. The archaeological manager: applying management models to archaeology. In Cooper, M.A., Firth, A., Carman, J. & Wheatley, D., (eds) *Managing Archaeology*. Theoretical Archaeology Group (TAG). London: Routledge, pp. 71–88.

Cooper, M.A. & Dinn, J.L., 1995. Computers and the evolution of archaeological organisations. In Wilcock, J. & Lockyear, K., (eds) *Computer Applications and Quantitative Methods in Archaeology 1993*. BAR International Series 598, pp. 89–94.

Cooper, M. & Richards, J., 1985. Computers and the Institute of Field Archaeologists. *Archaeological Computing Newsletter*, Vol. 4, pp. 9–10.

Dobson, M., 1990. What Shall we Teach Them? Computers and Archaeology Undergraduates. *Archaeological Computing Newsletter*, Vol. 24, pp. 17–19.

Evans, D., 1985. Computerisation and Information (Mis)Management. *Archaeological Computing Newsletter*, Vol. 5, pp. 13–15.

Flude, K., 1984. Setting up an archaeological computer system – an introduction. In Martlew R., (ed) *Information Systems in Archaeology*. New Standard Archaeology. Gloucester: Alan Sutton Publishing, pp. 31–44.

Flude, K., 1985. Computers and Archaeology. *Archaeological Computing Newsletter*, Vol. 5, pp. 18–20.

Gaines, S., 1984. The impact of computerised systems on American Archaeology: and overview of the past decade. In Martlew R., (ed) *Information Systems in Archaeology*. New Standard Archaeology. Gloucester: Alan Sutton Publishing, pp. 63–76.

Greene, K., 1988. Teaching Computing to Archaeology Students. *Archaeological Computing Newsletter*, Vol. 14, pp. 21–24.

Henderson, J., 1991. The use and abuse of computers. In Ross, S., Moffett, J., & Henderson, J., (eds) *Computing for Archaeologists*. Oxford: Oxford University Committee for Archaeology Monograph No. 18, pp. 201–205.

Hodder, I., 1999. *The archaeological Process – An Introduction*. Oxford: Blackwell Publishers Ltd.

Huggett, J., 1986. Book Review: Archaeology and Computers (by Powesland and Haughton). *Archaeological Computing Newsletter*, Vol. 8, pp. 21–23.

Huggett, J., 1989. Computing and the Deansway Archaeology Project. *Archaeological Computing Newsletter*, Vol. 18, pp. 1–7.

Huggett, J., 1993. Ranter's Corner: Democratising archaeological Knowledge with computers. *Archaeological Computing Newsletter*, Vol. 35, pp. 7–10.

Huggett, J., Lock, G., Spicer, D., Kvamme, K. & Stančič, Z., (eds) 1998. The Half-Centenary Editorial: The Future's Not What It Used To Be. *Archaeological Computing Newsletter*, Vol. 50. , pp. 1–2.

Kvamme, K., 1989. Geographic Information Systems in Regional Archaeological Research and Data Management. In Schiffer, M.B., (ed) *Archaeological Method and Theory*, Vol.1. Tucson: The University of Arizona Press, pp. 139–204.

Lang, N., 1999. Public Heritage in the Age of Decline. In Dingwall, L., Exon, S., Gaffney, V., Laflin, S. & van Leusen, M., (eds) *Archaeology in the Age of the Internet. Computer Applications and Quantitative Methods in Archaeology CAA 97*. BAR International Series 750, pp. 227–234.

Lock, G., 1984. Computerised Post-Excavation Work at Danebury Hillfort. *Archaeological Computing Newsletter*, Vol. 1, pp. 2–5.

Lock, G., 1985. A new direction or a new distraction: a pragmatic assessment of computer applications in archaeology based on work at Danebury hillfort. In Cooper, M.A. & Richards, J.D., (eds) *Current Issues in Archaeological Computing*. BAR International Series 271, pp. 35–46.

Lock, G., & Spicer, R.D., 1985. Real and imaginary limitations of micro-computers in archaeology. In Cooper, M.A. & Richards, J.D., (eds) *Current Issues in Archaeological Computing*. BAR International Series 271, pp. 103–122.

Lock, G., & Wilcock, J., 1987. *Computer Archaeology*. Shire Archaeology.

Marciniak, A., & Raczkowski, W., 1992. Polish archaeology and computers: an overview. In Reilly, P., & Rahtz, S., (eds) *Archaeology and the Information Age – A global perspective*. One World Archaeology 21. London: Routledge, pp. 47–51.

Martlew, R, 1984. *Information Systems in Archaeology*. New Standard Archaeology. Gloucester: Alan Sutton Publishing.

Martlew, R., 1988. New technology archaeological education and training. In Rahtz, S.P.Q., (ed) *Computer and Quantitative Methods in Archaeology 1988*. BAR International Series S446(ii), pp. 499–504.

McVicar, J.B. & Stoddart, S., 1986. Computerising an Archaeological Excavation: The Human Factors. In Laflin, S., (ed) *Computer Applications in Archaeology 1986*, pp. 225–227.

Moffett, J., 1989. Computer Perceptions in Archaeology 1. *Archaeological Computing Newsletter*, Vol. 20, pp. 11–16.

Moffett, J., 1991a. Computers in archaeology: approaches and applications past and present. In Ross, S., Moffett, J. & Henderson, J., (eds) *Computing for Archaeologists*. Oxford: Oxford University Committee for Archaeology Monograph No. 18, pp. 13–39.

Moffett, J., 1991b. The Archaeological Computing Newsletter – An Assessment. *Archaeological Computing Newsletter*, Vol. 26, pp. 8–10.

Murray, D.M., 1995. The management of archaeological information – a strategy. In Wilcock, J. & Lockyear, K., (eds) *Computer Applications and Quantitative Methods in Archaeology 1993*. BAR International Series 598, pp. 83–87.

Orton, C., 1992. Quantitative Methods in the 1990's. In Lock, G.R. & Moffett, J. (eds) *Computer Applications and Quantitative Methods in Archaeology 1991*. BAR International Series S577. Oxford: Tempus Reparatum, pp. 137–140.

Palmer, S., 1989. Computers, Planning and Management. *Archaeological Computing Newsletter*, Vol. 19, pp. 1–2.

Perkins, P., 1992. The Computers in Teaching Initiative Centre for History with Archaeology and Art History (CTICH). *Archaeological Computing Newsletter*, Vol. 30, pp. 1–3.

Rahtz, S., 1993. Ten Commandments for Archaeological Computing. *Archaeological Computing Newsletter*, Vol. 36, pp. 1–2.

Reilly, P. & Rahtz, S., (eds) 1992. *Archaeology and the Information Age – A global perspective*. One World Archaeology 21. London: Routledge.

Richards, J., 1985a. Into the black art: achieving computer-literacy in Archaeology. In *Computer Applications in Archaeology 1985*. London: University of London, Institute of Archaeology, pp. 121–125.

Richards, J., 1985b. Training Archaeologists to use Computers. *Archaeological Computing Newsletter*, Vol. 2, pp. 2–5.

Ross, S., 1991a. Systems engineering for archaeological computing. In Ross, S., Moffett, J. & Henderson, J., (eds) *Computing for Archaeologists*. Oxford: Oxford University Committee for Archaeology Monograph No. 18, pp. 41–53.

Ross, S., 1991b. Archaeological Computing and System Design. In Ross, S., Moffett, J. & Henderson, J., (eds) *Computing for Archaeologists*. Oxford: Oxford University Committee for Archaeology Monograph No. 18, pp. 11–12.

Rush, D., 1985. Training for Computing. *Archaeological Computing Newsletter*, Vol. 3, pp. 5.

Ryan, N.S., 1988. A bibliography of computer applications and quantitative methods in archaeology. In Rahtz, S.P.Q., (ed) *Computer and Quantitative Methods in Archaeology 1988*. BAR International Series S446(i), pp. 1–27.

Scholtz, S.C. & Million, M.G., 1981. A Management Information System for Archaeological Resources. In Gaines, S.W., (ed) *Data Bank Applications in Archaeology*. Tucson: The University of Arizona Press, pp. 15–26.

Scollar, I., 1982. Thirty years of computer archaeology and the future, or looking backwards and forwards at the same time while trying not to twist one's neck. In *Computer Applications in Archaeology 1982*. University of Birmingham: Centre for Computing and Computer Science, pp. 189–198.

Scollar, I., 1999. 25 Years of Computer Applications in Archaeology. In Dingwall, L., Exon, S., Gaffney, V., Laflin, S. & van Leusen, M., (eds) *Archaeology in the Age of the Internet. Computer Applications and Quantitative Methods in Archaeology CAA 97*. BAR International Series 750, pp. 5–10.

Stewart, J., 1999. Has 25 Years of Computing Provided Greater Physical and Intellectual Access to Archaeology? In Dingwall, L., Exon, S., Gaffney, V., Laflin, S. & van Leusen, M., (eds) *Archaeology in the Age of the Internet. Computer Applications and Quantitative Methods in Archaeology CAA 97*. BAR International Series 750, pp. 19–23.

USB Research Informatics. 1999. *NRC/NAS Ranking of Graduate Research Programs*. URL: http://www.research.sunysb.edu/research/nrcdata.html

Valenti, M., 1998. Computer science and the management of an archaeological excavation: the Poggio Imperiale project. *Archaeological Computing Newsletter*, Vol. 50, pp. 13–20.

van Leusen, M., Champion, S., Lizee, J. & Plunkett, T., 1996. Toward a European Archaeological Heritage Web. In Kamermans, H. & Fennema, K., (eds) *Interfacing the Past. Computer Applications and Quantitative Methods in Archaeology CAA 95* Vol.II. Analecta Praehistorica Leidensia 28. Leiden: University of Leiden, Publications of the Institute of Prehistory, pp. 507–515.

Voorrips, A., 1984. Data catchment analysis and computer carrying capacity. In Martlew R., (ed) *Information Systems in Archaeology*. New Standard Archaeology. Gloucester: Alan Sutton Publishing, pp. 45–53.

Watkins, C., 1999. Any Time, Any Place, Anywhere. In Dingwall, L., Exon, S., Gaffney, V., Laflin, S. & van Leusen, M., (eds) *Archaeology in the Age of the Internet. Computer Applications and Quantitative Methods in Archaeology CAA 97*. BAR International Series 750, pp. 195–199.

Wilcock, J.D., 1973. A general survey of computer applications in archaeology. In *Science and Archaeology: Computer Applications in Archaeology* 1. Stafford: George Street Press, pp. 17–21.

Wilcock, J.D., 1981. Information Retrieval for Archaeology. In Gaines, S.W., (ed) *Data Bank Applications in Archaeology*. Tucson: The University of Arizona Press, pp. 9–14.